P9-BEE-638

Understanding Interest Rate Swaps

Mary S. Ludwig

McGraw-Hill, Inc.
New York St. Louis San Francisco Auckland Bogotá
Caracas Lisbon London Madrid Mexico City Milan
Montreal New Delhi San Juan Singapore
Sydney Tokyo Toronto

Library of Congress Cataloging-in-Publication Data

Ludwig, Mary S.
    Understanding interest rate swaps / Mary S. Ludwig.
        p.   cm.
    Includes index.
    ISBN 0-07-039020-7 :
    1. Interest rate futures.   2. Swaps (Finance) I. Title.
HG6024.5.L83   1993
332.63'23—dc20   92-39058
                                              CIP

Copyright © 1993 by Mary S. Ludwig. All rights reserved. Printed in the United States of America. Except as permitted under the United States Copyright Act of 1976, no part of this publication may be reproduced or distributed in any form or by any means, or stored in a data base or retrieval system, without the prior written permission of the publisher.

2 3 4 5 6 7 8 9 10 11 12 13 14 BKMBKM 9 9 8 7 6 5 4 3

ISBN   0-07-039020-7

The sponsoring editor for this book was David J. Conti, the editing supervisor was Jane Palmieri, and the production supervisor was Suzanne W. Babeuf. It was set in Palatino by McGraw-Hill's Professional Book Group composition unit.

Appendix B consists of EITF Abstracts Issue No. 84-7, "Termination of Interest Rate Swaps," and EITF Abstracts Issue No. 84-36, "Interest Rate Swap Transactions." Copyright by Financial Accounting Standards Board, 401 Merritt 7, P.O. Box 5116, Norwalk, Connecticut 06856-5116, U.S.A. Reprinted with permission. Copies of the complete document are available from the FASB.
Appendixes C, D, and E consist of ISDA's Master Agreement, Definitions, and Standard Letter Agreement Confirming a Swap Transaction. These materials are reprinted with the permission of the International Swap Dealers Association, Inc.

   This publication is designed to provide accurate and authoritative information in regard to the subject matter covered. It is sold with the understanding that the publisher is not engaged in rendering legal, accounting, or other professional service. If legal advice or other expert assistance is required, the services of a competent professional person should be sought.
                        —from a declaration of principles jointly adopted by a committee
                        of the American Bar Association and a committee of publishers

This book is printed on recycled, acid-free paper containing a minimum of 50% recycled de-inked fiber.

To my husband, Benedict Ludwig, who wishes at this point that I had never heard of an interest rate Swap.

Contents

3. How Rates Are Set   **35**

4. Financial Institutions and Credit   57

10. Other Derivative Products: Sounds Complicated but It's Not

11. Other Types of Interest Rate Swaps

Preface

Many leading business publications have carried articles and editorials about the latest potential crisis to hit the banking system: Swaps. Not many understand these new financial products that for the most part did not exist a decade ago. Swaps didn't exist when I went to graduate school, and until very recently they were not included in the curriculum of most business schools. Although regulators in a number of countries have been concerned about the lack of regulation of Swaps and most other derivative products, Jerry Corrigan cast the first public stone in January 1992 when he declared in a speech to the New York State Bankers Association, "High-tech banking and finance has its place, but it's not all it's cracked up to be.... I hope this sounds like a warning, because it is."

The press loved it. The market makers hated it. In a March 25, 1992, article, *The Wall Street Journal* reported, "For their part, many derivatives traders were outraged by Mr. Corrigan's speech; they protest that he made their market out to be the 'financial version of crack,' as one lawyer angrily put it." So who's right? Both sides have certain legitimate concerns.

The crux of the problem is the fact that Swap products are so new and that the markets have grown so fast that only the few people intimately involved with these products on a day-to-day basis understand them enough to be comfortable with them. The interest rate Swap market is around $3 trillion, up from zero in 1980. That means anyone who completed his or her formal education before 1980 received no training in Swaps (or most other derivative products). The reality is that anyone who completed his or her formal education before the late 1980s never heard of interest rate Swaps or derivative products in a classroom setting.

The 1980s was a decade of unheard-of financial innovation. Products never seen before sprung up, and markets for them grew phenomenally. It's no wonder that concern over this largely unregulated market exists. But the products are not as difficult as you might imagine. Many, in fact, are quite similar, and others are simply the combination of two or more. Those who say there is only one concept in finance—present valuing—might not be right, but the comment is not as off-base as it might at first seem.

Many of the products described in this book are based on present value techniques. The people who understand this basic concept (and for those who don't, it's been spelled out) are on their way to understanding the interest rate Swap market. The derivatives market is composed of a few "building blocks." Understand those few basic building blocks, combine them in a variety of ways, and you're on your way.

I received an MBA from New York University in 1977. My complete formal education in anything remotely related to interest rate Swaps and derivatives consisted of a half-semester course on futures. Of course, the only futures traded then were commodity futures, and the only reason I took the course was that I worked for Continental Grain Company at the time. My boss at Continental Grain taught the course, and I was determined to prove that a woman could do just as well as a man in this field. Anyway, in quick order I managed to get an A in the course and get myself transferred to Continental Grain's Treasury Department. That course was the end of my association with futures—or so I thought.

Ten years later, as I was leaving my third and last interview for my current job at Olympia & York, the treasurer called after me, "Do you know anything about futures?" "Only a little," I responded. "I did work for Continental Grain a number of years ago. But there were no financial futures then."

"Good," she said, or something to that effect. "If you understand commodities, financials will be no problem for you." I nodded, in ignorance, and didn't give it another thought. We were wrong, by the way. Although it wasn't excruciatingly difficult to advance on the learning curve, it wasn't that simple either. I can cook a little, but no one would ever ask me to stand in for Julia Child.

This book is an attempt to bring the reader up on the learning curve and then a little further. It assumes no previous knowledge of the Swap market and goes from there. Those who have some basic understanding might wish to skim Chapter 1, "What Is an Interest Rate Swap?" and perhaps Chapter 3, "How Rates Are Set."

If you're reading to get a basic understanding of the way the market works, you may be content to leave some of the math to me. But redoing the math and redrawing the diagrams is recommended for all. It will greatly enhance your understanding of the concepts presented.

Although there are many numbers and diagrams, and the reader is urged to replicate them all, there is also an attempt to give a flavor of the market. You are given an inside glimpse of what goes on in the markets and also some of the lines traders may try and feed their corporate clients. Corporate customers are given recommendation on some strategies that may work best for them; market makers get a look at what happens on the other side of the desk.

The book is aimed at those who wish to become proficient and active market participants as well as to those who are a few steps removed from the day-to-day activity but who need to understand the way Swaps work. Senior executives will benefit from a thorough reading of this book because it answers many of the basic questions they may have but are reluctant to ask. Accountants, auditors, and analysts working for corporations and financial institutions will be better equipped to handle these new financing techniques in their day-to-day responsibilities if they understand the basics of the market. A good part of the hysteria about the Swap market is owing to a lack of knowledge. A little understanding of how the market works will alleviate some of the unrealistic concerns, thus allowing those concerned about the market to focus on the few areas that might truly deserve their attention.

The book starts with a chapter that presents the subject of interest rate Swaps in a very basic and accessible way. Key concepts and market terminology are introduced. The chapter contains several very simple examples and introduces the readers to diagrams that they are encouraged to draw themselves. Chapter 2 traces the development of the Swap and derivatives market from its inception to the present. It reviews the famous (at least in Swap circles) case in England where municipalities were allowed to walk away from millions of dollars of losses on their Swap positions. What happened at Drexel, the Salomon Treasury bidding scandal, the Resolution Trust Corporation's use of Swaps, the effects of the credit crunch in 1991, and the first attempt to foreclose on a Swap are some of the events discussed.

Chapter 3, which is a continuation of the first chapter, shows the reader how rates are set on Swaps. It discusses the rate setting on what's referred to in the trade as plain vanilla Swaps, and it includes several charts, which readers are encouraged to redraw, and calculation of rates that readers can do themselves.

The reader is then given a break from calculations and diagrams by Chapter 4 on financial institutions and how banks and financial institutions run their shops. Assignments, documentations, ISDA, lines, relationships, and Swap desk reputations are all discussed. Chapter 5 presents a number of real-life applications. An overview of the Financial Accounting Standards Board rulings is included in Chapter 6. (Copies of several FASB rulings can be found in Appendix B.) Chapter 7 talks about the cashflow method of looking at Swaps and the mark-to-market approach, explaining which is correct and why. The concept and procedures for marking a Swap to market along with the unwinding of Swap positions are also explored in detail in Chapter 7. Chapter 8 takes a look at some pricing refinements to the basic plain vanilla techniques described earlier. These techniques are necessary in certain circumstances, which are spelled out for you.

Chapter 9 takes an in-depth look at Swaptions, while Chapter 11, on other types of interest rate Swaps, discusses some of the more than two dozen Swap choices. Don't panic—remember the building-block approach. Most Swaps involve looking at the plain vanilla Swap from a different angle. Chapter 10 on derivative products and Chapter 12 on other types of Swaps offer some simple real-life applications.

The final two chapters address risk and the future. Chapter 13, "Managing Risk: Setting Up a Risk Management Program," shows corporate end users (and market makers as well) how to evaluate the appropriateness of certain products and how to set up a risk management program within their company. Because Swaps are so new, many companies do not have formal programs in place to monitor them. End users who don't fully evaluate all the risks associated with the product may find that they have traded one risk for another. Chapter 13 shows you how to make sure you don't do that. Chapter 14 offers a look at the future, from my perspective and from the dealer's side of the desk.

Those who think that the Swap market will fade away need to think again. As we go to press, a new market maker has emerged. The Chicago Board of Trade has announced that it will enter the market toward the end of 1993.

Most, if not all, major business publications carry articles about the expanding Swap market. Some are quite good. But they all assume a certain level of knowledge on the part of the reader. After reading this book (even if you don't do the more complicated math), you will be able to follow those articles as well as identify those that are faulty.

By the time you're finished, you will not only know what "marking to market your Swap portfolio by interpolating on-the-run securities using a zero coupon yield curve" means, you'll know how to do it.

Mary S. Ludwig

Acknowledgments

Like most of the rest of the financial community, I completed my formal education before Swaps and most other derivative products were included as part of the business school curriculum. Yet, I've been able to accumulate quite a bit of knowledge in this area. For that, I'd like to thank the many fine Swap market participants I've driven crazy along the way for answering my many, many questions. If I tried to mention everyone, the list would be too long, my publisher would object, and I'd probably leave someone very important to me out. (And then I'd feel terrible.)

But a special thanks goes to Debbie Orlando, Director, Barclay's Bank PLC, and Neil Winter, Vice President, Merrill Lynch Futures, for helping me with both material and contacts—and, of course, my colleagues at Olympia & York who are probably among the best, if not *the* best, group of professionals in the world.

Thanks to David Conti, Editorial Director, Business McGraw-Hill, for getting McGraw-Hill to say yes. And to Jane Palmieri, Suzanne Babeuf, and the editorial-production staff for making this book look so good.

And to my niece Christine, who warned me that I better not be working on this book when we went away again. Don't worry, Christine, it's done!

To the two lights of my life, Ben and Lara, a special thanks for keeping the interruptions to a minimum.

Finally, to my husband who graciously spent most of our last vacation on Martha's Vineyard in the company of two six-year-olds while I madly worked at completing this book—thank you.

1

What Is an Interest Rate Swap?

Let's look at Ben Johnson, Treasurer of Plymouth Industries Inc. Plymouth Industries is a real estate company. It owns a building that is completely leased (rented), and all the leases run for 10 years. Ben Johnson knows exactly how much rent his building will generate each year. He can estimate his expenses associated with the building pretty well also. So he has a very good idea of how much cash will be available to cover his debt service—that is, interest payments.

Ben Johnson goes to his local bank to refinance the mortgage on his building. The bank offers him an interest only loan for 10 years at the prime rate. Ben's interest payments will go up or down each month depending on whether the prime rate goes up or down. Now, if interest rates go down, Ben Johnson is a happy man. If they go up a little, he can live with it. A problem arises when the prime rate goes way up—say to 20 percent, as it did in the late 1970s. Then Ben's building will not generate enough cash to cover his interest payments.

For this reason Ben Johnson prefers to get a fixed-rate loan even if it is a little higher than the current prime rate; he doesn't want to wake up in the middle of the night worrying about higher interest rates. So Ben asks his banker to consider a fixed-rate loan, that is, a loan where the interest rate does not fluctuate during the life of the loan. His banker says "no" but suggests he call a Swap dealer. (Later in the chapter I'll discuss why the bank won't make a fixed-rate loan.)

Diagrams

Before we find out what happens with the Swap dealer or trader, we're going to diagram Ben Johnson's transaction so far. A *diagram* is a picture that shows the cashflow between two or more parties. *All* professionals involved in any manner with the Swap market diagram their transactions, sometimes even the very simple ones—the ones referred to in the business as "plain vanilla."

Figure 1-1 shows the interest payments or what's referred to as the "cashflows" or sometimes simply the "flows." You'll note that a box is drawn to represent each party and an arrow is used to show in which direction the payment will flow. The diagram shows Plymouth Industries paying the bank the prime rate. If the bank had been paying the company, the arrow would have pointed the other way.

The payment shown in Figure 1-1 is called a *floating rate,* because it changes or "floats" every time the prime rate changes. Some floating rates can change as frequently as every day. We've now got the first part (also referred to as the first leg) of our transaction.

The Solution

The banker has suggested to Ben Johnson that he try and use the Swap market to "fix" the rate on his loan. Ben calls several financial institutions that run Swap desks (more about this later) and gets bids from them. The first offers to "swap" prime for 10 percent, the second for 10.1 percent, and the third for 10.25 percent. (In a real life situation, the bids would be much closer—say 10.01 percent, 10.015 percent, and 10.012 percent.) Naturally, Ben Johnson accepts the 10 percent bid. Why naturally? Because he wants to "lock in" the lowest possible rate as that is the rate he is going to pay.

What Ben has swapped are interest payments at the prime rate for interest payments at a fixed rate of 10 percent. His Swap and his loan are two separate transactions. Most of the time they will be done with two separate financial institutions. However, it is not unusual for the lending area of a bank to make a loan and the capital markets area of the same bank to provide the Swap facility. Many of these financial institutions will be banks, but investment houses, insurance companies, and others are entering the field.

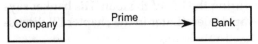

Figure 1-1. Floating payment diagram for the borrower.

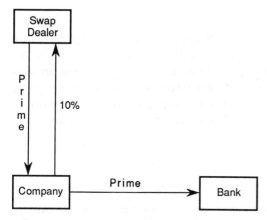

Figure 1-2. Company Swap diagram.

Each month, Ben will pay the bank the prime rate as we diagrammed in the first part of the transaction. Then there will be the Swap part of the transaction (Figure 1-2). In this leg, the Swapping institution will pay Plymouth Industries the prime rate, which will cancel out Plymouth Industries' payment to the bank. Then Plymouth Industries will pay the Swapping institution 10 percent. These three payments will effectively "lock in" Plymouth Industries' rate at 10 percent and effectively give it the fixed-rate loan it wanted in the first place.

Synthetic Fixed Rate

We just saw that Plymouth Industries effectively locked in a rate of 10 percent. This can also be viewed as synthetically creating a fixed-rate loan. Ben Johnson has taken two components from two separate markets (his floating-rate loan and his Swap) and by combining them has created a third instrument (a fixed-rate loan). This is done all the time when there are two different entities (the bank and the company) with different needs. (The bank needs to make floating-rate loans, and the company needs a fixed-rate loan.)

There are many occasions when a borrower will be able to obtain lower fixed-rate financing by synthetically fixing his or her rate through the Swap market. Borrowers with access to the Swap markets should compare the fixed rate their banks offer with the synthetic rate they can create themselves by combining a floating-rate loan with a Swap. This will be explained in Chapter 3, "How Rates Are Set."

Counterparty

The financial institution with which Plymouth Industries did the Swap is known as the Swap *counterparty*. (And Plymouth Industries is the Swap counterparty for the financial institution.) When Swaps are discussed, the counterparties are very, very important. Market participants will talk about counterparty credit, counterparty limits, and so on. In the case of assignments, discussed in Chapter 7, all counterparties are not equal.

Paying Rates versus Receiving Rates

In a Swap transaction, Ben Johnson is known as the *payor*. As already indicated, Ben would be interested in paying the lowest possible rate. The Swap counterparty who is receiving the fixed payment is known as the *receiver*. The terms *payor* and *receiver* always refer to the payor and receiver of the fixed rate. And as common sense would indicate, the payor always wants to pay the lowest possible rate, and the receiver always wants to receive the highest possible rate. Like any other market where there is a buyer and a seller, one party wants to receive a high price and the other wants to pay a low one.

Swap Desk

In order to get the best rate, Ben Johnson should call the Swap desk at several financial institutions to get quotes for his Swap. What are Swap desks and who has them? Loosely put, a Swap desk is a group of individuals who run a Swap portfolio for the financial institution. Not every commercial bank runs a Swap desk; many investment houses and several insurance companies run them. Many foreign banks run big Swap desks. As the credit rating of many U.S. banks drops, U.S. banks are being squeezed out of the Swap market and are being replaced by European and Japanese banks.

The Swap desk will give you a price (level) for your transaction. (What they do on the other side of the transaction will be described in Chapter 4, "Financial Institutions and Credit.") After getting several prices from several different desks, you will decide which is best and execute your trade.

U.S. Dollar Interest Rate Swap

The Swap we have been discussing is a U.S. dollar interest rate Swap. The payments will be made in U.S. dollars, and the interest rates are

U.S. interest rates. Swaps can be done in other currencies and based on other countries' interest rates. Although the U.S. dollar interest rate Swap market is the largest interest rate Swap market, transactions in other currencies are increasing rapidly.

Why Banks Want
Floating-Rate Loans

Ben Johnson would not have had to go to the Swap market if his bank had been willing to give him a fixed-rate loan. But the bank wasn't. Banks fund themselves in two ways. Their first source of funding comes from deposits from people like you and me. The CDs, passbook savings accounts, and money we leave in our checking accounts are their preferred sources of funding. If that is not sufficient to meet their needs, and it usually is not, they then go out into the marketplace and borrow money. This might be done through the issuance of commercial paper (short-term IOUs) or the issuance of longer-term notes or bonds.

Banks (especially savings and loans (S&Ls) that are not serious players in the Swap market) got burned badly in the 1970s when interest rates rose dramatically. Many of them had made fixed-rate loans, especially long-term mortgages, at rates below 9 percent and were forced to fund them at rates closer to 15 percent. This resulted in a negative cashflow, and in some cases, serious negative cashflow. This mismatch of assets and liabilities has made banks quite leery of fixed-rate loans. Banks learned from their mistakes and now try to match assets and liabilities. They've found new mistakes to make (like poor real estate loans. They're correcting that problem though—they've all but stopped lending to real estate companies—but that's another story.) Banks now try to match their assets with their liabilities. Most banks do not leave themselves open to the risk of higher interest rates. If interest rates go higher, not only will banks have to pay their depositors more, but they will earn a higher rate on the loans they've made. They've transferred this risk to the borrower.

Why Couldn't the
Bank Swap?

But, you ask, why doesn't the bank just Swap the floating payments it receives from the borrower for a fixed rate in the Swap market? The bank could do the same thing that Plymouth Industries did. And some do. But, in these days of tightening credit, banks are in the driver's seat. And some think, why should they? It's not their problem, it's the borrowers. (This is an oversimplification. If the borrower goes bankrupt, it will become the bank's problem very quickly.)

The second reason why a bank might be reluctant to do a Swap has to do with its allocation of credit. Just as a bank limits the amount it will lend any one borrower, it also sets limits on the amount of Swaps it will do with any one counterparty. Without going into all the details, the bank limits the total amount of business it will do with any one entity. So a Swap could take away from other business the bank might want to do with a counterparty. This is sometimes referred to as using double credit. (If this is not 100 percent clear, don't worry; it will not affect your understanding of Swaps.)

What If the Bank Swapped

To get a better understanding of a Swap transaction, let's look at this transaction from the bank's viewpoint if it had given Ben Johnson the fixed-rate loan and swapped it to floating in the Swap market. The bank calls three counterparties and tells them the bank wants to receive fixed. The bank receives the following quotes: 9.8 percent, 9.9 percent, and 9.75 percent. Because the bank is going to receive the fixed rate, it chooses the highest rate.

The first leg of the transaction will be the company's paying the bank the fixed rate. Let's use 10 percent as we did in the earlier example (see Figure 1-3). Then we add the second leg of the transaction, the Swap. In this, the bank pays the Swap counterparty 9.9 percent and receives prime. At first glance, this seems like a better transaction for everyone involved. The bank is paying 10 basis points less than it is receiving from the company. This savings could either be kept entirely by the bank or shared with the company. Maybe the bank could charge the company 9.95 percent. Then they'd each come out ahead of the game—except for one problem.

It was mentioned earlier that banks limit the total amount of business they do with any one entity. This Swap (and in the bank's eyes, an unnecessary Swap) would eat into that limit. (Figure 1-4 is a bank Swap diagram.) In addition, banks have to allocate a certain amount of capital for each transaction (keep in mind that capital costs the bank money).

Payment to bank	(Prime)
Payment to Swap dealer	(10%)
Payment from Swap dealer	Prime
	(10%)

Figure 1-3. Company interest payment diagram.

Figure 1-4. Bank Swap diagram.

And who is going to pay for that? Not the bank and not the Swap counterparty. The borrower. This cost will be spread over the life of the loan and will be reflected in a higher fixed rate charged to the borrower. In some instances the bank may charge even more than the cost of reserves, adding on something for their cost of administering the Swap.

Anyway, let's say the bank decides it needs an extra 25 basis points to cover its costs. If the bank is receiving 9.9 percent, it will need to charge the company 10.15 percent (9.9 + .25). Having the bank do the Swap would result in the company's paying a higher fixed rate. Sometimes, however, companies have no choice but to have the bank do the Swap. Many smaller companies, along with those whose credit ratings are not sterling, do not have access to the Swap market. When we discuss credit in this and other chapters, you'll see that Swap market participants are very picky about those with whom they do business.

Figure 1-5 shows how the transaction would look if the bank, instead of the company, did the Swap. The bank has created the floating-rate loan it desired. Unfortunately, Plymouth Industries ends up with a higher rate on its loan.

More about Diagrams

As mentioned earlier, diagrams are an integral part of the Swap market. I've always found that the things I've learned best are those that I actually do myself. If you are new to the Swap business, you might want to draw these diagrams yourself. Go back to the beginning of this chapter and begin to read. Cover each diagram. Draw the diagrams yourself after reading the facts. You'll see how easy it is to get the arrows going in the wrong direction.

If the material presented so far seems fairly basic, you might try drawing the diagrams in the rest of the chapter before looking at them. Don't be discouraged if you get an arrow or two going in the wrong direction. Even the pros do.

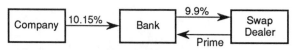

Figure 1-5. Bank Swap diagram with costs passed on.

A Look at the Other Side of the Coin

Borrowers are not the only ones who are concerned about the movement and direction of interest rates. Let's visit with Nora Lewis, the portfolio manager for Shenandoah Corporation. Nora Lewis's problem is a little different. Shenandoah owns some bonds that pay 9 percent. Nora is concerned that interest rates will rise, and not only will her bonds lose value, but the portfolio's performance will look poor when compared to market indices. Figure 1-6 shows the first leg of the transaction—the company's receiving 9 percent from the bond issuer.

Nora Lewis calls several Swap desks and gets several quotes. She wants to pay the fixed rate and receive the floating rate. She gets three quotes: 8.9 percent, 9 percent, and 9.1 percent. Naturally, she will pick the lowest rate because she is going to pay the fixed rate.

Figure 1-7 shows the diagram for the whole transaction. You will note that the floating index in this transaction is Libor, not prime. In most Swap transactions, the floating index is Libor, not prime. The term *Libor* stands for London Interbank Offer Rate, sometimes referred to as the Eurodollar rate. All plain vanilla Swaps use Libor as the floating index. Many floating-rate bank loans made to large customers who may use the Swap market are based on Libor.

The next thing to focus on is the fact that the fixed rate Nora Lewis receives from the bond issuer is not the same as the rate she will pay her Swap counterparty. In this case, she is lucky. She'll receive 10 basis points more than she has to pay. (You'll also note that if she had executed her Swap at 9.1 percent, she'd have to pay out 10 basis points more than she received.)

Figure 1-6. Floating payment diagram for the investor.

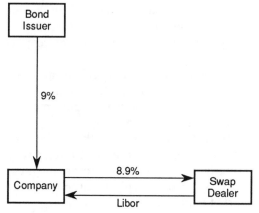

Figure 1-7. Investor Swap diagram.

Reset Date

The floating leg of a Swap must be reset or recalculated periodically. Let's look at an interest rate Swap with a fixed rate swapped against six-month Libor. The day that the Swap was executed, a Libor contract was also selected and, assuming a spot start, both the fixed rate and floating rate begin to accrue. Now in our simple example, the floating rate must be reset periodically usually to coincide with the tenor of the floating leg. Thus the floating leg of a Swap against six-month Libor is reset every six months and a Swap against three-month Libor is reset every three months. Since Libor is set two business days before the contract starts, the reset date is two days before the beginning of the new period.

Cashflows

Let's look at Shenandoah's cashflows. Shenandoah will receive 9 percent from the bond issuer. It will pay 8.9 percent to the Swap counterparty from whom it will receive Libor. Nora Lewis has converted the company's interest income to a floating rate of Libor plus 10 basis points (9.0% − 8.9% + Libor). The effective rate on Shenandoah's investment is Libor plus 10.

Who Uses Interest Rate Swaps?

The two simple examples presented so far indicate that both borrowers and investors have legitimate needs for the Swap market.

Borrowers can use the Swap market not only to lock in costs, but also to unlock their costs should they expect rates to fall. A borrower with a fixed-rate loan, who feels that interest rates have peaked might choose to "unlock" his or her fixed rate and let the interest expense float down. (Of course, if the borrower is wrong in his or her outlook, the interest expense will float up.)

Similarly, investors who feel that interest rates have peaked can "lock in" fixed rates and sit back and smile as they watch rates decline.

Swaps can also be used to lock in current rates in anticipation of future borrowing needs. We'll see how that works in Chapter 5.

The Swap market is also used by Swap dealers and others who take positions and speculate on the future direction of interest rates, Swap spreads, or both. In fact certain (many?) traders view customer business as a nuisance, getting in the way of what they really want to do—take positions based on their own market expectations.

Borrowers versus Investors

You will note as you read through this book, and most other literature about Swaps, that most of the examples revolve around borrowing, not investing. This is because the Swap market is used heavily by borrowers and to a much lesser extent by investors. This will be made even clearer when you read Chapter 2, "History of the Market." You'll note that most of the major developments in the marketplace were driven by borrowing phenomena.

Borrowers with access to the Swap market will calculate where they can get the best rate. If they want a floating-rate loan, they will calculate the floating rate they can get from their lender and compare that to the floating rate they can get by issuing a fixed-rate debt and then swapping it to floating, or vice versa.

Notional Amount

The preferred size for each Swap transaction is $25 million. Smaller trades are done, and much larger trades are also done. In fact, certain institutions prefer large trades. The size of each transaction is referred to as the *notional amount*. When a dealer asks you what the notional amount of your proposed trade is, he or she is asking you how much you want to do. Typically, if you are trying to lock in a rate, your notional amount will be the same amount as your loan or investment.

However, if you have a large amount, you may want to use several different Swap houses, and the transaction may be done in several different pieces at several different points in time. You might want to average in.

For example, a $100 million transaction might be broken into four pieces (sometimes referred to as *tranches*). Each tranche may or may not have the same notional amount, but the sum of the notional amounts for all four tranches would add up to $100 million. Typically, the tranches would have the same maturity.

What Moves Swap Spreads?

We all, theoretically anyway, understand a little bit about what moves interest rates. What moves Swap spreads is not so easy to understand and is open to much debate. But here is a very rudimentary explanation.

Swap spreads of different maturities are affected by different phenomena. Conventional wisdom and Swap market tradition tell us that spreads (at all maturity levels) have an inverse relationship to the level of interest rates. Pretty simple actually. As rates go down, spreads go up, and vice versa.

This relationship did not hold up during most of 1991. Both rates and spreads plummeted. With nearly everyone expecting lower interest rates, corporates stayed out of the market, waiting for lower rates. This, combined with the incredibly low rates on the floating side, forced spreads close to historical lows. (Some say that perhaps the whole structural level of spreads has shifted downward.) What has become patently clear from this experience is that Swap spreads, as with most goods, are subject to the laws of supply and demand. With so little demand on the part of corporates to fix rates, the level of spreads (price) shifted downward.

Longer dated (i.e., five or more years) Swap spreads are typically driven by customer business. As corporates issue new debt, they typically use the Swap market to fix the rate. This will cause the spreads to rise if many companies come to market at once. When there is little new issuance of debt (or those issuers choose not to fix), longer-term spreads will decline. Along the same line, if corporates become convinced that rates are going to rise, they may come to the Swap market, forcing spreads upward.

Short-term spreads are driven to a lesser extent by debt issuance. These spreads are tied to the Eurodollar futures markets.

Affect of Credit Crunch on Swap Spreads

One thing that drives spreads is supply and demand. If financial institutions are cutting all but their very best customers out of the Swap market, the demand has been cut. Even if this cut is an artificial cut and these corporates would like to do some Swap business, the decrease in demand is there. The fact that many corporates have been cut off from the Swap markets by lack of credit has had an affect on the level of spreads. As indicated before, lack of demand will drive spreads lower—and the market doesn't differentiate why the demand is not there.

U.S. Dollar Interest Rate Swaps

All the examples in this book, unless otherwise noted, will refer to U.S. interest rates. Obviously, interest rate Swaps are available in many other currencies. Japanese borrowers can swap their fixed-rate yen borrowings for yen Libor, Canadians for Canadian Libor, and so on. These Swaps work the same way as U.S. Swaps, except payments are made in local currencies, not U.S. dollars (unless the interest rate Swap has been combined with a currency Swap as well).

Market conventions for the payments may vary. For example, floating payments for U.S. dollar Swaps are generally calculated on an actual number of days and a 360-day year basis. Yen floating rates are calculated on an actual number of days and a 365-day year basis. This point is not meant to confuse the issue but to show the reader that before entering into a Swap in any currency, he or she should confirm with the counterparty all relevant terms. Some of these market conventions will be explained in Chapter 8, "Other Refinements in Swap Pricing."

Expanding the Theory

As we'll discuss a little later in the book, the first Swap was not an interest rate Swap but a currency Swap. Financial markets feed on one another. A concept developed in one market is quite frequently borrowed by another. The concept is modified to meet the needs of the particular market. A simple example of this might be the concept of options. First we had stock options on individual stock. Now we can buy or sell options on futures contracts, baskets of stock, and, as we'll see later, even Swaps.

The theory behind Swaps, the exchange of one type of a payment for another, is spreading to other markets. Commodity Swaps have become quite popular, especially where the underlying commodity is anything related to oil. These Swaps are cash settled, making them much cleaner than futures (no fear of having to take or make delivery), and are being written in growing numbers.

The theory has also expanded to equities, where we now have money managers and others involved with equities writing Swaps related to equity indices instead of simple interest rates. Who knows what will be next?

2
History of the Swap Market

One might say that the interest rate Swap market developed as an offshoot of the foreign exchange market. The first Swaps, which were currency Swaps, were done in the very early 1980s. (Currency Swaps with the same currency on both legs of the transaction are known as *interest rate Swaps*.) In the beginning the market was quite awkward because the Swaps were done on a completely matched basis, and they typically were brokered. Because there was no hedging, just matching the two transactions was not completed with the ease or timeliness that we see in the marketplace today. There was also no standardization of documentation, and each party had its own means and techniques for evaluating the creditworthiness of the potential counterparty.

In August 1981 this fledgling market received the impetus it needed to attain legitimacy. The World Bank, with its large borrowing needs, was often able to borrow most cheaply in U.S. dollars. The size of its borrowings often would be too large for the European markets it desired to enter. For example, the World Bank might need to borrow Swiss francs, but the size of the borrowing could not be absorbed easily by the Swiss market. In 1981, the first currency Swap involving two prestigious creditworthy counterparties—IBM and the World Bank—was arranged. This transaction gave the market the legitimacy and impetus it needed to attract other creditworthy participants. The IBM/World Bank currency Swap is believed to be the first Swap ever.

The market began in a small way, by today's standards. In 1982, there was only $5 billion notional amount of Swaps outstanding. Most, if not all, of that was done in 1982. A year later the market had grown to $20 billion, and the market doubled the following year. Compare that with almost $2 trillion notional amount outstanding for currency and interest rate Swaps at the end of 1989 and almost $3 trillion a year later.

In the mid-1980s, with rates at lower levels in the United States, investors began to look with great interest at the much higher yields in New Zealand and Australia. You may remember that a number of funds began pushing investments in these two countries. At the same time, borrowers in New Zealand and Australia were attracted to the single-digit borrowing rates available in the United States and in certain European countries. Borrowing or investing in a currency different from the ultimate repayment currency can expose the borrower or investor to additional risk that can more than eat up any profits or savings if the repayment is not hedged. Thus, the interest differentials around the world gave the currency Swap market a boost.

Evolution of the Interest Rate Swap Market

In the early 1980s, with interest rates high and the United States in recession, borrowers had a difficult time getting long-term fixed-rate funding. Banks, in fear of even higher rates, had learned from the S&L debacle of the 1970s and were reluctant to lend at a fixed rate for long periods of time. Investors also were reluctant to lock in fixed rates for long periods of time. They, too, were concerned that rates would go higher and that they would "miss out" on it. This put all but the very best credits in a position of borrowing short term at a floating rate (sound familiar?)—not a place where most borrowers, who also remembered even higher rates, wanted to be. An interest rate Swap was a natural extension of the currency Swap market. Although we don't know what the first interest rate Swap was, we know that by 1982 there was an interest rate Swap market.

Fixed-rate payors of reasonable credit quality were able to obtain funds at a better rate in the Eurobond market than from a domestic bond issuance. Those desiring floating rates were then able to swap these obligations in the interest rate Swap market to obtain a lower floating rate—sometimes even sub-Libor. Swap dealers began to follow new Eurobond issuance in an effort to forecast the direction of spreads. Meanwhile, those who did not have access to fixed-rate financing were able to swap their floating obligations for a fixed rate in this market.

Interest Rate Futures

The mid-1970s had given those concerned about managing their interest rate exposure the first tool to address this problem—interest rate futures. These vehicles were first traded (and continue to be so traded) on the same exchanges that traded commodity futures. GNMAs (Ginnie Maes) and Treasury bills were among the first interest rate contracts traded. Treasury notes, Eurodollar futures, and other interest rate contracts were quickly developed. These contracts were based on underlyings with longer maturities.

With the exception of the Treasury bond contract, most allow cash settlement. This helps simplify the life of the hedger—no problems with delivery, short supply of collateral in the marketplace, or trying to figure out the "cheapest to deliver" underlying. Despite the obvious benefits of interest rate futures as hedging vehicles, there are some disadvantages: The complete lack of customization, daily settlement, and relatively short lives of the contracts are a few.

Expansion of Interest Rate Futures

Interest rate futures have become the most popular contracts traded. As of this writing, the Chicago Mercantile Exchange (the CME or the Merc) has announced plans for a massive expansion, and that interest rate and currency futures will have trading pits on their own floor when the construction is completed. No more sharing a floor with commodity pits.

And trading is no longer limited to those few hours when the markets are open. Thanks to technical advances undreamed of a generation ago, round-the-clock trading is now available.

Swap Futures Contracts

Swap futures contracts, first introduced in the early 1990s, have proved less successful than other interest rate contracts. Two contracts were introduced originally—a three-year and a five-year contract. The three-year contract has been delisted and replaced with a ten-year contract.

ISDA

In May 1985, ISDA, the International Swap Dealers Association, was formed. It was formed by representatives from several international market participants active in both the interest rate Swap market and the currency Swap market. The formation of ISDA and the work it has done are one of the primary reasons that the market has matured to the point it has and is as liquid as it is. It is hard to find a market participant who has anything bad to say about ISDA because ISDA has been solely responsible for getting documentation of Swaps standardized.

ISDA and Documentation

Before ISDA, documentation was done on a case-by-case basis with each detail being negotiated each time two new institutions decided to do business. Not only was this time-consuming, but it sometimes got in the way of the real business, not to mention the legal costs for preparing and negotiating new documentation. Now all market participants use what's referred to as the ISDA master and negotiate only a schedule. The schedule contains those items that differ from the master. Most companies and financial institutions have a few standard items that they always negotiate either into or out of the master.

A copy of the latest ISDA master appears in Appendix C. A quick look at it will make most realize why many market participants are so thankful for ISDA. A thorough reading of the master is recommended for all serious market participants. The days of letting documentation slide or perhaps even unwinding the transaction before the documentation is really worked on are probably gone forever.

In addition, there is also an ISDA standard confirm which many use. The confirm spells out the details of each trade governed by the master. A new confirm is sent for each trade. Again, having a standard confirm makes business much easier and fluid for market participants.

Additional ISDA Business

Membership in ISDA has expanded from the original market makers who founded the institution to include corporations, software firms, and law firms. Over 140 institutions are now members. Officers and directors of ISDA are from the large market participants.

ISDA states that its "primary purpose is to promote practices conducive to an efficient Swap market and to foster high standards of business and commercial conduct." That is just the beginning. It also conducts seminars around the world, formulates position papers on issues relevant to its members, and has developed a number of fine publications in addition to the master. When the Caps, collars, floors, and options market developed, ISDA was right there. It has developed standard addenda to its master to cover these products. It is safe to say that the Swap market would not be where it is today without ISDA.

ISDA's headquarters is in New York. To obtain additional information, write to ISDA at 1270 Avenue of the Americas, New York, NY 10020, or call (212) 332-1200. The people at ISDA are extremely helpful.

Marketplace Development

Interest rate Swaps now dwarf currency Swaps by approximately three times the notional amount of interest rate Swaps outstanding. This gap has the potential to grow even bigger by 1999, when the European Community adopts a uniform currency (assuming they do).

In the early 1980s, most interest rate Swaps involved the exchange of a fixed-rate payment for a floating-rate payment, most typically Libor. And even today, the lion's share of interest rate Swaps is fixed for floating. However, a market for Swaps with the exchange of one floating payment for another, say Libor for commercial paper, developed in the mid-1980s. These typically are referred to as floating/floating Swaps or *basis Swaps*.

Unlike in today's Swap market, the big players in the early days tended to be the American commercial banks, certain investment bankers, and many S&Ls. This changed when the S&Ls got into financial difficulties and the market became intensely credit sensitive. The S&Ls have largely faded out of the picture, as have many American commercial banks. Many of the original players are finding it difficult to compete in a market that has become overly credit conscious. Their place is being taken by the large, highly rated European and Japanese banks, many of which are not household names. The investment bankers remain big players.

Security Pacific, once a premier player in the market, saw its franchise fade as its credit rating fell. However, many on the original Security Pacific team have been snapped up by other market players—DKB, Deutsche Bank, Lehman Bros., and Citibank, to name a few.

As hedging and financing strategies become more sophisticated, the institutions that can arrange the financing and imbed in those financing, hedging strategies involving both interest rate and foreign exchange components will attract the largest market share. The investment bankers, along with a few of the major U.S. commercial banks with decent credit ratings, have a real shot at becoming the big players in the 1990s in this growing market niche. Bankers Trust and Merrill Lynch are two names that come readily to mind in this category, although they are by no means alone.

Swaps and Christmas Clubs

How did those beginning players get started in Swaps? What do Swaps and Christmas clubs have in common? Nothing, unless you're Rich George, Vice President—Global Swap Group for Merrill Lynch Capital markets. In 1986, Rich was a bright young corporate lending officer for Canadian Imperial Bank of Commerce (CIBC) on the West Coast. He was approached by the bank to market a new product that was the wave of the future—interest rate Swaps. It seemed like a great opportunity, and although the bank was a little vague on details (like where Rich's office would be), Rich jumped at the opportunity. The next thing he knew, he was sitting on the platform of one of the bank's retail branches on the corner of Flower and 7th—10 feet from a teller's window. Not exactly the busy trading floors with screens and phones and computers and trading assistants that we today associate with a Swap trading and marketing operation. And certainly not the support that Merrill Lynch provides Rich today.

For the first few months in his new job, Rich solicited Swap business in between retail requests to open checking accounts and Christmas clubs. Because there were no screens, he was forced to call brokers just to get Treasury yields and spreads. When he called me in those days to solicit business, he never told me he was putting me on hold to call a broker to get a quote!

The profits were good—three or four basis points instead of the one or two that Swap dealers squeeze out today. Of course, the dealers had to work much harder as they ran a completely matched book. No hedging or averaging and certainly no position taking. And when two parties were finally lined up, there could be further negotiations to work out an agreement on all the details. And it was not always easy to find a willing and able counterparty. Rich tells a story about one of his first bosses who once stayed up all night shopping around the globe for a counterparty for a $50 million seven-year transaction. Today that trade could be hedged in the Treasury market in a matter of minutes (if not seconds). So, I guess they did have to work a little harder. But the profits and intrigue of this new instrument soon led many into the business.

Hiring

En Masse Hiring

Not all desks evolved the way CIBC's did. As in other parts of the financial world, sometimes a whole group of specialists were hired. Sometimes there was a formal arrangement where a number of people from the same institution were hired by a second institution, as was the case in 1991 when DKB hired Denise Boutross and a dozen others to start up its Swap group. Other times it was less formal; one person, usually a more senior person, would be hired and over the next few months would in turn hire a number of former colleagues. Before you knew it, half the old group was working at the new institution.

Boutique Hiring/Merging

As the derivative markets evolved, a number of small boutiques opened up and began to thrive. Many of these smaller organizations developed proprietary computer models that allowed them to profit from small nuances in the market. Although they were quite profitable, many did not have the capital to play in a really big way. After all, you can make much more money if you have several hundred million to trade with, than if you "only" have several million. A number of these small firms, although quite low key, developed excellent reputations.

In order to get the capital and backing to do the trading they wanted, several of the boutiques formed alliances with larger institutions. The most famous was the merging of the O'Connor group with Swiss Bank. Many market participants predict that most boutique operations will either merge with a larger firm or eventually disappear.

Non–U.S. Dollar Interest Rate Swaps

As might be expected, the lion's share of interest rate Swaps done in those first few years were U.S. dollar interest rate Swaps—that is, a fixed rate based on a spread over the comparable Treasury note for U.S. dollar Libor. (Unless otherwise indicated, *Libor* in this work refers to *U.S. dollar Libor*.)

In the late 1980s, activity in interest rate Swaps denominated in currencies other than U.S. dollars took a giant leap forward. In 1987, roughly 75 percent of new interest rate Swaps were denominated in U.S. dollars. Prior to that, non–U.S. dollar interest rate Swaps were virtually nonexistent (a slight exaggeration, of course). By 1989, this percentage dropped to 65 percent, and six months later, it approached 50 percent. These drops in market share do not indicate a drop in activity in U.S. dollar interest rate Swaps, as the numbers seem to imply. Rather they indicate a tremendous growth in total interest rate Swap activity. As a matter of fact, total interest rate Swap activity more than doubled between 1987 and 1989. Interest rate Swap activity increased another

50 percent in 1990, while currency Swap activity was up another 33 percent. Activity in 1991 showed no increase over 1990.

Although as of this writing figures for 1992 are not available, it is expected that when the final figures are in interest rate Swap activity will show a decline. This reflects the effect of the credit crunch and the overwhelming reluctance of certain corporates to lock in fixed rates as both rates and spreads fell during the year.

Most of the non–U.S. dollar interest rate Swap activity is in three currencies: yen, sterling, and marks. Interest rate Swap activity in the Australian dollar has begun to grow. Activity in other currencies is minimal. It should be apparent (and I want to stress the point, in case it's not) that non–U.S. dollar interest rate Swaps are very different from currency Swaps. The later involves the exchange of a fixed rate for a floating rate denominated in a currency other than U.S. dollars, and the later involves the exchange of two different currencies.

Tenor of Swaps

The tenor, or average length, of a Swap has probably decreased in the last few years. In the early days, the average tenor was five to seven years. There are a few players willing to go out for 30 years (at exorbitant rates), but on average the tenor of most Swaps has decreased. Although 30-year Swaps were not done in the early days, 10-year Swaps were done without blinking an eye. Today, in order to do a 10-year Swap, a corporate must have an excellent credit rating (AA or better). Even for an institution with an excellent credit rating, certain Swap houses prefer to avoid this activity. Most interest rate Swaps today have a tenor under seven years, with the largest share going to the under-five-year maturity.

Plain Vanilla Swaps

In the early days, Swaps were stand-alone products. They were usually not directly tied to a financing or asset. This has changed. Certain market players pride themselves on bringing extra value to a transaction because they can tie the two together and imbed the Swap in the transaction. However, there still remains a large market for the plain vanilla transaction.

Secondary Market

As with other financial instruments, it didn't take long for a secondary market to develop. A market for unwinds and assignments began to develop almost immediately. Once traders figured out how to hedge a transaction in other financial markets (mainly with Treasury notes originally, but eventually with interest rate futures), the Swap market became more liquid. No more phoning all around the world just to close one trade. Now, instead of running a completely matched book (transaction by transaction), dealers were able to introduce more sophisticated hedging techniques and hedge the entire book—or less than the entire book, should the dealer wish to take a position.

The development of these new hedging techniques, along with the secondary market, gave dealers the ability to fine-tune their book. The evolution of the market also gave rise to a decline in spreads. Once the market became established and competitive, the difference between the bid and offer on transactions narrowed.

Derivative Products

FRAs

Shortly after the Swap market began, a market for a new derivative product sprung up. In 1983, the FRA (Forward Rate Agreements) began to emerge. As with many other derivative products, most of the activity is in U.S. dollars. And as with most other derivative products, the large bid offer spreads available in the early days have disappeared—especially for those contracts written with shorter tenors.

Caps

Anyone issuing floating-rate debt is concerned about rising rates. There's always that nagging fear that you could be wrong about the direction of rates. Even if you're right, there's always the chance that something totally unrelated to interest rate markets will happen and cause rates to skyrocket. Those intimately involved with bond markets will remember that the markets went crazy in the hours immediately after the 1991 attempted coup in Russia. By the time the U.S. markets opened, the markets had calmed down, but overseas markets saw bond prices move several points in immediate reaction to the news.

In 1987, as the stock market crashed, it was impossible to get live bond prices off normally reliable screens. Even good dealers had trouble holding a price for more than a second or two. In fact, when the stock market first started its 500-point decline, rates rose quickly. Anyone who went long bonds that day made a tidy profit if the positions were held for a short while. And, of course, rates rose when Iraq invaded Kuwait in 1990.

These are the types of unpredictable political events that can cause markets to react violently. These are the types of things that make floating-rate debt issuers very nervous. Many floating issuers are happy to pay a fee to cap their interest rate exposure. It gives them the best of both worlds. In 1985, the market for this product—Caps—developed quickly. Just as the Swap market achieved a certain legitimacy owing to the IBM/World Bank Swap, the Cap market had a big trade that helped establish it.

Twenty large U.S. banks floated a $2.75 billion floating-rate issue. The issue contained an option that capped the interest rate. The issuers "stripped" the Cap feature from the notes and sold them for an up-front fee. S&Ls were the biggest buyers of this first "sale" of Caps. It is not hard to understand why this product would be a godsend to S&Ls concerned about funding fixed-rate mortgages with floating-rate deposits. Unfortunately, the S&Ls' Caps did not help solve their problems when rates fell and their customers rushed to refinance their fixed-rate mortgages—but that's another story.

As corporates began to use Cap options, banks began not only to run matched books in them, but to trade them.

Floors

Just as borrowers were concerned about high rates, investors were concerned about low rates on their investments. This gave rise to the sister product, usually discussed in the same breath as Caps, known as floors. The market for this product is much smaller, and quite frequently floors are sold in an attempt to reduce the cost of a Cap. The uses for these products are discussed in much greater detail in Chapter 10, "Other Derivative Products."

Evolution of the Cap and Floor Market

Although the first Cap trades involved Caps on U.S. dollar interest rates, it was natural that this activity would spread to interest rates in other countries. The first real boost to the non–U.S. dollar Cap market came in 1989 when activity in deutsche mark Caps and floors grew as a result of German unification. It was around this same time that the market for Caps and floors denominated in yen also took off as Japanese banks began to speculate using these products.

As with Swaps, the bulk of the activity remains in the less-than-five-year maturities. Longer than that, these options can get quite expensive.

Commodity Swaps

Financial futures lack certain attributes that make interest rate Swaps more attractive to managers hedging interest rate exposure.

Commodity futures also have similar drawbacks. Commodity Swaps (i.e., the swap of a fixed-rate payment for a market price payment) first became available in 1986. The commodity Swap allows a producer or end user to lock in a current price or to float and get a market price at the time the contract matures. The commodity Swap, very much modeled on interest rate Swaps, allows customization needed by market participants.

Although longer tenors are available, the average length of a commodity Swap appears to be around two years. The first commodity Swaps were related to oil, and the bulk of activity still appears to be related to these commodities despite the possibility of structuring a transaction around any commodity imaginable.

Swaptions

Swaptions (an option on a Swap) did not become a popular tool for hedgers and interest rate speculators until the late 1980s. Although Swaps, both currency and interest rate, had become very popular by the mid-1980s, the Swaption market did not take off until market participants showed how the Swap market could be used to strip out the value of puts and calls imbedded in certain debt issues. Inefficiencies in different markets allowed smart financial engineers to arbitrage between two markets and extract value. Needless to say, this arbitrage opportunity did not go on for very long.

However, it did give the Swaption market the boost it needed, and it was not long before Swaptions were being traded just as Swaps and Caps and floors were. The U.S. dollar market is the largest for Swaption activity, but the deutsche mark and sterling markets are growing. Swaptions have become such a big part of any derivatives manager's portfolio that Chapter 9 has been devoted to the discussion of Swaptions.

Equities

In 1982, the first stock index futures were introduced on the Kansas City Board of Trade. The following year, the Chicago Mercantile Exchange introduced the most popular stock index future—the S&P 500. Contracts on other indices followed quickly. There are now contracts on most, if not all, major indices traded on most major exchanges around the world. Not only do these contracts provide money managers with a wonderful hedging tool, but speculators love them.

Although options on individual equities have been around for quite some time, it was not until the futures market began trading the stock indices that it was possible to buy or sell options on various indices. This has become quite popular. It has given the average person the means to go long or short the market without the millions of dollars necessary to buy a basket of stocks that replicates the index.

The typical development of many classes of derivatives appears to be first a futures contract, followed by options on the futures, followed by Swaps, and then options on the Swap (Swaptions) and the Caps and floors. In the equity class, we are at the Swap stage. The first equity Swaps are beginning to be transacted. A few years from now, we'll probably talk about the early 1990s as the inception of the equity Swap market. We're still waiting for that first big trade.

Innovative Uses of the Swap and Derivatives Market

Financial experts have long arbitraged inefficiencies among markets. With the development of the Swaps market, it was only a matter of time before that market became another tool to be used in the game of let's make a buck without taking any risk. Several strategies developed. Most played well for a short period of time. Once market participants learned what was being done, the inefficiencies soon disappeared. And then it was time to look for the next inefficiency. And there will be more. One of the first was the monetization of the Cap features imbedded in the floating-rate notes issued in 1985, which were discussed earlier. Here we look at another.

Monetizing Call Features in Callable Bonds

In the late 1980s, borrowers found that by utilizing the Swap option market, they were able to take advantage of inefficiencies in the way the bond market valued the call feature in bonds. The market was charging too low a price for allowing the borrower to include call features in a bond offering. Sophisticated borrowers (or their investment bankers) figured out that they could monetize the value of the call features imbedded in their bond offerings by selling Swaptions in the over-the-counter market. Initially, borrowers were able to realize impressive savings through this type of structure. (This structure will be discussed in Chapter 10, "Other Derivative Products.") However, as investors (maybe they had the same investment bankers?) began to more accurately value these bond offerings, the savings diminished.

Defaults

The Swap market was hit with its first serious default in 1989 from the least likely counterparty—a government entity. Before that, defaults in the Swap market were minimal. Britain had legislation that limited the number of Swaps into which building societies (British mortgage banks) and mutual insurance companies could enter. There was no legislation governing municipalities in this area. That was the problem. The building societies and insurance companies were limited to the total of their liabilities. The regulating authorities believed that the Swap market could be used to hedge liabilities but not for purposes of speculation.

The municipality of Hammersmith and Fulham had debts of £350 million. However, its Swap portfolio totaled £6 billion—almost 20 times as large as its debt portfolio. Unfortunately for Hammersmith and Fulham's counterparties, these Swaps were out of the money to the municipality. The courts ruled that not only had Hammersmith and Fulham exceeded the implied limits, but that municipalities had no authority to enter into Swap contracts at all. Moreover, they ruled that the local authorities had exceeded their authority and that the contracts were null and void. Although all municipalities were affected by the ruling, Hammersmith and Fulham was the only one playing in the Swap market in a big way. One wonders if Hammersmith and Fulham would have been allowed to cash out these contracts had it been in the money!

Effects on the U.S. Market

Needless to say, the large default by a government entity shook up the market. Swap dealers became more cautious about getting documentation completed. Corporates can expect the financial institutions, acting as their counterparties, to ask to see resolutions from their boards of directors authorizing the use of Swaps. Sometimes this may be an extension of a borrowing authorization. Corporates whose authorizations are fuzzy when it comes to Swaps should consider getting updated authorizations from their boards. This protects not only the counterparties, but also the officer authorizing the Swap activity for the firm.

Drexel Burnham Lambert

On the heels of the British debacle in early 1990 came word that the investment banking firm of Drexel Burnham Lambert was going under. Drexel was a big player in the market. When it went under, it was believed to have a Swap book of $25 billion with 300 different counterparties. Its downfall caused market participants to take a serious look at another venerable practice: netting and the effects of defaults on netting.

Netting

In 1989, Congress recognized the validity of netting and in the following year authorized netting in bankruptcy situations. This was a big step in the Swap markets. It allowed banks to net their Swap exposures with one counterparty. Netting decreases the counterparty's risk; therefore, the amount of capital a bank must reserve for its Swap portfolio can be reduced. This allows banks more flexibility; they can also write more Swaps with the same counterparty as long as the exposures net. This is important in the dealings between market makers; it is less important to corporates. Of course, corporates benefit indirectly when market makers have more flexibility and lower capital costs.

More important to corporates is the fact that in bankruptcy all Swaps with the same counterparty can be netted to one exposure. Unfortunately this was not law when Drexel experienced its problems. The lack of ability to net presented a serious problem. Let's see why.

Terminations

Many Swap master agreements have termination clauses. A variety of things can trigger an immediate termination of a Swap. An event of default triggers a termination in most Swaps. So do certain other things, such as bankruptcy, missed payments, and so on. If a Swap is terminated early, the Swap must be marked to market (the same as if the Swap is being unwound). Typically this results in a payment from one party (the party to whom the Swap is out of the money) to the other (the party to whom the Swap is in the money). This appears reasonable except for one thing: Many Swap agreements have in them limited two-way payment clauses.

Limited Two-Way Payment

An interesting concept! The limited two-way payment clause, included in many Swap agreements (including most, if not all, of Drexel's) penalizes a defaulting party. If a Swap is in the money when the default takes place, the defaulting party forfeits the unwind premium. Remember, a default triggers the termination of the Swap. Now common sense tells us that if a party knows it is going to default on an in-the-money Swap, it could and should simply unwind it. But this is easier said than done. Drexel is believed to have had in the area of 2000 Swaps on its books. Drexel's downfall was quick, and the market was well aware of what was going on, making it nearly impossible for Drexel to unwind its winning contracts at reasonable levels.

Now one may question why Drexel agreed to such a clause in the first place. The answer to that is quite simple—it never expected to be the defaulting party.

Full Two-Way Payment

Many market participants prefer full two-way payments, allowing payment to the in-the-money party regardless of which party defaults. This is viewed as being eminently fairer to both parties. Interestingly enough, most Swap dealers today allow full two-way payments among themselves but try and insist on limited two-way payments with their corporate customers. Corporates should resist including this clause when negotiating a master.

So, What Happened to Drexel?

There is some honor among some Swap market participants. Roughly 70 percent of Drexel's counterparties who weren't technically obligated to pay Drexel did so anyway. This gave Drexel the cash it needed to make partial payments on its Swaps that were out of the money. Drexel paid out roughly 70 cents on the dollar. The market estimates that Drexel lost $10 million on nonpaying Swaps. Many of Drexel's Swap traders and salespeople ended up getting jobs at other Swap houses. Many got jobs rather quickly. This must say something about their abilities and reputation in the marketplace.

The RTC and Swaps

In the S&L bailout, the Resolution Trust Corporation (RTC) got some pretty unusual assets: a $9 billion notional amount of off–balance sheet derivatives—not only plain vanilla interest rate Swaps, but currency Swaps linked to yen-denominated collateralized bonds, Caps, floors, and Swaptions. Not exactly what the RTC thought it would be getting in the thrift bailout. In 1991, the RTC was able to unwind $8 billion of this portfolio without disrupting the market and without losing value.

The RTC tried a novel approach. First it marked each Swap to market and used cash to bring the Swap to par with the original counterparties. Then the Swaps were bid competitively in the market for assignment. It is believed that a good portion of the S&L business was originally done with Salomon Brothers and Merrill Lynch, although by no means were they the only counterparties involved.

After some initial wrangling with the original counterparties about who would be acceptable on assignment, the RTC came up with a list of close to 40 acceptable counterparties. By getting competitive bids from numerous counterparties for each assignment, the RTC obtained the best prices possible and is believed to have saved American taxpayers somewhere between $5 and $10 million. Remember that the next time your Swap dealer suggests that you leave an order and don't shop around.

Risk Evaluations

As the 1980s came to an end, and a new, more somber era began, the Swap market began to discuss risk in a semiserious way. The default by the municipality of Hammersmith and Fulham in 1989 shook the whole market. Dealers who had long joked about letting documentation slide were forced by their credit departments not only to complete documentation, but to submit their customers to serious credit evaluation before entering into transactions. And the evaluations were tough. Many customers sharing long-standing relationships with the Swap departments were turned away for credit reasons both real and imagined. The credit crunch did not discriminate.

Regulators

Around the same time, many regulators became concerned because here was a market, which participants bragged had $3 trillion notional amount outstanding, that was virtually unregulated. In the United States, the Commodity Futures Trading Commission was rebuffed for its attempt to monitor the Swap business. Those institutions pushing mark-to-market Swaps might just give the regulators the entrée they need. After all, what do mark-to-market Swaps remind you of? Because mark-to-market Swaps are a small part of the business, futures regulators lacked the necessary ammunition to institute regulations. But that doesn't mean they will remain unregulated.

Both the SEC and the Federal Reserve Board have voiced their concern. The most vocal has been Jerry Corrigan from the New York Fed. (More about this in Chapters 6 and 13 discussing risk.) There will probably be some regulation at some point in time. Although 99 + percent of market participants are responsible, there's always the chance that someone, somewhere, probably inadvertently, will do something that could hurt the market. And although some of the stories will make your hair stand up, the only ones that will be hurt are those institutions that hire and then fail to monitor these people.

Most other financial markets have traders who take unauthorized positions; a few Swap traders do so too. While these traders make money or lose only a little, everyone looks the other way. But when one of these traders loses a big number, management pretends to be shocked and the trader is very quietly fired. Indeed, everything is kept very quiet, and the institution who hired the trader and then failed to monitor trading activity correctly is the only one hurt. However, there is always the chance that improper trading activities go completely unnoticed and that the institution goes for a big number, which is usually owing to poor monitoring and few controls.

This lack of controls is frightening because an institution could get hurt in a big way through ignorance rather than greed. You may remember the incident in the mid-1980s when Merrill Lynch was rumored to have lost several hundred million dollars because a confirmation had allegedly been "filed" in a trader's (not a Swap trader) desk. Although this story is an extreme example of the losses that can happen when not enough attention is given to controls, smaller losses can hurt smaller institutions.

It should be noted that the unauthorized positions discussed here and in other parts of this book are exactly that—individuals taking unauthorized positions. I am not referring to those individuals who are paid (usually quite handsomely) to take positions for their companies. Such traders are authorized to take positions within specified limits, and these limits are sometimes quite high.

Risk Police

Perhaps in response to the Merrill Lynch incident just described or in recognition of the need to monitor its trading activity, Merrill Lynch has invested a good deal of money, time, and talent in what is known affectionately as the "Risk Police." All trading activity is monitored in a comprehensive proprietary system. Each trading desk has limits that are continually monitored, and those limits may be further broken down at the discretion of the head of the trading desk.

Each time a Swap is done, a trade sheet is filled out by hand by the individual who did the trade. These handwritten sheets are kept long after the information is put into the system. A variety of monitoring reports are generated from the system. As new products are developed, new modules are added. The system is quite impressive, and Merrill should be congratulated on its development.

Do Swaps Have Value?

In 1992, when Olympia & York first ran into financial difficulties, what was the first asset that anyone tried to foreclose on in the United States? Not a piece of real estate or some stocks or bonds, but an interest rate Swap. Morgan Guaranty announced its plans to foreclose on the interest rate Swap and even went so far as to advertise for an auction of it in *The Wall Street Journal*. As of this writing, the foreclosure action has been delayed (hopefully forever).

What is interesting about this whole event involves not only the notoriety surrounding the issue, but the fact that in-the-money Swaps have value and that they are sometimes used as collateral. Chapter 11, "Other Types of Interest Rate Swaps," talks about collateralized Swaps. The O&Y transaction is almost the complete opposite. Instead of pledging assets to collateralize a Swap, the Swap was pledged to collateralize the loan.

Regulators and Capital

One of the things that has regulators so worried is the capital adequacy of the institutions engaged in the Swap business. Because Swaps are off–balance sheet items, they do not have the same capital requirements as on–balance sheet items. This is of special concern to the Fed. Mr. Corrigan has expressed his concern that the next big crisis in the banking community will involve derivative products. Some of the early activity on the part of S&Ls' use of derivatives to manage their interest rate exposure proved that there is risk associated with these products, especially if not used correctly. (For a more detailed explanation of what went wrong with the S&Ls' initial use of derivative products, read Chapters 6 and 13 on risk.) Fortunately, as time passes, most market participants have become better educated.

Off–balance sheet activity can leave the participating institution with more liabilities than appear at first glance on the balance sheet. And, as stated already, off–balance sheet activity has less stringent capital requirements. It was estimated that one of the big Swap players would have had triple the assets and liabilities on its balance sheet in 1991 if it had had to report all this activity on the balance sheet. Those are some pretty scary numbers for an institution that doesn't know what it's doing. However, this institution is one of the most respected in the business. But it becomes understandable why Mr. Corrigan gets so upset about the lack of regulation.

Mr. Corrigan is not alone in his concern. He's just the most vocal. Regulators from other central banks are also concerned. One note before talking about the concerns of most central bankers. The Fed is only responsible for the activity of those institutions that it regulates. Thus, the Fed is not responsible for the activity of investment bankers or insurance companies. Although insurance companies (with a few exceptions) are not big players in the Swap market, investment bankers are.

The Basle Accord

The Basle Accord is a complex agreement that became effective at the end of 1992. The central bankers involved in the accord are concerned about capital adequacy and bank credit risk. In calculating capital requirements, this off–balance sheet derivative activity will be considered. (Later chapters will take a look at how the Swap market has been used in some cases as a financing vehicle.) The capital requirements will be determined according to the risk associated with the activity. For purposes of calculating capital requirements, Swaps must be marked to market. Unfortunately, netting is only to be allowed in cases where two offsetting Swaps have been written with the same institution. Although this is a start, and a much needed one, it does nothing to monitor the activity of a large part of the market.

Netting in Bankruptcy

Because Swaps are a relatively new instrument, they do not fit into many of the existing frameworks for things like financial statements, accounting, taxes, and bankruptcy. Each of the appropriate regulatory agencies is attempting to deal with the relative issues. Certainly bankruptcy laws designed years ago did not anticipate Swaps and what would happen to a bankrupt party who was a counterparty in a Swap or, more specifically, more than one Swap. Bankruptcy courts in the United States have ruled that in cases of bankruptcy, Swaps written with the same counterparty can be netted.

Systemic Risk

Could the downfall of one institution bring down the whole market? Probably not. Although some regulatory help was needed when Drexel went under, that scenario does not appear likely to happen again. As institutions become more credit conscious, many of the problems that have concerned the regulators seem less likely to happen. And as time passes, many of the original Swaps written during the free-wheeling early days have either been unwound or have expired. The system was probably more at risk from these Swaps than from those being written today. However, that does not mean that if the economy improves, the tight credit constraints won't gradually disappear. Maybe the regulator for this business will end up being ISDA. Who knows the business better? One thing seems clear: A market this size will not go unregulated forever. The election of Bill Clinton seems to point in that direction.

Merrill Lynch's AAA Facility

In recognition of the effects of the credit crunch, Merrill Lynch, who was rated A2, designed an innovative vehicle to deal with this fact. When everyone started focusing on credit, Merrill Lynch found itself locked out of doing business with the very top rated credits—some of the very clients for whom they raised money. One of the big innovations in the late 1980s was the ability of many big Swap houses to help a client raise money and marry into that financing the appropriate derivative product. Although in most instances Merrill was still able to raise the money, it could not do the derivative business with those clients who had credit rating restrictions on prospective derivative business.

Merrill came up with a facility that was capitalized to the point where the rating agencies gave it their top rating. This took a lot of work and a good deal of capital. The only clients that this facility now trades with are those rated AA or AAA.

1991

Nineteen ninety-one will probably be remembered as one of the worst years in the Swap markets. The credit crunch hit in a big way, forcing many corporates out of the market. This left less business for the remaining dealers. At the same time, the market tiered. The AA and AAA banks had fewer and fewer counterparties with which to do business—on the corporate side and as competitors.

It will also be remembered as the year when both spreads and rates fell—something that was not supposed to happen. The end of the year saw interest rates at levels not seen in 20 years. The yield curve was extremely steep, keeping many of the traditional fixed-rate payors out of the market. Why lock in 7 percent when you could pay 4 percent Libor. You could always lock in later, and you would probably have saved enough currently to more than offset a slightly higher rate later on.

And 1991 will be remembered as the year of the Salomon Treasury scandal. Although it paid dearly (in more ways than one) for that episode, don't count Salomon out yet. Salomon was forced to make many changes as a result of that affair. One of the changes was a reduction in the size of the firm's assets—from $134 billion on June 30, 1991, to $97.4 billion by the end of the year. This put a crimp in some of Salomon's business activity, but not all of it.

A 1992 *Wall Street Journal* article reported that while decreasing its stock and bond portfolio by $50 billion, Salomon increased its derivatives portfolio by $140 billion. The largest part of this increase came in the second part of the year. This increase is possible because Swaps are still considered off–balance sheet items. Remember, Salomon is not regulated by the Fed and, thus, is not subject to the same regulation and capital requirements as commercial banks. Salomon does not have to reserve as much capital for each Swap transaction as commercial banks will have to do. Given its funding constraints, Salomon simply looked for an alternate route to carry out its business.

1992

January started out with Mr. Corrigan's stinging remarks about risk in the derivatives markets—just what an already shrinking market needed. The U.S. economy began emerging very slowly from a recession that had taken its toll. No one expected a robust recovery, nor increasing rates. This was bad news for the Swap market. One way to increase activity is to have people concerned about rising rates. Then the traditional fixed-rate payers will flock to the market and market activity increases. The only talk about interest rates in 1992 centered around whether or not the Fed would ease again, causing interest rates to decline—not what the market needed for activity to increase. Nineteen ninety-two may just end up being remembered by market participants as the year that was as bad as 1991.

Closing Thoughts

As you read through this book, you'll notice that the topic of risk comes up over and over again. For the corporate analyst, it is important to fully understand not only the products being used, but also all the risks associated with them. And Swap dealers are going to be forced, whether they realize the importance or not, by regulators to deal with the issue. Activity such as was described at Salomon can be very profitable and is probably monitored very closely, but it makes the regulators very nervous.

3
How Rates Are Set

This chapter was written from the perspective of the end user—the corporate customer. It provides Swap dealers with a view of how they themselves are viewed and evaluated by their customers. Corporate swappers are directed on how to get quotes. They are also advised on what to watch for and what to avoid in potential Swap partners.

Chapter 1 recommended that several quotes be obtained before executing a Swap. These quotes are for the fixed side of the transaction. The floating side floats and is reset periodically, usually every six months or every three months and sometimes every month. Swaps are quoted in two ways: as an all-in rate and as a spread. Before looking at both of these, we need to talk about the composition of the Swap rate. The fixed rate on a Swap has two components: a Treasury component and a spread component.

Swap Rate Components
Treasury Component

The Treasury component is the yield on the comparable Treasury note or bond. For example, if you want to do a 10-year Swap, the yield on the 10-year Treasury is used. For a five-year Swap, the yield on the five-year Treasury is used. This is pretty standard, and the Treasury yield that one Swap desk can get should be the same as the next Swap desk. This is because the transaction is hedged (matched) in the live Treasury market as the trade is being executed.

The Treasury market is very liquid, and there are no credit or quality issues. (If this doesn't make sense, just remember that everybody gets the same Treasury yield at the same time.) It's like sugar or salt or some other product where the brand doesn't matter. Despite this, some dealers are better at execution than others. Most dealers claim they're the best when it comes to execution. You'll get a feel for who's the best executor if you are active in the market. And if you're not, you can look at the annual Euromoney polls and see who gets top grades for speed and accuracy of execution.

Spread Component

To the Treasury component is added a spread component. Each Swap desk may have different spreads. They'll be close, but this is where Swap desks differentiate themselves. The desk that wants to do a certain piece of business will offer a more attractive spread. Similarly, the desk that doesn't want to do a certain piece of business, will offer an unattractive spread. (Why a desk would or would not want to do a trade will be discussed in Chapter 4, "Financial Institutions and Credit.")

Typically, the shorter the time frame, the lower the spread. I said typically, not always. Just as we have inverted yield curves (when short-term rates are higher than long-term rates), we can have inverted Swap spread curves. At the time of this writing, two- and three-year Swap spreads are higher than 7- and 10-year spreads, which are approaching historical lows.

Swap Rate

Once you have your two components, you add them together. Now the spread won't change, but the Treasury will be changing constantly as the market moves. Let's take a snapshot view of one moment in time

	Treasury	*Spread*
2 years	7.40%	+50
3 years	7.60%	+55
5 years	7.90%	+60
7 years	8.05%	+75
10 years	8.20%	+80

Figure 3-1. Treasury and spread quotes—indicative.

and look at a few quotes. Figure 3-1 shows some indicative rates. You'll note that in the chart both the Treasury yield and the Swap spreads increase as the maturity of the transaction increases. In a "normal" environment, this will always be true. However, from time to time the environment will not be "normal."

Figure 3-2 shows the all-in Swap rate. This rate is obtained by adding the Treasury yield to the Swap spread (i.e., 7.40% + .50 = 7.90% for a two-year transaction). When obtaining Swap quotes, there are two ways to get them.

Obtaining Quotes
Spread

A Swap quote can be given as just a spread. For example, in Figure 3-1, a quote for a two-year transaction would be quoted as 50 (or + 50 or 50 over the Treasury). A spread quote is usually good for a long period of time—sometimes all day. However, when something drastic happens, the quote can change quickly. The stock market's falling 200 points in an afternoon, war, and the resignation or appointment of an important monetary official are the types of drastic actions that can move markets rapidly.

All-In Rate

Another way of quoting is for the Swap desk to give an all-in rate. For the two-year transaction in Figure 3-2, the Swap desk may quote 7.90 percent. However, because the Treasury market is moving constantly, the trader may tell you that he or she will have to give you a live quote (or freshen up the quote) when you get ready to trade. The quote you've been given is just an indication. If you're not told that the quote is good for some short period of time—say five minutes—be suspicious, be very

```
2 years  → 7.90%
3 years  → 8.15%
5 years  → 8.50%
7 years  → 8.80%
10 years → 9.00%
```

Figure 3-2. Swap rates—all-in.

suspicious. The trader has built in some leeway, and we all know who is going to pay for that leeway.

The Best Way

It's best to get your quotes using the spread method. Remember, the Treasury market is very liquid, and that's where the dealer is hedging his or her transaction. By comparing spreads, you'll be comparing apples and apples and will be able to determine who's giving you the best price. If you have access to Telerate screens or one of the other live systems, you will be able to watch your screens and determine the exact time when and at what level your trade should be executed.

Negotiate the Spreads

The Treasury levels are what they are, but there is usually a little flexibility in the quoted spread. You can negotiate a slightly better spread than what is first quoted to you. If you've gotten several quotes, it is often possible to get one or more traders to improve on their price. Each trader usually wants desperately the trade. (Many are paid a bonus—and usually a large bonus—based on the money they make for their firm.)

Yield versus Rates

As in most transactions, the yield on the Treasury note, and not the rate, is what's important. In the case of our Treasuries, that's the yield to maturity. These figures, which are quoted in the newspapers every day, are the numbers on which the Swap rates are calculated. The initial issuing rate on the instruments has little relevance.

Let's look at a simple example. On August 5, 1991, a seven-year Treasury note (maturing July 15, 1998) had a coupon of 8.25 percent but a yield to maturity of 7.89 percent. In calculating a fixed rate for a seven-year Swap, the 7.89 percent would be used. Similarly, on the same day, a five-year note (maturing July 15, 1996) had a coupon of 7.875 percent and a yield to maturity of 7.614 percent. Yield to maturity calculations can be easily computed using a financial calculator such as the Hewlett Packard 12C. If you don't know how to do the calculations, consult the manual that came with the calculator. You'll also note that I have referred to Treasury notes not Treasury bonds. Any Treasury instrument with a maturity between 1 and 10 years is a note, and because most Swaps are under 10 years in maturity, the term *note* is used.

On-the-Run Treasuries

We've talked about using a Treasury note of comparable maturity to calculate fixed rates. Unless you swap on the same day as the Treasury auction (four times a year for most maturities relevant to Swaps), you'll never have a perfect maturity match. The relevant time periods in the Swap markets are two years, three years, five years, seven years, and ten years. Four times a year, there is an auction for each of these notes. The most current is called *on-the-run* and is used for Swap calculations.

In the previous example, the bond maturing on July 15, 1998, was the seven-year on-the-run Treasury note on August 5, 1991. That note would be the on-the-run issue until the next seven-year auction— October 15, 1991. Even though on August 5, 1991, the July 15, 1998, note is not quite a full seven years, it would be used for all seven-year calculations. Most of the trading in the Treasury market involves the on-the-run issues because there is greater liquidity in the on-the-run issues. On-the-run issues are also referred to as *benchmark issues.*

One last comment, even though many Swap desks quote four-year transactions, there is no four-year on-the-run issue. The yield for the four-year issue is always calculated by *interpolating* between the three- and five-year issues.

wi Bonds

A week or two before October 15, 1991, a new *wi* (when issued) seven-year *bond* will start trading and may be used for Swap calculations. This is something that should be pointed out to the counterparty with whom you are doing business. Make sure that your counterparties are quoting you based on the wi bond and not the old bond. Why is this so important? As was pointed out earlier, most of the trading involves on-the-run issues. The wi bond is about to become the on-the-run issue. On-the-run issues trade at a better price and, therefore, have a lower yield than the old issues. This differential can turn into as much as four or five basis points in a few days. If you are paying fixed, you will want to get the lowest possible rate and can do this by trading off the wi bond.

If the Swap desk insists on trading off the old bond, make sure the price differential is reflected in a lower Swap spread. In reality you don't care what the Swap desk trades off as long as you get the best price. The Swap spreads should reflect the issue. And don't let someone try to tell you it's only a basis point or two difference. That may be true, but make sure the basis point or two is in your favor. In today's rate environment, a basis point on a $100 million 10-year transaction is worth $65,000.

The only time the *wi note* cannot be used for Swap calculations is for specialized Swap transactions tied to a particular issue. This often happens with *spreadlocks*.

Interpolation
Treasuries

Quite frequently the maturity of the Swap desired will not match the Treasury note maturity exactly. A borrower or an investor who is hedging will desire a Swap to the exact maturity of the item being hedged. If the maturity desired is very close to an on-the-run issue, the yield to maturity (hereafter referred to simply as *yield*) will be used in the calculation. Let's look at a simple example where the desired Swap maturity is 6.25 years on August 5, 1991, and we'll use our previous numbers.

Note maturity	Yield
7/15/96	7.61%
7/15/98	7.89%

Now, 6.25 years from August 5, 1991, takes us to November 5, 1997, for the final maturity for the Swap. In order to get the exact yield to use in the calculation, you will need to interpolate between 7.61 percent and 7.89 percent based on the time outstanding. Let's go through the math:

$$730 \begin{bmatrix} 7/15/96 \\ 11/5/97 \\ 7/15/98 \end{bmatrix} \quad 252 \quad \begin{bmatrix} 7.61\% \\ ? \\ 7.89\% \end{bmatrix} \quad .28\%$$

where 730 represents the number of days between 7/15/96 and 7/15/98.

252 represents the number of days between 11/15/97 and 7/15/98.

.28% represents the difference between 7.89% and 7.61%.

The proportion of .28% that will be subtracted from 7.89% is 34.5% (252 ÷ 730). It is the proportionate share of the rate attributable to the time that this Swap will not be outstanding in relation to the seven-year note yield. The 34.5% proportionate share of the .28% is .0966 (.28 × .345), which will be subtracted from 7.89%, giving us 7.7334% (7.89 − .0966) to use in our Swap calculation as the Treasury component for a 6.25-year Swap on August 5, 1991. Your financial calculator can be used to calculate the number of days.

You also could have figured out the number of days from July 15, 1996, to November 5, 1997, taken the proportion of that to 730, and multiplied that by .28 percent. Then you would add your result to the July 15, 1996, rate of 7.61 percent. Either way, you would have come up with the same answer.

Swap Spreads

The interpolation method just discussed is usually only used on the Treasury portion. Although it is possible to interpolate spreads in the same manner, this is rarely done. Usually a spread will be quoted for the maturity desired for a variety of reasons having to do with the way the dealer is running his or her book and the curve of the spreads. Just like yield curves for rates, the curves for spreads are sometimes not quite normal. Finally, some dealers may try to squeeze out an extra basis point for themselves by using a spread that is a little higher or lower than would be indicated if you were doing a Swap of an odd maturity. Question any spread quoted about which you are not comfortable, and, as in any transaction, get quotes from a few people.

A Word about Calculations

All the calculations that can be done on a financial calculator can also be done using Lotus or any other computer spreadsheet program. If you intend to fully understand Swaps, you will need to become proficient with financial calculators or spreadsheets. You'll need to handle YTM (yield to maturity), number-of-days, and NPV (net present value) calculations in your sleep. I use an HP12C, as I mentioned earlier, even though Hewlett Packard has come out with more sophisticated calculators. Most pros use the 12C. In fact, Hewlett Packard intended to discontinue the 12C once it came out with its more sophisticated programmable calculators, but there was too much protest from the financial community. One trader went out and bought a dozen 12Cs to be ready for the rest of his career. Because of the demand, Hewlett Packard continues to make the 12C, which sells for around $70.

Half the Story

In the examples presented so far, we've only looked at one side of the picture. The Swap market is like the futures market: For every long trade there has to be an equal and opposite short position; that is, for every payor of the fixed rate there is a receiver of the fixed rate. All transactions are two sided. Every day, each Swap desk sets a bid and an offer for each maturity. The typical daily Swap quotes for any Swap desk would look like Figure 3-3.

Each day the quotes are revised to reflect the desk's book, its particular bias, competition, supply and demand in the marketplace, and so on. The quotes rarely change during the day. Sometimes in a slow market, the quotes don't change for days. However, if something happens that makes the market move rapidly in one direction—for example, a 200-point drop in the DOW or an attempt on the president's life—the spreads may be updated during the day. Sometimes just a rumor about the health of the president can move the market. Events overseas can also have an impact on our market. The quotes are not set in stone and can usually be negotiated.

Two-Sided Pricing

The Swap quotes given in Figure 3-3 show two-sided prices or a bid and an offer. Your price depends on whether you want to pay the fixed rate or receive the fixed rate. Using the quotes in Figure 3-3, we see that if an institution wished to pay the fixed rate, it would use a spread of 48 for two years; if the institution wished to receive the fixed rate (i.e., pay the floating), it would use a spread of 40 when calculating the fixed rate it would receive.

An easy way to remember which side of the bid offer quote to use in your calculations is to realize that you will be using the one that offers the lesser advantage to your position. So, the borrower who is trying to lock in a fixed rate on his or her loan will always be charged the higher spread. Similarly, the investor looking to lock in a high yield by receiving the fixed rate (and paying the floating rate) will always receive the lower spread.

```
2-year → 40–48
3-year 42– 50
5-year → 45–55
7-year → 48–58
10-year → 50–60
```

Figure 3-3. Swap quotes—two-sided.

Two-sided pricing applies not only to the Swap spreads, but to the Treasury note component as well. Those familiar with the bond market know that bonds are also quoted with a bid and an offer. For example, on August 16, 1991, the 8¼s of July 1998 were quoted as 103.05–103.07. This means that if you wanted to buy the Treasury notes that matured on July 15, 1998, you would have to pay 103.07, and if you wanted to sell them, you'd get 103.05. Bonds and notes are quoted in 32nds. Thus, the "05" and "07" represent $\frac{5}{32}$ and $\frac{7}{32}$.

When you pay the fixed rate on a Swap, you pay the Treasury rate plus a spread. When you receive the fixed rate on a Swap, you receive the fixed rate plus a spread. In calculating your Swap rate, use the bid side of the Treasury price if you are going to pay the fixed rate, and the offer side of the Treasury price if you are going to receive the fixed rate. See, for example, Figure 3-4. The higher price implies lower yields.

Receivers and Payors

In the discussions so far, I have referred to institutions as paying the fixed rate and receiving the floating rate, or paying the floating rate and receiving the fixed rate. This terminology is cumbersome. Market participants simply refer to payors and receivers. When the shortened terminology is used, it *always* refers to the fixed rate. Thus, when you call a Swap desk and say, "I want to receive in 10 years. What's your spread?," you want to pay the floating rate and receive the fixed rate in 10 years. If the quotes in Figure 3-3 were being used, the spread would be 50 over. And if you had said that you wanted to pay in five years, the spread would have been 55 over.

Computing the Fixed Rate

Computing the fixed rate for your Swap is not difficult once you have the right components. Simply add the components together, making sure you use the correct side of the prices. For example, if you were doing the calculations using the numbers in Figures 3-3 and 3-4, you would pay 8.23 percent (7.65 + 58) and you'd receive 8.12 percent (7.64 + 48) if you wanted to pay the floating rate.

Price	Yield
103.05	7.65%
103.07	7.64%

Figure 3-4. Treasury yields—seven years.

Note: A common mistake made when calculating YTM on a financial calculator is the failure to convert the 32nds part of the Treasury price to a decimal before entering the price in the calculator. In the preceding examples, the price of 103.05 would be entered as 103.15625 and 103.07 as 103.21875.

Up-Front Fees

As a matter of common practice, no *up-front fees* are paid to enter a Swap. In the early days of Swaps, up-front fees were occasionally paid by companies to financial institutions that arranged these transactions. These fees, when paid, were small—almost always less than 1 percent of the notional amount.

On the rare occasion when they are paid today, the fees are for the purpose of writing down the fixed rate on the Swap if you are paying the fixed rate (and writing it up, if you are receiving). For example, if the fixed rate using normal calculations were 7.75 percent for five years, a $1 million up-front payment might cause the rate to be lowered to 7.5 percent. This rated reduction is obtained by spreading the effect of $1 million over the five years at current interest rates.

All-In Effective Rate

When looking at the all-in effective rate of a floating-rate loan (or for any transaction) that has been swapped to fixed, it is important to look at all the pieces. Let's look at a five-year floating-rate bank loan at Libor + 100 that has been swapped to maturity. (The 100 represents 100 basis

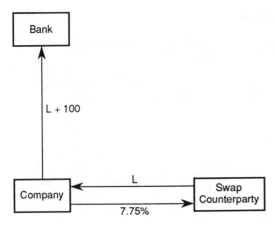

Figure 3-5. Diagram of floating-rate loan swapped to fixed.

points, or 1 percent.) In Figure 3-5, the fixed rate on the Swap is 7.75 percent and it is swapped for Libor. *Note:* The capital letter L will be used to represent Libor going forward.

Now let's look at the companies' cashflows associated both with the loan and the Swap (Figure 3-6). (Outflows are represented as negative numbers and inflows as positive numbers.) You will note that the Libor payment on the loan is offset by the Libor payment received on the Swap. The effective rate for the loan after the Swap is the fixed rate on the Swap *plus* the spread on the original loan. Many forget to add the spread on the original loan when calculating the effective rate. Swaps are always done against Libor flat, so the spread must be added back.

Netting

Swap payments are usually netted. For example, in the Swap just discussed, the fixed portion was at 7.75 percent. If the floating piece for the period was at 6 percent, the company's 7.75 percent payment would be reduced by the 6 percent payment it was receiving from the Swap counterparty, resulting in a payment of 1.75 percent to the Swap counterparty. In addition, the company would have paid its bank 7 percent (the 6 percent Libor + the 100 basis points). The net result for the company would have been 8.75 percent (7 percent to its bank and 1.75 percent to its Swap counterparty).

Swaps with Maturities Longer Than 10 Years

In our discussion so far, the longest maturity for a Swap appears to be 10 years. And that is as far out as the "established" market will quote. As a matter of course, some institutions prefer not to go out longer than seven years. However, several firms (notably, at this writing, AIG and Salomon) will quote a price for longer transactions.

These are specialized prices on a deal-by-deal basis and cannot be easily checked with other market makers. They also reflect the additional

Loan	(L + 100)
Swap	L
	(7.75%)
	(8.75%)

Figure 3-6. Company's cashflow.

risk owing to the length of the transaction and the difficulty in matching it. These additional risks are reflected in wider bid offer spreads. And should you wish to unwind these transactions, in all probability you will be limited to unwinding with the original counterparty—unless the maturity of the Swap at the time you wish to unwind it is less than 10 years.

You might wish to negotiate an unwind mechanism before you enter into the transaction. This will prevent hard feelings owing to what both parties may feel are unreasonable expectations on one party at the time of unwind.

Exchange of Principal
Concept

In certain types of Swaps, especially foreign exchange Swaps, there will be an exchange of principal on the day the Swap starts. (That is, if it were a U.S. dollar Swap for yen, one party would give the other a certain number of dollars, and the party receiving the dollars would give a certain number of yen to the other party, usually based on the spot exchange rate. See also Chapter 12 on foreign exchange, or currency, Swaps.) In an interest rate Swap, there is no initial exchange of principal. This is usually specified in the Swap documentation.

Relationship between
Treasury Yields and
Swap Spreads

Just as the yields on the Treasury notes go up and down, Swap spreads also fluctuate. They may not move at all for days on end, and then, in the course of an active day, they can move several times. The latter is very rare. More typical is the situation where the spreads drift in one direction. Unlike the yields on the Treasury notes, which, while drifting in one direction, will move up a little and then down a little, spreads *tend* to move steadily, albeit slowly, in one direction.

The spreads also tend to move in the opposite direction of the yields. If the yields on the notes are increasing, expect the spreads to decrease. Notice the use of the word *tend*. Although this inverse relationship is true most of the time, it is not always so. Witness the first half of 1991. While rates on the 10-year note fell from 8.25 percent at the beginning of the year to 7.25 percent by the summer, spreads also declined from 75–80 to 47–53, approaching historical lows. This was owing in large part to the lack of demand on the part of fixed-rate payors and wreaked havoc with many financial models.

Monitor Both the Treasury Yields and the Swap Spreads

In order to obtain the best possible rate on your Swap, it is important to monitor both the Treasury yields and the Swap spreads. As discussed earlier, both the Treasury yields and the spreads move. You can get the desired rate on your Swap by movement in either the Treasury or the spread. Let's look at a simple example. Suppose you have a target of 8 percent to fix rates on your portfolio. The Treasury is currently at 7.5 percent and spreads are at +75, giving a Swap rate of 8.25 percent. If you just watch the Treasuries, figuring you'll fix when the note drops 25 basis points, you may be in for a surprise. In a "normal" environment, when the note gets down to 7.25 percent, the spreads might have shot up 5 to 10 basis points, leaving you a little short of your target. If your time frame had been the first half of 1991, and you were looking to pay fixed on your debt portfolio, you would have been in for a pleasant surprise. Spreads would have dropped 5 to 10 basis points, allowing you to lock in at 7.90–7.95 percent.

However, if instead of looking to pay a fixed rate on your portfolio, you were looking to receive a fixed rate, you would have had a nasty surprise. You would have received a little less than the anticipated 8 percent. And, in the prior example, if you had watched both the Treasuries and the spreads, you would have been able to lock in your fixed rate of 8 percent earlier.

Big moves in rates can be partially offset by moves in the opposite direction of the spreads. Typically, this is what happens (although, as we've discussed, this is not always true). For those institutions that trade Swaps on an active basis, this can be especially frustrating; you can be right about the direction and magnitude of yield changes only to see your "profits" eaten up by inverse moves in the spreads (which will be discussed in detail in Chapter 7, which discusses unwinds).

Spread Guidelines

First, spreads move in an inverse relationship to rates *most of the time*. However, just as we periodically have inverted yield curves, there will be spreads that from time to time move in the same direction as rates.

Second, in times of unexpected political events or wild happenings in the financial markets, expect spreads to both widen (i.e., the difference between the bid and the offer will increase) and "pop" (i.e., increase). Examples of such situations include the 1987 stock market crash, the mini crash in 1989, the invasion of Kuwait in 1990, and the coup in Russia in 1991.

Third, usually the longer it takes for the Swap to mature, the higher the spreads will be. As with all the preceding rules, this also is not always true.

What Is Hedging?

I'd like to digress a moment and talk about hedging. The term has been used quite a bit and never fully explained with regard to Swaps. Hedging, broadly defined, is a mechanism whereby the hedger limits his or her risk. It is a transaction that is equal in size or opposite in direction to the item being hedged. The hedger rarely eliminates the risk completely, but he or she does limit it. The reason that the risk is rarely eliminated is that a hedge is seldom a perfect match.

The farmer who is concerned about the price he might get next year for his corn, can use the futures market to "short" his corn position. If he is correct and the price of corn drops, the lower price he receives when he sells his crop will be offset by his profits on his short corn futures position.

Similarly, the Swap dealer will take an equal and offsetting Treasury position when putting a Swap on his or her books. Thus, when you fix your rate, the dealer will go out and sell Treasuries to hedge the position. If you want to receive the fixed rate instead of paying it, the dealer will buy Treasuries. He or she will hold these Treasury positions on the books until he or she is able to execute a Swap going in the opposite direction. When the dealer matches that trade, he or she will unwind the Treasury trade. On shorter maturity trades, the dealer may use the futures market to hedge the position.

The market maker can hedge the Treasury component of the Swap rate in the futures or note market, but there is no effective hedge for the spread.

Matched Books

The lack of hedging ability of the Swap spread is one of the principal reasons that financial institutions run a matched book. As discussed earlier, they make their money from the spreads on the transaction (not the Swap spreads, but the spread between the bid and the offer quotes).

Most do not take positions. The market makers ideally like to match their books as quickly as possible. In a slow market, this is not as important as in an active market. The problem is that spreads can "pop" in either direction on a moment's notice. Who expected Iraq to invade Kuwait or the Russian coup? These political events affect not only the financial markets, but also the Swap spreads.

Occasionally you will get a call from your Swap market maker who has a special deal "just for you." Usually this means the financial institution has a position that it has either been carrying for a while or is larger than it is comfortable with and is attempting to get off its books. Remember, spreads can't be hedged. Usually these quotes are a little better than the market and can sometimes be negotiated even a little more.

But, is it a special offer "just for you"? Probably not. The financial institution has probably started with its most valued customers (who are not necessarily the ones who give the most business) and is working its way down the list. If the deal is better than the market (and you'll be able to judge that if you monitor the market daily), you're probably near the top of the list.

Getting Many Quotes

When you are getting serious about doing a transaction—that is, you expect to trade in the next hour or so—call several of your best contacts and ask them for indications on the spreads. You'll want to tell them that although you've asked for indications, they should be prepared to trade at the spreads quoted. Let them know that you'll set the Treasury level after you've agreed on a spread. If they hesitate to do this (and unless the market is very, very active, they shouldn't), ask them for a quote good for 15 to 30 minutes.

Once you've got all your quotes lined up, eliminate the dealers whose quotes are either too far off or who, if their quote is not the best from your past experience, are reluctant to improve their quote. You should be left with two or three. More than that is unmanageable. Then call them all back, including the person who gave you the best quote, and ask them if they can improve at all. Most of them will. Once you've gotten all your final quotes, decide with whom you are going to do the trade. If your time frame is short, don't call the other two back until you've executed your trade. That way, if anything goes wrong, you have a fallback position. Sometimes your decision will include other factors besides the actual price quoted. There may be business reasons why you will want to do a trade with one entity. And you definitely want to consider the whole relationship. (More on this in Chapter 4,

"Financial Institutions and Credit.") Once you've decided with whom you will do this Swap, you are ready to execute your trade.

Executing a Trade

There are two ways of getting a trade done. The first involves actively monitoring the transaction; the second involves leaving an order. The Swap dealer with whom you execute your trade will much prefer that you leave an order. However, you might be more comfortable monitoring the transaction. Regardless of the method you choose to execute your trade, make sure you go over every detail of the Swap. This should also be done when getting your quotes on the spreads. Don't assume anything. A good dealer will repeat these details back to you. If you've been talking about the same transaction for several days or weeks, go over the details before you get ready to bid. If you're getting quotes from several people, it's easy to forget one detail with one of the dealers. For that reason, it's not a bad idea to make a little list of the details for yourself. Figure 3-7 is a sample list.

Leaving an Order

The simplest, and believe me least stressful, method of executing a Swap is to simply leave an order. After confirming the spread level at which your trade will be executed, decide on a Treasury yield and leave an order with your Swap dealer. Or just tell the dealer the all-in level that you'd like. Usually these orders have a specific time limit (i.e., one hour, or until the close of business the same day) or are "good till canceled." This relieves you of the responsibility of closely monitoring your transaction, freeing you to attend to other matters. When the transaction is executed, you'll get a phone call confirming your transaction. What could be simpler? What could go wrong? Plenty!

Amount
Start date
Maturity of Swap
Name of payor
Floating-rate index
Fixed-rate day count
Agreed-upon spread

Figure 3-7. Sample Swap details.

First, if your order is a little stale (i.e., it has been around for a while), it could get overlooked. This is especially true if your order was supposed to be passed overnight (more on this later). Second, Swap traders may take advantage of your absence and use the opportunity to make an extra basis point or two for themselves. On a 10-year trade for $25 million, this would amount to something around $16,500 for each basis point ($66,000 on a $100 million trade). What's the difference, you ask, as long as you get your rate? You might not get your rate. Your level may have been the top (or bottom) of the market and you've missed your trade. Your Swap wasn't executed. And better for that basis point to go into your company's pocket, especially if you receive any bonus compensation.

Monitoring the Trade

A better method, at least in my opinion, is to monitor the market and make the call for execution yourself. To do this you will need a live Treasury screen similar to a stock quote tape. Live Treasury quotes are provided on services such as Telerate and Reuters by certain dealers. The screen will show live Treasury prices and will continually update them. Once you've decided on the note yield you need, convert that back to a note price, as most of these services provide their quotes in the form of prices not yields. Then you can watch the note trade, and when it approaches your level you can call the Swap dealer.

As mentioned already, you should call several Swap desks and get quotes on the spreads from them all. This might not be a bad time to review with the dealer the details of your trade. You'll try and negotiate the best spread, and when you've agreed upon the spread with one dealer, you can turn your attention to the Treasury note yield portion of your quote.

The dealers will hate you for this. But, as an old boss of mine once told me, "You don't come to work to make friends." When the market gets very close, say several *ticks* (32nds) away from your level, call the broker and place your order. You can do one of several things. Either leave the level and tell the broker that he or she has an open order for five minutes or ask if you can remain on the phone while the broker tries to execute the transaction. Don't ask to remain on the phone unless the market is moving rapidly or the market is right on top of your price.

Occasionally you will see your level on the screen but the dealer will not execute your trade, which means one of two things: The dealer may be playing games trying to pick up a little extra for himself or herself, in which case you are justifiable in raising a fuss. Or more likely, especially if you're on the phone demanding every 30 seconds to know if you're done, the dealer has not been able to get your trade done because of the size. While you're monitoring your trade, also keep an eye on the size of the orders placed and the rapidity at which the trades go off. If the orders are only for $1 million here and there and they are sitting on the screen for several minutes or longer, the dealer is probably telling the truth. You can call around to several other dealers and ask them if anything got done at your levels. This should happen very rarely and usually on a very slow afternoon. If you feel you have not been treated fairly, you should respond in an appropriate manner—take your business elsewhere.

Leaving an Order Overnight

Most major Swap dealers have Swap desks not only in the United States (principally in New York), but also in Tokyo and London, and sometimes Hong Kong. This allows them to execute for you any time of the day or night. Most "pass their book" overnight. The book goes first to Hong Kong, then to Tokyo, then to London, and then back to New York. This allows you to leave an order overnight and have it executed whenever your level is hit—even if that's 3 a.m. where you live.

The disadvantage of this is the same as any other order you might leave. However, if your level hasn't been hit by close of business and you think your level may be hit overnight, this may be your only alternative (unless you have a screen in your home and don't mind monitoring the situation from there). You have a little control because the next morning you can call other dealers to find out the highs and lows hit overnight in the note market overseas.

Confirms

The minute your order has been executed, the dealer will call you back to confirm. He or she will say something like "Done for 25 million at 102 or at 7.74 percent," and you'll reply something like "Done." There is a very important reason for this. Most financial institutions tape the phone calls of their employees involved in financial transactions. This is for their protection, but it protects you as well. If a discrepancy arises and you feel you are correct, don't hesitate to ask them to replay the tape. Because transactions of very large size are handled over the phone, the financial institution needs to protect itself against unscrupulous customers who might decide to renege on an unprofitable trade. It also can be used to settle legitimate disagreements. These tapes are only looked at in cases where a problem arises.

After the trade has been confirmed verbally over the phone, you will be sent a written confirmation. These confirmations enumerate all the details of the trade and are signed by an officer (sometimes two officers) of the institution and will need to be signed by an officer of your company. For your own protection, avoid having the person who executed the Swap sign the confirmation. If your firm requires two officers' signatures, then the person responsible for the trade could also sign. These confirmations are fairly standard in format and have usually been agreed on in negotiations of a master Swap agreement (this will be discussed in the section on documentation in Chapter 4). Confirmations should be telexed or faxed to you the same day or the day following the execution of the trade. Review them as soon as they come in because they frequently contain mistakes.

Learn Which Market Makers Will Take Advantage

Any institution involved in the marketplace develops a reputation. After you've been involved for a while, you'll become familiar with the reputations of these organizations. Not all the reputations will be bad. Some, in fact, are quite excellent not only for their speed and accuracy of execution, but also for the backup support they provide. Many provide excellent newsletters, and some will even provide a portion of the research you may need for a special project. (This will be discussed in detail in Chapter 4, "Financial Institutions and Credit.") It won't take long for you to realize which dealers really will get you the best execution on your trade. When you first set up a relationship with an institution, you'll be told that you've chosen the best. You, of course, will reserve judgment until you can see for yourself.

Certain institutions have developed a reputation for taking advantage of the customer. You will learn which ones they are and either not deal with them or watch them carefully when you do.

Matching Payments

In an ideal situation, a corporation that is using the Swap market to hedge an asset or a liability will have a perfect matching of payments. For example, if the Swap market is being used to convert the rate on a loan, the Swap payment dates will ideally correspond to the interest payment dates on the underlying loan. This is not always possible, especially when you are using a Swap that has a floating component of six-month Libor. But most Swap dealers will customize the Swap to meet the special needs of the customer. This will be discussed in detail in Chapter 8, "Other Refinements in Swap Pricing."

Sometimes the mismatch of payment dates will not bother the corporation. It figures that in the long run it will even out. Other times, it may prefer mismatched payment dates. In a falling rate environment, a company with some flexibility on its loan may decide to make one-month Libor elections on the underlying loan despite the fact that it is receiving six-month Libor on its Swap. When a company thinks that rates are going to start rising, it may then make a six-month election on its loan.

A company can choose to live with these inherent mismatches in the portfolio or can eliminate them by customizing its Swap. As indicated before, the mechanisms for doing this will be discussed in Chapter 8.

Graphs

In reading about Swaps, you will quite frequently see *graphs*. They are common when reading about Swaptions (options on Swaps). To understand the kinds of graphs you're likely to see, let's look at a few simple ones here. Figure 3-8 shows both a fixed-rate loan and a floating-rate loan.

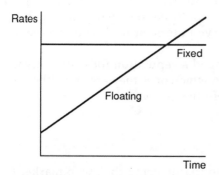

Figure 3-8. Fixed- and floating-rate loan graph (assumes positive yield curve).

Pricing Short-Dated Swaps

Swaps with a tenor of under two years are sometimes hedged in the futures market rather than in the Treasury market. The quote will still be given to the customer as a spread over Treasuries, but this spread is calculated based on the futures market. It involves doing a strip of (usually) Eurodollar contracts. As the futures markets become more liquid in the far dates, some dealers are using this market to hedge transactions as far out as four years.

4
Financial Institutions and Credit

My good friend Debbie Orlando, Director at Barclay's Bank, says, "In this business, all I have is my reputation." The reputation of both the financial institution and the individual Swap person are very important in attracting business. Let me give you two examples.

Reputation

Individual

There are generally two types of traders in the Swap market (and most other financial markets): those who look to establish a long-term relationship with the client and those who look to take advantage every chance they get. The relationship people may make a little less on each trade, but they more than make it up in volume. And who do you think gets those trades where everybody is quoting the same price? It doesn't take long for a firm to get a reputation in the marketplace and the traders who try to take advantage end up with less. Let me give you a few real life examples.

At one point in time, the firm I worked for did a lot of hedging in the futures market. A good portion of this business settled with Merrill

Lynch. The broker at Merrill Lynch, Neil Winter, provided us with a great deal of research support. Whenever we needed figures for a project and couldn't find them elsewhere, Neil would find them for us. As our business needs changed, our futures activity with Merrill dropped off. Our relationship with Merrill's futures area dwindled to nothing. After a while we stopped calling Neil because it didn't seem right to ask for information when we were giving Merrill no business.

One day Neil called me. He said, "You don't call me any more. I suspect the reason you don't call me is that we're not doing any business these days." When I confirmed this he said, "Well don't worry about it. If you need something, please call me. We'll do business again sometime in the future. Don't worry about it." So, I didn't worry about it and took him at his word. And several months later, Drexel ran into problems, and we needed to move accounts out of Drexel. When I was called at 9 p.m. at home and told to try and get new accounts open somewhere so we could move our business from Drexel, who do you think I called?

And let me tell you about Security Pacific. Security Pacific called on us in an attempt to do some Swap business. The firm made a professional presentation and offered us help in any analysis whenever we needed it. So, when we couldn't find numbers we needed, and we were too embarrassed to call Neil, we called Security Pacific. When the market finally cooperated, and interest rates were at a level where we wanted to fix, we began a massive Swap program. As I started calling banks to get quotes, I had a thought. We had to give some business to Security Pacific, even if its rates were not quite as good as the rest.

However, I was not sure my company would go along with this idea. As I was heading to see the treasurer, she ran into my office. "I was just coming to see you," I said. "I want to give some of the business to Security Pacific, even if they don't have the best rates. Unless their rates stink, let's give them something."

"That's what I was coming to tell you," she replied.

Security Pacific's rates were good, and it would have gotten the business anyway, but Security Pacific ensured its place in our portfolio by its excellent service and good prices. The good prices got Security Pacific a bigger piece of the pie.

Institution

Obviously in the first examples just given, the good reputations of the individuals involved reflected well on the institutions that employed them. This is part of the way an institution earns its reputation. Service quality certainly makes the difference when two institutions are competing for the same piece of business and both have essentially the same price. Just as Merrill Lynch and Security Pacific have earned good reputations, others have earned bad reputations.

The bad reputations are usually earned by those dealers who try to take advantage of the customer. They look not at long-term relationships but, rather, at making the most profit on the current trade. Because the financial business is gossip driven, word travels fast. Traders who brag about "taking a certain customer for a ride" would be horrified to realize that this has a way of getting back to the customer. Of course, these proud traders should also take a second look at the transaction to make sure the customer was the one who was taken advantage of.

Warren Buffett recognized the importance of a firm's reputation when he became interim CEO of Salomon Brothers. One of his first publicly stated objectives was to improve the firm's reputation, which improved just by the announcement of Mr. Buffett's new position with the firm. Salomon may have needed Mr. Buffett even without the Treasury scandal. Not too many tears were shed by Salomon's competitors when the scandal broke. And more than one trader claims to have been told by Salomon, "We are the market." Given the recent Treasury scandal, more than one market participant has been known to retort, "Now we know why!" This is probably not fair, but it does go to show how important a firm's reputation is.

Credit Quality

The second part of a firm's reputation is dictated by its financial conditions. Top-of-the-line personnel will not be able to compensate for a poor credit rating when it comes to doing Swap business. Until the last few years, the financial condition of the Swap counterparty was not the major concern that it is today. Of course, up until the last few years, most large financial institutions (with the notable exception of BankAmerica) had reasonably good credit ratings. The drop in the credit ratings of the large U.S. banks corresponds to their fall from prominence in the world Swap market. The ideal Swap counterparty for most companies is an institution rated AA or better. This lets out most, if not all, investment houses and all but one major U.S. bank.

Not only are corporations concerned about the creditworthiness of the financial institutions with whom they swap, but the financial institutions are evaluating the creditworthiness of their corporate counterparties. They, too, are becoming quite selective about those with whom they will do business. Although Swap desks may want to do certain transactions, their credit committees are telling them that they cannot. Customers with whom they formerly have done a good deal of business are being turned away. The market appears to be tiering into two tiers.

The top tier, consisting of the corporate customers of the very highest credit quality, can go about their Swap business as before. This top tier is not very large. Then there is the rest of the marketplace. These companies either do not have Swap lines or, if they do, the conditions surrounding them are quite stringent. These conditions will be discussed in detail in Chapter 11, "Other Types of Interest Rate Swaps."

In addition, financial institutions are beginning to insist on documentation for all transactions. In the good old days, the industry joke was that if you put on a Swap and then reversed it in a short period of time, say a year or so, you might completely avoid completing the documentation (with the exception of the confirm). This worked with a majority of Swap market participants. (More on this in the discussion on documentation later in the chapter.) This is next to impossible today.

Breakdown between Trading and Marketing

As with many other financial products, the responsibility for trading the product and marketing the product is broken down between two different groups. The traders trade the Treasury notes and set the spreads for the Swap transaction. However, corporate customers rarely meet the traders. They will deal with the marketing staff who rarely introduces the traders to the customer. The marketing staff will give you the prices that they get from the traders and are also responsible for bringing in new business. When someone from the Swap desk calls on a corporate client, it is usually someone from marketing. Occasionally, especially if you do a good deal of business or have a special requirement, you will be introduced to the trader.

The trader and the marketer typically have different priorities. The trader wants to get the trade done for the largest profit, and the marketer wants to keep the customer happy. They are often at each other's throats. It is not uncommon to hear a trader accusing the marketer of working for the customer. And there are some traders who think that they don't really need the people who do the marketing. These typically are the traders with no bedside manner who would have no customers after six months if they had to handle the customer relations themselves.

Having said all these bad things about the traders, let me add that there are some very good traders who realize the value of long-term customer relations. You may get to know who they are. In fact, if the relationship is good and your regular contact is out, you may sometimes call the Swap trader directly. However, you may also be encouraged not to do this.

Importance of Customer Business to the Swap Market

What do all traders like to do? They like to trade, take positions, be right in the positions they take, and make a lot of money as a result of their trading. Taking care of customers is a distant second in most traders' priorities. This extends to many, if not most, Swap trading desks. That's why traders need people to handle the marketing side. Let's look at a typical conversation between a Swap trader and a marketer. Variations of this conversation take place every day on many Swap desks.

> MARKETER: My customer wants to...Can you give me a live price?
>
> TRADER: I don't care what your @#$%! customer wants to do. That doesn't fit with our position. Tell them to go @#$%! themselves.
>
> MARKETER: I have to give them a price. Give me a level where you can deal.

The trader then curses at the marketer and gives a quote 3 basis points over the market and adds: "Why don't you go work for the @#$%! customer. You care more about their business than ours."

The marketer says to the customer: "We're not too aggressive today." The marketer then gives the customer the quote and adds, "I think I can get them to improve a little if you want to deal. You know we value your business and want to help you wherever we can."

If the trader happens to overhear this exchange, another round of accusations may begin, sometimes before the marketer hangs up the phone. Many traders, but not all, resent the marketing staff because they feel marketing eats into their profits. Although they would not get a good deal of customer business without the marketing staff, many traders don't care. That's because they really want to trade and take positions based on their views—not take care of customers. Most financial institutions don't agree with this philosophy, so most financial institutions have separate marketing staffs to handle Swaps.

The Customer Is Always Right

Now pity the poor marketers. If their clients are at all sophisticated or knowledgeable about the Swap market, they will know where the market is and have gotten prices from several institutions. When the marketers relate the lousy price, the marketers will now have to experience the wrath of the customer. They are in an awkward position. Many customers, if they feel the trader is either trying to take advantage or pull a fast one, will let the marketer know exactly what they think of the price, the traders, and perhaps the institution as well. And sometimes they are no nicer than the traders. Because the marketers are interested in a long-term relationship with the customer in most cases, they must exercise all the restraint and tact that they can muster. Not a pretty spot to be in.

Usually it is better for the dealer to admit that the price is bad. However, many are reluctant to do this. One of the marketers I respect most is the woman who has said to me occasionally, "This is my price. I'm ashamed to give you this price but this is the best we can do today." The institution I respect the least is the one that, upon quoting a price which was so clearly an attempt to exploit the customer, goes on to explain why it was really a good price. It's one thing to have a bad price; it's another to openly and blatantly treat the customer like a fool.

If the customer wants to trade, the trader will be forced to execute the customer's transaction and then realign his or her book to adjust for this transaction. (We'll talk a little later in this chapter about when the trader might not want to do the transaction.) And the marketers are usually moderately successful in negotiating a halfway decent price on behalf of their customers. This, of course, does not lead to a harmonious relationship between traders and marketers. And in all but a few cases, this lack of harmony is kept from the customers' view.

To be fair, some customers can be just as unpleasant and unreasonable as some traders.

Brokered Transactions

If traders don't trade with customers, where will they trade? They'll trade with a Swap broker. These brokers get the present value of one basis point per year. The bid offer spreads in the broker market are much tighter (i.e., smaller) than in the customer market. Traders who trade in the broker market can do so without having to get their hands dirty dealing either with their own marketing staff or even with customers. And many marketers will tell you that many traders would rather give that basis point to the broker than to the marketer. Traders can and do use the broker market to hedge their Swap transactions. This will allow them to avoid using the Treasury market to hedge a transaction when executing a Swap. And if they hedge in the Swap market, they can lock in their profit and not worry about the spreads. Some Swap brokers include Prebon, Noonan, and Babcock—not exactly household names.

Although there may be an 8 to 10 basis point spread between the bid and offer quotes for a Swap trade for customers (which usually can be improved on by negotiating at the time of execution), there will only be a 3 to 4 point spread in the broker market. Of course, there's the additional one basis point that the trader will have to pay the broker, but it still is a much tighter market.

Interbank Transactions

Interbank transactions is an area that causes much friction between the trader and the marketer. Although the marketer is clearly responsible for all customer transactions and, therefore, the profits on trades done on behalf of customers must be split with them, transactions done with other banks present another problem. Some organizations have staffs specifically responsible for marketing to other banks. In these few cases, there can be no conflict. However, most institutions don't have such specialized staffs.

The traders at one institution may or may not talk to the traders at a second institution. Even if the two traders talk on a regular or semiregular basis, a trade with such an institution may be brought in by the marketer. If marketers bring in the trade, they will feel entitled to a fair share of the profits. However, traders may not feel inclined to share the profits because they also have a relationship with the institution. Many institutions have no hard-and-fast rules regarding interbank transactions. This leads to more animated discussions.

Relationships between Swap Traders and Treasury Traders

If traders are executing a Swap and hedging it immediately, they can do that either in the broker market or, as was noted earlier, in the Treasury market. As with their relationship with the marketer, Swap traders sometimes have an adversarial relationship with the Treasury traders, who are other people with whom to split part of the profits. In the case of Treasury traders, the traders are only getting the spread that they would ordinarily get on a Treasury trade. However, this relationship is rarely smooth.

Dealers Who Act as the Middleman

The Swap market that we have been talking about so far is the market that exists for top-rated companies and financial institutions. The major players are the big companies, big financial institutions, large sovereigns with good credit ratings, and supranationals. There is a second tier in the marketplace consisting of those customers who are either smaller or not as well known. Many of these are very fine companies with excellent credit. They have access to the Swap markets but to a much lesser extent. Their bank will act as a middleman or, as it is known in the Swap market, a price taker. This middleman will, of course, increase the cost to the ultimate end user—the customer.

Using a price taker will cost anywhere from one to five basis points to the end rate (i.e., the customer pays one to five basis points more if the customer is paying; if receiving, the customer will receive one to five basis points less. Many of the price takers are creditworthy regional banks acting on behalf of their customers. However, it is the bank's name and credit on the line, not that of the customer. So, if the customer defaults on the Swap, the bank is left with the transaction on its books.

When Do Traders Not Want to Trade?

A financial institution must allocate credit to Swap transactions. In lay terms, the end result of this credit allocation means that a trader cannot put an infinite amount of Swap transactions on the books. If the credit allocation is used up for the period (usually a quarter), the trader must unwind or assign away transactions in order to put new ones on his or her books. This could be a reason why a trade might not fit with the book. Traders have to hustle to take a position off in order to accommodate the customer. And why should they? It may not mean any extra profits for them (and those extra profits turn into larger bonuses in most institutions).

Another reason why traders won't trade is because the end of the bonus period is approaching and traders have locked up a good profit, thus ensuring a good bonus for themselves. They don't want to do anything to blow that bonus. So rather than take a position, they may prefer to do nothing until the start of the next period. These bonus periods can be as frequent as quarterly or as infrequent as annually.

Also, there are times when the market is dead. Traders know that they will have a difficult time laying off a position and are not comfortable in carrying it. This can happen the day before some economic news is expected. Or it can happen in a slow market, like the spring and summer of 1991. A customer with access to a screen will be able to tell this by watching the screen and seeing how infrequently the numbers change. And if the customer has a halfway decent relationship with the marketing people, the customer will know the market is dead. Their friends will be complaining to them that they're bored and desperate to do something, anything because the markets are so slow. After speaking on the phone with a trader for over an hour one slow afternoon, I asked "How's business?" His reply told the whole story: "Have I been interrupted at all by another phone call? When can you remember that happening before?"

And then there are the simple human excuses. Traders might not want to do a trade because they're tired, hung over, or because they dislike the customer or the marketer. And let me add a word in defense of some of the fine traders who do exist in the market—and there are a few of them. They may be tired or have used up all their capital or the market may be dead, but when they know the customer needs help, they hustle. They'll execute the trade at a reasonable rate in order to help the customer. Then they'll do what's necessary to cover their position— even if it means no extra profit for them.

Execution

We've already spoken about speed and accuracy of execution. This falls directly in the trader's lap. This is where traders distinguish themselves. Sometimes your Swap contact tells you that your transaction is done even though you know the market never reached your level. What happened? Usually one of two things. Most likely, the trader decided to make a little less on the trade and has given you the level you wanted. You've got your price and you should be happy. The trader may think your level will not be reached soon and doesn't want the trade walking away. If you're really lucky, the trader may have a trade on the books that he or she wants to offset. Remember, traders can't hedge the spread, and if they're worried about spreads moving against them, they're better off locking in a smaller gain than no gain.

Or the trader may be sticking his or her neck out and leaving the position unhedged for a minute. If the trader is afraid that you will give the trade to someone else, he or she may execute your Swap and go "naked" for a few minutes, hoping that the market will move so that he or she will be able to lock in a favorable price. Most traders are not supposed to do this, but some do. Traders who are not authorized to leave a position unhedged, even for five minutes, are taking a big risk. If the market moves against the trader, he or she can incur a big loss quickly.

In either case, the corporate customer does not really care what risks the trader takes in hedging the position, but the trader's management may care. It is not unheard of for traders to take positions during the day and close them before the close of business. The positions don't show on the financial institution's books and it would be very difficult to prove later. This is especially true for hedging done in the futures markets. However, as financial institutions become more sophisticated in their monitoring techniques, this may happen less frequently. In Chapter 2, the section on risk police explains how one institution, Merrill Lynch, monitors its portfolio. Although the system was not set up specifically to monitor Swap traders, it does.

Newsletters

Certain Swap dealers send their valued customers periodic newsletters. Most of these are weekly. They contain the pertinent Swap-related data for the week and may contain some commentary on the week just passed and/or the week to come. The best of these are faxed to the recipients so that they will be received on a timely basis. I get a very nice one from a prestigious bank that is printed nicely on good paper and then mailed. The problem is that by the time it arrives in my office, the information is out of date and virtually worthless. The written commentary is only as good as the writer.

Effects of the Credit Squeeze

Owing to their deteriorating credit ratings, U.S. banks are being squeezed out of the market. One of the reasons given for the merger of Chemical Bank and Manufacturers Hanover Trust Company was the intent that the merger would improve the ratings of the combined institutions. Both of these institutions had impressive Swap desks in the beginning days of the Swap market. As their credit deteriorated, corporate clients began to take their business elsewhere. It is expected that once all the cost efficiencies of the merger are worked into the corporate structure, the new entity will receive a higher rating from the credit agencies. The improved rating of the new institution will allow the new institution to compete in the Swap marketplace once again.

The merger of BankAmerica and Security Pacific should work in a similar manner. BankAmerica did not have a real presence in the Swap market because of its prior poor rating and problems. However, its ratings were improving while the ratings of the other big U.S. banks were declining. On the other hand, Security Pacific has one of the best reputations for service and overall Swap capability in the market. Its declining ratings, however, were starting to affect its business. Once the cost efficiencies of the merger work their way into an improved credit rating for the new institution, the new institution will be set to become the major player that BankAmerica should have been and Security Pacific was. There is only one problem. Many of the people who gave Security Pacific its fine reputation have left the bank and have taken positions elsewhere. Only time will tell on this one.

Mergers

Are these two mergers the only ones, or will other big banks merge? The consensus seems to think that there will be other mergers. This can only help make the market stronger. Market share lost by U.S. institutions to foreign banks will have to be won back. This will not be easy. There may be fewer Swap dealers in the market, but the ones that remain will be stronger.

Assignments

There has been a good deal of discussion about the credit rating of Swap counterparties. Why should a corporate customer care with whom it does the Swap? Isn't it like a loan where the focus is on the rate not the lender? There is an additional factor in evaluating Swap counterparties. Many Swaps are not kept on the books of the original counterparty until maturity. The counterparty may have never intended to keep the Swap on its books, or its interest rate outlook may have changed. In either case, many customers unwind transactions before maturity. This can be done in one of two ways. (The math associated with an unwind will be discussed in detail in Chapter 7 on unwinding a Swap.)

The party wishing to unwind a transaction will usually start by going to the original counterparty and asking for a price to unwind the transaction. Depending on where interest rates and Swap spreads have gone since the original transaction was done, the price may be either positive or negative. In other words, the party who wants to unwind may either have to pay to terminate the transaction or may be paid upon termination.

If the customer is not satisfied with the price offered, he or she may go to other Swap market participants and ask for a price. The first thing the other market participant will want to know is the counterparty named on the Swap you are trying to sell. This is where the credit rating of your counterparty is of vital importance. If the counterparty's rating is not as high as the rating of the party to whom you are trying to sell them, one of two things will happen. The "buyer" may refuse to bid on the trade, or the bid offered will reflect a discount based on the lower credit ratings of the counterparty.

Additionally, even if the credit rating is acceptable, you may not get a bid. If one party has too much business already on its books with the counterparty of the Swap you are selling, they may decline to bid. The trader will tell you that he or she is full up on that name. This will happen periodically and there is nothing you can do about it. Finally, after you've found someone to buy your Swap, you will have to check with the original counterparty to make sure that the Swap dealer you are attempting to sell the Swap to is acceptable to them.

Unless the assignment clause is clearly written in your master Swap agreement, the original counterparty may have the right to refuse to allow certain assignments. Most assignment clauses limit assignments to AA-rated institutions, and some allow the counterparty to reject assignments if it is filled on the name.

Financial institutions can be very funny about assignments. Everyone has a certain amount of pride, and most are not crazy about being assigned although most will take assignments. If these situations are not handled tactfully, you can end up with some very angry people. I've seen two financial institutions with identical ratings refuse to take each other on assignments. Each felt that although its ratings were the same, it was marginally better than the other. And I've seen an institution complain when assigned to a clearly superior credit-rated institution because it wasn't consulted properly.

Assignments happen every day. Even the corporate customer who puts on a Swap intending to leave the Swap in place until maturity needs to be concerned. He or she may get a call from the Swap counterparty requesting an assignment of his or her position. If the requesting party is an institution with which the customer has a good relationship, it may want to accommodate its partner. And even if the institution doesn't, it may have no choice. Anyone who had a Swap on his or her books with Drexel Burnham Lambert found itself needing to understand assignments.

Liquidity in Market

Just as a Swap trader can go into the marketplace any time of the day or night to hedge a transaction, the corporate customer with a Swap portfolio can trade any time of the day or night—that is, a corporate with a good credit rating. As discussed earlier, the corporate can unwind its transaction with the counterparty with which it originally did the Swap, or it can assign the Swap to a new counterparty. As long as the credit rating of the counterparty is good, it will be able to find someone to assign it to. In this instance, the creditworthiness of the Swap counterparty is of importance and the creditworthiness of the selling institution is of little concern. But suppose the credit of the counterparty is not so good or the counterparty is over its limit with most major market participants. This occasionally happens.

The institution wishing the assignment can put a Swap on its books with the same parameters as the original Swap, except going in the opposite direction. For example, if the institution wished to unwind a Swap where it was paying a fixed rate with seven years' remaining life, it could do a Swap where it would receive the fixed payment for seven years. If the payment and reset dates were matched, the institution would have achieved the same thing as an unwind with the exception that the up-front cash payment would not be made but would be spread over the remaining life of the Swap. This is occasionally done anyway. (In the annuities section of Chapter 8, this will be discussed in detail.) Instead of eliminating the Swap, the institution would now have two Swaps on its books. But because they offset each other, it would be of no real importance except for one issue: double credit.

Using Double Credit

By holding two Swaps on its book, the company will have used up credit with two Swap counterparties instead of using credit with no one. That might not be a problem for an institution with unlimited access to credit, but it is a problem for most institutions. Most banks allocate a certain amount of credit to a particular company, and then the account officer responsible for the relationship allocates that credit to the various lines of business. A bank might not only do Swap business with a company, but it might also lend the company money and do foreign exchange. All of these use credit.

And they all get added together. The addition is not straightforward, and different things get allocated a different amount of credit. For example, a five-year Swap uses half the credit that a 10-year Swap uses. And short-term foreign exchange contracts use very little. Anyway, by keeping two Swap contracts alive, the corporate client will have used up quite a bit of credit. Most are reluctant to do this as it will affect other business the company may wish to do.

That is in addition to the administrative work connected with keeping the two Swaps alive. Payments have to be calculated, made, and received, and the associated accounting must be done. From an operations standpoint also, most companies would prefer not to keep the two Swaps alive.

Matched Book

We've discussed how Swap desks match the transactions on their books. This is called running a matched book, and that is what most

Swap desks are empowered to do. Any trader who takes positions even for a few minutes is probably overstepping his or her authorization.

Swap Lines

Many institutions will allocate credit to a variety of lines of business. The credit that has been allocated to a particular company will be translated into a Swap line. As you might expect, the longer the Swap line, the more credit it will use up. Let's look at a simple example. A company might be given a $100 million 10-year Swap line. Most, if not all, financial institutions will translate this into a $200 million five-year line. However, a $200 million five-year line is not necessarily the same as a $100 million 10-year Swap line. The financial institution granting the Swap line may not wish to grant the company credit for that long a period of time.

Generally speaking, lines can be translated into larger lines with shorter maturities, but not necessarily the other way. The only exception to this would be if the translation resulted in an amount outstanding that was larger than the financial institution's limits for one customer. For example, a financial institution willing to do a $100 million 10-year Swap might not wish to have a $1 billion one-year Swap with one counterparty. The $1 billion exposure might be too large for one counterparty.

It is not uncommon for credit for a particular line of business to be borrowed from another line. You'll hear dealers saying things like "I lent part of my line to foreign exchange," or "We borrowed the credit from the lending group until we can get a Swap line approved."

Certainty of Swap Lines

Swap lines are like uncommitted lines of credit. You have no guarantee that they will be there when you need them. And although most lines of credit are there for the institution when needed, the same cannot be said about Swap lines. Part of this problem is attributable to the fact that the lines traditionally have been unofficial. In many instances, the corporation will not even know what its line is. In the good old days, most reasonable credits could do as much as they wanted with a variety of institutions. (This, of course, is a slight exaggeration—but you get the point.)

If a line has not been used in a while, the financial institution may pull the line to review the creditworthiness of the counterparty to whom it has granted the line. More likely, when a corporate customer hears this excuse when it goes to execute a Swap, the financial institution has changed its mind about doing business with the company.

This happened so many times during the credit crunch in 1990 and 1991 that certain Swap dealers decided not to check with their credit departments about the availability of lines that had been in place for years. Swap dealers saw their credit departments pull Swap lines when they went before them to have customers' lines increased. Swap dealers who thought they were doing their corporate customers a favor by going to their credit committees to have their lines increased were dismayed to see the lines pulled. Once burned...

Documentation

It is not possible to talk about Swaps without talking about documentation. It is probably the thing about Swaps that people who are connected with the marketing, trading, and execution of Swaps, hate the most. The documentation can be broken into two main categories: the master, which governs the whole relationship, and the confirm, which details each individual transaction. Although there are many instances (as time goes on, however, fewer and fewer instances) when a master agreement never gets done, there always is a confirmation, even if the two sides don't agree on the form of the confirm. The figures (both rates and dollar amounts) associated with each transaction must be verified.

There used to be a standing joke in the industry that if you did a transaction and unwound it quickly enough, say within 12 to 18 months, documentation would not have to be done. More than one Swap dealer has half jokingly suggested to me that we unwind so we don't have to get our hands dirty doing documentation. What is this documentation that everyone hates so much?

Master Swap Agreements

The first part of the documentation, the part that should govern the whole Swap relationship between the two parties, is called the master agreement. Until the summer of 1992, the master agreement was the ISDA document, which was updated in 1987 and again in 1991. In the summer of 1992, a new master was published. The master, along with the 1991 ISDA definitions, governs these transactions. Copies of the 1992 master and a good portion of the 1991 ISDA definitions are included in Appendixes C and D. They spell out every detail of the relationship. All terms are defined, and the form of the confirm is included in the definitions. Ideally, this master is negotiated before any transactions are executed. As suggested already, the master is not always negotiated before a Swap is entered into. So why all the fuss if everyone uses the ISDA standard agreement?

Schedules

To the master, each institution attaches what is known as its schedule. The schedule contains all the additions and deletions to the master. Schedules can be quite lengthy and the source of much negotiation between the two parties. Some financial institutions take a hard line and say, "This is our schedule. We use it in all transactions. If you want to do business with us, you will use it also." Others say this and then bend a little during negotiations. And with others, they expect to negotiate the schedule. There are some items on which institutions won't be flexible; others are open for discussion. And some of the additions to the schedule can be quite interesting.

Here's a sample of what can, if necessary, be negotiated. Olympia & York is a large real estate development company owned by the Reichmann family. Because the Reichmanns are orthodox Jews, all negotiated agreements, including all Swap agreements, define the term *business day* as including not only the standard banking holidays but also 12 religious holidays. So, just as payments cannot be made on July 4 or December 25, they cannot be made on the 12 holidays specified in the O&Y agreements. At first, Swap traders who had never done business with Olympia & York were surprised, but no bank has ever objected to the inclusion of this clause. Although the O&Y "business day" clause is only one example of the special clauses to be negotiated into a schedule, it gives you an idea of the things that can and often are negotiated.

The 1992 version of the master contains a schedule that includes many of the items that are typically negotiated into a schedule.

Confirms

The form of the confirmation is usually negotiated as part of the negotiation of the master. It is usually not a big deal. Sometimes, when a master has yet to be negotiated, the confirm will contain a few unique clauses to ensure that the master will contain clauses important to one or both of the parties. This could include things like the O&Y definition of *business day*, but more often the master contains clauses that a parent company might give such as a guarantee or a statement about the timing of the negotiation of a master or the delivery of financial statements or net worth maintenance. If one party has a point that is of vital importance to it and no master is in place, the point should be negotiated and included in the confirm.

Most institutions use the ISDA standard confirm with few modifications (see Appendix E).

1992 ISDA Documentation

Included in Appendix C is a copy of the new 1992 ISDA Master Agreement. You will note that the master has a schedule to be attached that includes many of the points typically negotiated into masters. For the purpose of this text, the Local Currency—Single Jurisdiction Master has been included. There is also a Master for Multicurrency—Cross Border transactions. The type of business you intend to do with the proposed counterparty will dictate the master you'll use. As you might expect, the Local Currency—Single Jurisdiction Master is shorter.

A second document, the 1991 ISDA definitions, is also included. This document is intended to be used in conjunction with the master. Any disagreements of terms spelled out in the definitions document should be addressed in the schedule. You will also note that a sample confirm is included in the definitions.

ISDA—1992 and Beyond

ISDA, in its ongoing attempts to allow counterparties to document a growing number of derivative products, continues to standardize documents for use by market participants of all sorts. At the same time it published its new master in 1992 for use in interest rate products, several other documents were published. These include a 1992 FX and Currency Option Definitions, a 1992 U.S. Municipal Counterparty Definitions and Schedule, and an Equity Index Option Confirmation.

ISDA also is planning to publish two more documents. The User's Guide to the Standard for Agreements will be published by the spring of 1993 and the ISDA Commodity Derivative Definitions will be published by the end of 1993. The latter should be very useful to new market participants to whom much of the documentation process may appear somewhat confusing.

How Financial Institutions Allocate Credit

Most financial institutions jealously guard their mechanisms for allocating credit. Theoretically, the bank does a thorough review of the company's financials and, in conjunction with that review, makes some subjective determinations. It is these subjective judgments that have gotten some banks into a lot of trouble. It is also these subjective judgments that are responsible for the credit crunch in 1991.

Swaps are off–balance sheet items, so credit is not allocated on a dollar-for-dollar basis. As already noted, banks are secretive about how they allocate credit, but you can estimate that the institution will allocate 2 percent of the notional amount per year for Swaps. So a $100 million 10-year Swap will use up $20 million worth of credit allocation— that is, if a bank is willing to do a 10-year transaction in the first place. Most would prefer to do a $200 million five-year transaction.

This trend will probably change in response to regulators' concerns and will certainly change for commercial banks as the Basle Accord is implemented.

Credit Considerations When Doing a Swap

Although pricing is certainly a consideration when deciding with which institution to execute your Swap, the 1990s has brought a new focus to the counterparty issue. Counterparties are evaluating the credit of their potential Swap partners in a thorough manner not seen before in this marketplace. Not only are they evaluating the credit rating given by the major rating agencies (S&P and Moody's), but they are also evaluating other related credit issues. For example, even a hint of the possibility of a problem or potential downgrade can make it difficult for a financial institution to do Swap business.

The reverse can also be true. Although Security Pacific has an excellent reputation in the Swap market, most market participants had expected them to be downgraded shortly before the merger with BankAmerica was announced. It is expected that the merger with an institution of higher credit rating and the eventual upgrade of the combined institutions will help preserve Security Pacific's place in the market.

Moreover, a firm's reputation in the Swap marketplace can play an important part in the customer business it wins. When making the decision about with whom to do a particular trade has been narrowed down to two institutions, the one that is more cooperative will generally win the business. Some institutions have a reputation that is so bad that their customers hate giving them business and do so only when they have to. Others have such good reputations that companies will go out of their way to try and give them the trade.

Because many Swap transactions do not stay on the firm's books until maturity, the ease with which a transaction will be able to be assigned, should the company wish to unwind, is of key importance. If the financial institution has a good credit rating and reputation, the Swap can be assigned without much trouble. If the reverse is true, it can be difficult to assign the Swap. This is important as it does not tie a company to one institution's pricing. If your counterparty does not want to do a transaction on a certain day, you will want to be sure that you can assign the Swap and get a good price should you wish to unwind. Being able to assign a Swap easily ensures that an institution will be unable to hold you captive to poor pricing. But if an institution has a poor reputation, other firms may tell you that they prefer not to take your counterparty because it is difficult to deal with that party.

Or even worse, if your counterparty has done so much business on the street, most other institutions may be "full up" on that name. You will then be captive to your original institution's below-market pricing. And this institution may realize it and take full advantage of it. Of course, if the organization you wish to assign is difficult to deal with, the "full up" response may be a polite way of saying no.

Managing a Swap Portfolio

Financial institutions manage their Swap portfolio just as they do other portfolios. No longer do most run a completely matched book (although there are a few out there who still do). The portfolios are rebalanced on a daily basis in most cases. Most desks take positions within preauthorized limits. It is difficult if not impossible to hedge Swap spreads. Some desks will speculate in them and will be happy to add positions that reflect their biases. But when they are asked to put on positions that go against these biases, the traders have to hustle.

A Way Around Credit Restrictions

In Chapter 11, "Other Types of Interest Rate Swaps," we'll discuss a number of Swap types that will help those with less than stellar credit ratings get access to the market. These include things like the collateralized Swap and the mark-to-market Swap.

In early 1992, Merrill Lynch came up with a response to the issue of having a credit rating less than AA. Because Merrill Lynch was rated A, it found itself (as do other market makers in the same boat) excluded from doing business with corporate clients who insist on dealing only with those institutions rated AA or AAA. To get around this, Merrill Lynch set up a separate credit-enhanced facility that was rated by the rating agencies. It received the coveted AAA rating and will deal only with institutions rated AA or AAA. Goldman Sachs followed their lead several months later.

As regulators remain concerned and vocal about credit quality and the lack of regulation of the Swap and derivatives market, it's a good bet that the market makers will continue to watch the credit quality of their corporate counterparties.

5

Some Practical Day-to-Day Applications

The strategies discussed in this chapter utilize only interest rate Swaps. Later in the book, we'll look at other strategies, including more advanced products. You'll notice that at different companies, the risk management for the firm is handled by people with different functions. Depending on the size of the company, it may be the controller or the treasurer, or an assistant treasurer or an assistant controller, or the chief financial officer or, at a large company, a financial risk manager who does nothing but monitor and evaluate financial products and strategies. Although some of the real short-term activity could be handled in the futures markets for smaller transactions, there are some disadvantages to that. The futures markets require day-to-day management, a daily mark to market and exchange of cash based on this evaluation (although there are some Swaps that also require mark to market), and allow no customization. The futures market may be useful for smaller trades, but it falls down by comparison to the over-the-counter (OTC) Swap market that allows individual customization and financial innovation as your company may desire. Let's look at Swaps in action.

Synthetic Fixed-Rate Loan

Kate Lyons, the Treasurer of Amerand Corporation, became concerned that rates were going to rise. Specifically, she was concerned about a $300 million floating-rate loan that the company had at a rate of Libor + 75. The company had budgeted $25 million for interest expense for the next three years. The company had experienced several unexpected downturns, and each department head had been instructed not to go over budget. If the interest expense exceeded $25 million, Kate Lyons would be forced to cut expenses elsewhere. When Kate had discussed this plan with the president, he had told her to do what she had to do to bring in her budget, even if it meant no raises or bonuses for her staff or herself.

The $25 million implied an interest rate of 8.333 percent ($25 million ÷ $300 million) or a Libor level of 7.5833 percent (8.333 percent less 75 basis points). Because Libor was running around 7.25 percent, the Amerand Treasury staff weren't in immediate danger, but expecting rates to rise, Kate Lyons entered the Swap market and locked in her interest expense. She was able to do a three-year Swap at 7.5 percent against Libor (see Figure 5-1). The effective rate on her loan was 8.25 percent (see Figure 5-2 to review the cashflows).

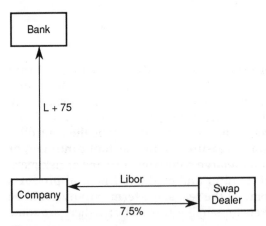

Figure 5-1. Synthetic fixed-rate diagram.

Interest	(L + 75)
Swap—floating rate	L
Swap—fixed rate	(7.50%)
Effective rate	(8.25%)

Figure 5-2. Synthetic fixed-rate cashflows.

Remember, to get the effective rate on a floating-rate loan that has been swapped to fixed, you must always add back the spread on the original loan. Using the Swap market, Kate Lyons ensured that she would bring in her interest expense below budget. In fact, she guaranteed that each year the company would come in $250,000 under budget on their interest expense. [This figure is arrived at by multiplying $300 million by 8.25 percent ($24,750,000) and subtracting the result from $25,000,000.] When she pointed this out to the president and asked whether this money could be used to augment the skimpy raises of her staff, he agreed to give her a portion of it for one-time staff bonuses.

Synthetic Floating-Rate Loan

TransEuro was able to place a $450 million Eurobond for seven years at a fixed rate of 8.5 percent. When it issued the bond, Ed Smythe, the Treasurer, was quite pleased because he had expected rates to rise. And for a while he was right. However, after about a year and a half, rates started to fall. Six months later, with five years remaining on the loan, Ed became convinced that rates would continue to fall for some time. He decided that he would like to convert his loan into a floating-rate loan. His bank was willing to lend him on a floating basis. However, the original loan had some very hefty prepayment penalties and TransEuro did not wish to pay these penalties. Ed's banker suggested a synthetic floating-rate loan using the Swap market to convert his loan.

Figure 5-3 diagrams TransEuro's cashflows. You will note that because the loan had a remaining life of only five years, the Swap was

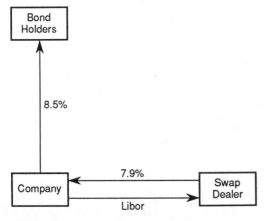

Figure 5-3. Synthetic floating-rate diagram.

Loan	(8.5%)
Swap—fixed rate	7.9%
Swap—floating rate	(L)
Effective rate	(L + 60)

Figure 5-4. Synthetic floating-rate cashflows.

done for five years instead of the original seven. You will also note that the company continued to make the debt payments on the Eurobond.

Figure 5-4 shows the company's cashflows after completing the five-year Swap at 7.9 percent. The company turned its 8.5 percent fixed-rate loan into a synthetic floating-rate loan of Libor + 60. If, after a few years, TransEuro had wanted to go back to a fixed-rate loan, it could by simply reversing its Swap position. If it were correct on its call on the direction of interest rates, it would even make money by reversing the Swap, effectively lowering its interest rates even further. This will be discussed in detail in Chapter 7 on unwinds.

Financing Alternatives

The Swap market gives borrowers an alternate mechanism for locking in the best rates on their debt financing. Crasco wanted a floating-rate loan to finance the construction of a new plant. After shopping around at several banks, the best rate it was able to obtain was Libor + 90. Anne O'Dorian, the Assistant Treasurer for Crasco, noticed that if she could float a public offering at 8.25 percent and swap it at 7.5 percent, the company would save 15 basis points per year. Because this was to be a three-year loan for $200 million, the savings of $300,000 per year would save the company almost $1 million over the life of the project.

Figure 5-5 shows what Crasco's potential debt and Swap structure will look like. Anne's management agreed with her proposal, and the company arranged for the public offering.

Figure 5-6 shows the company's cashflows. Through use of the Swap market, Crasco effectively borrowed at Libor + 75 instead of Libor + 90 as the banks were offering. And the Swap market gives Crasco the same flexibility to go back to fixed as it did TransEuro should Crasco change its mind about the direction of interest rates.

Sub-Libor Financing

Most floating-rate Libor loans are made at a spread over Libor. Most institutions are content with this, and as long as they can keep this spread low, they are happy. What's low depends on the times, the company,

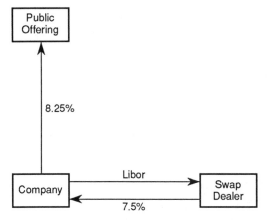

Figure 5-5. Public offering swapped to floating diagram.

Public offering	(8.25%)
Swap—floating rate	(L)
Swap—fixed rate	7.50%
Effective rate	(L + 75)

Figure 5-6. Public offering swapped to floating cashflows.

and the lending institution. At one point in the mid- to late 1980s, certain real estate developers were able to borrow at Libor + ⅜. Anyone who has read a newspaper in the last year or so knows that developers can no longer borrow at such low rates. Now the table has turned, and just getting a bank to lend to a real estate developer is an achievement. Yet some borrowers have been able to borrow below Libor through use of the Swap market.

One of those institutions is Hershet International. When Ian Shanley, the Assistant Treasurer for Hershet, went to the bank to get a floating-rate loan, the best rate he was offered was Libor + 75. This was not bad given the times, but Hershet felt that because of its excellent credit rating it should have been able to borrow at a better rate. Ian felt that rates had topped out and was determined to get a floating-rate loan so that Hershet could take advantage of falling rates. Yet Libor + 75 seemed high.

Hershet made a public offering in the Eurobond market and was able to lock in 7.25 percent for five years. Most people would have been satisfied with this, but not Ian Shanley. As he expected, rates fell. Six months after the public offering, Hershet was able to enter the Swap

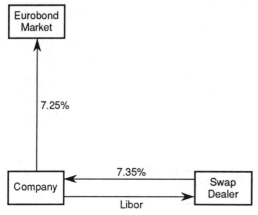

Figure 5-7. Sub-Libor Swap diagram.

Interest on Eurobonds	(7.25%)
Swap—fixed rate	7.35%
Swap—floating rate	(L)
Effective rate	(L − 10)

Figure 5-8. Sub-Libor Swap cashflows.

market and receive 7.35 percent while paying a floating Libor rate (see Figure 5-7).

For the first six months of the loan, Hershet paid a fixed rate of 7.25 percent. For the remaining four and a half years, Hershet paid Libor − 10. See Figure 5-8 for a calculation of Hershet's rate.

By being patient and waiting for rates to drop, Hershet was able to save 85 basis points—the 75 on the best floating-rate offer Hershet received and 10 earned by the synthetic sub-Libor rate.

What to Do When You Think Rates Are Going to Fall

Early in 1991, Nancy Lewko, Chief Economist for Gen Falls Ltd., called for lower interest rates. Knowing her track record (she was rarely wrong in the past), Gen Falls' Treasurer David Cinto evaluated the company's $1 billion debt portfolio. The company had maintained a 50–50 mix between fixed and floating rates. After careful thought, he decided to convert half of the fixed portion of the portfolio to floating, giving the company a 25–75 mix. Over the course of several days, using several different Swap dealers, David swapped $250 million of the company's fixed-rate debt to floating. His only regret one year later was that he did not convert the entire floating portion.

If Nancy had called for higher rates, he would have converted part or all of the floating portion to fixed as we'll see in the next example.

What to Do When You Think Rates Are Going to Rise

As just mentioned, if Gen Falls' economist had called for higher rates, the treasurer would have used the Swap market to convert a portion of Gen Falls' floating-rate debt to a fixed rate. The fixed-rate debt currently on the books would have been left alone. These interest rate decisions would have to be integrated into the company's total financial planning. If a floating-rate loan had a remaining life of two years, then the Swap fixing the rate would have to be for two years. If, however, the company would have an option at the end of that period to extend the loan for another five years, and it intended to exercise that option, it might want to enter into a seven-year Swap. Then again, if Gen Falls wasn't sure whether there would be a business need for that loan, it might want to consider only a two-year loan. Finally, even if there was a chance that the loan might not be needed, but that the Swap could be used to hedge a different financing, a longer tenor might be chosen if the company liked the rate that could be locked in.

Partial Swaps

Sometimes the Swap chosen might not match exactly the loan whose rate it was altering. The Swap could differ from the loan in either tenor or notional amount. There are a variety of reasons for this. Swaps can be used to alter the fixed/floating mix in a portfolio. Sometimes this fine-tuning can result in a loan that is half swapped from floating to fixed, with half remaining floating (or vice versa). At other times, an anticipated repayment of the underlying financing (whether owing to a sale of the related asset or to a more attractive financing) would leave the counterparty with a naked Swap position that it did not wish to hold. And at other times, a steep Swap yield curve may induce an interested party into fixing in a shorter maturity than the underlying debt.

Using a Partial Swap in a Steep Yield Curve Environment

Brikon Corporation was able to obtain a 10-year loan at Libor + 100 from its local bank. When Brikon suggested that it preferred a fixed-rate loan, it was promptly introduced to the bank's Swap group. The Swap

2-year	→	5.25%
3-year	→	5.50%
5-year	→	5.75%
7-year	→	6.75%
10-year	→	7.75%

Figure 5-9. Swap yield curve (partial Swap).

dealer showed Brikon an array of rates that were currently available in the Swap market.

Brikon studied the rates shown in Figure 5-9. It did not wish to pay the extra 200 basis points that the Swap dealer demanded in order to lock the rate in for 10 years instead of five. "Who knows where rates will be in five years? Who knows if we'll still have the loan?," wondered the treasurer of Brikon. Besides the money saved in the first five years could be invested, and if rates were higher in five years, the savings plus the investment returns on those savings could be used to pay a higher rate. A rough calculation shows that Brikon would be able to pay approximately 280 basis points more for the last five years and still come out even. And the treasurer could envision certain economic scenarios where rates would be lower. Also, at the point when the Swap matured in five years, Brikon would be looking at putting on another five-year Swap (not a 10-year). All things considered, the treasurer decided to lock the rate through an interest rate Swap for only the first five years.

Brikon's effective rate on the loan was 6.75 percent (5.75 + 100) for the first five years. At the point that the loan and five-year Swap were originated, the rate for the second five years would float. Brikon would have several alternatives as time goes on to decide what to do with the second portion. Brikon might at some point during the first five years purchase an option (called a Swaption, see Chapter 9) to fix the rate for the second five years. Or, if the yield curve flattened and it still wanted to fix, a forward start Swap might fit the bill. And then, if Brikon became convinced that rates were falling, it might simply float.

Sale/Refinancing

Scorion's problem was different than Brikon's, but the solution was identical. Scorion had a floating-rate loan at Libor + 75 for a warehouse that the company would need for only another two years. The work done at that facility was being transferred to a new facility being built in the adjoining county. Knowing that construction always runs into problems and never finishes on time, Scorion had scheduled the warehouse for sale in three years. The loan had five years to run but was prepayable. However, Scorion became convinced that rates were going to rise and rise quickly, and it wanted to protect itself.

The solution to Scorion's problem was to do a Swap for three years rather than five. Doing a three-year Swap enabled the company to lock in its rate for the three remaining years that it expected to have the loan on its books. If everything went according to plan (and when does that ever happen?) and it was able to not only complete the new warehouse but to sell the old one within the three years allotted, it would be perfectly matched. Scorion would not have to be concerned about a naked Swap that would possibly be out of the money. Because the yield curve was positive, Scorion also paid a lower fixed rate using the three-year rate rather than a five-year rate.

The only possible fly in the ointment would come if the new construction or anticipated sale took longer than three years. At that point, Scorion would have a floating-rate loan which, if it was correct in its interest rate assumptions, would have forced the company to pay rates higher than it would have liked.

Fixed/Floating Mix

Very rarely is someone so convinced of an interest rate projection that he or she wishes to put their entire debt portfolio either all fixed or all floating. Most companies strive for a mix and will, depending on their outlook, either increase or decrease the allotted percentage of debt in either category. A company that was totally unsure of the direction of rates might opt for a 50–50 mix between fixed and floating. One that thought rates were going to increase would increase its fixed allocation, and one that thought rates were going to fall might increase its floating allocation. Before the advent of the Swap market, the only way to alter this mix was through refinancing and perhaps a little tinkering with the futures markets. This could get quite messy.

Evencam had a debt portfolio of $400 million consisting of four $100 million loans. The company did not have a strong view on the direction of rates and had been sitting with half the portfolio fixed and half floating. The company had all its loans floating, but had used the Swap market to fix the rate on half. The management committee decided that with the uncertainty of an upcoming U.S. election, along with the country's slow recovery out of a recession, there was a chance that rates might rise. It decided to increase the portion of its debt that was fixed to 60 percent (and thus decrease the floating piece to 40 percent).

This 10 percent change would require altering the rate on $40 million. But each of Evencam's loans was for $100 million. One of the nice things about using the Swap market is that the Swap is separate from the underlying loan. Swap dealers don't care if you're hedging all or part of your debt. For that matter, they don't care if you have any underlying debt at all. So Evencam's assistant treasurer fixed the rate on a $40 million piece of one of their loans. If, at some later date, the committee decides that Evencam wants the fixed portion to increase to 75 percent, then another $60 million piece could be done.

6

Financial Institutions and Risk Management

"High-tech banking and finance has its place, but it's not all it's cracked up to be.... I hope this sounds like a warning, because it is," said E. Gerald Corrigan, president of the Federal Reserve Bank of New York, in a speech to the New York State Bankers Association in January 1992. Mr. Corrigan voiced the fears and concerns of many regulators about the growing derivatives market. The market has grown from virtually nothing to several trillion dollars in a decade. No wonder some are concerned.

In a March 25, 1992, article, *The Wall Street Journal* reported, "For their part, many derivatives traders were outraged by Mr. Corrigan's speech; they protest that he made their market out to be the 'financial version of crack' as one lawyer angrily put it." So who's right?

What Could Go Wrong?

Whenever there's a lot of money on the table, it can be tempting. And there's a good deal of money on the derivatives table. First of all, let's be realistic. There is no way that a financial market of this size (Swaps alone are believed to be $4 trillion notional amount at year-end 1991) is going to be allowed to operate unregulated. Most market participants behave in a very professional manner. However, just a few unethical, or even uneducated, individuals could undermine the market. The market is probably more at risk owing to ignorance than to fraud. Let's take a look at some trouble spots, which have the potential to cause trouble for the market makers or for their corporate clients who use the products. A few have the potential to cause trouble for both.

Flaws in the Domino Theory

Let's face it, some of Mr. Corrigan's fears are not unfounded—not in all cases, but in more than we'd like to admit. In many instances, there is nothing to worry about, and some banks and financial institutions monitor their risk in an admirable manner. Others don't. But much of the potential risk is to the individual institution, not the system. Most market makers either run a matched book or take positions based on preapproved exposures. The default of one party on one payment does not start a domino effect. Let's look at a very simple example. If one of the leading market makers does not receive an expected payment, it is not going to turn around and default on its obligation to someone else related to the first missed payment. It is getting paid to take that risk. It will be out of pocket for the missed amount at least initially, but it can then pursue the offending party within whatever legal means previously agreed upon in the master agreement.

Even taking a worse case scenario, with an out-of-the-money Swap with several more years to run, the market maker is out of pocket. This is what market makers are paid for. If they did not make good simply because someone else stuck them, they'd be out of business. They would then be the offending party subject to legal redress allowed in the master with the second counterparty. It is analogous to the bank who takes deposits and then lends that money to others. When one of the bank's borrowers misses a payment, the bank does not turn around and not pay interest to one of its depositors. In recent years, Swap market makers have gotten very picky about credit for this very reason. The institutions that are less credit conscious stand more to lose as do those institutions that are lax or ignorant about true credit risks.

Looking at a Swap from a Cashflow Viewpoint

Whenever a Swap is executed, unless there is a severely inverted yield curve, the fixed rate will be higher than the floating rate. The fixed-rate payor will be out of pocket for the first period. Both counterparties know this. It's how interest rate Swaps work. (It's also dangerous for those who are rewarded for short-term gains.) In the environment where the yield curve is steep, the fixed-rate payor can be out of pocket a significant amount. Let's look at a simple extreme example from the summer of 1991.

Six-month Libor was at 5.5 percent. The all-in fixed rate on a 10-year Swap was 8.05 percent on the day in question. Now 8.05 percent might look like a good rate for 10 years, but look at the initial cashflows. For the first six-month period, the payor would pay $1,006,250 (on a $25 million Swap) and receive $687,500. This nets to an outflow of $318,750. Both parties know this on the day they execute the Swap. If the receiver is naïve (and there are naïve Swap dealers in the market), he or she may decide not to match the book. Why should he or she? The receiver has a huge positive carry in his or her favor. And if the receiver does this not on $25 million, but on $250 million or more, his or her initial cashflow will be even greater. The cashflow for the period looks great—which should be great for the receiver's bonus. Right?

Looking at a Swap from a Mark-to-Market Viewpoint

When the accountants come in at year-end, they mark all securities to market. Now let's assume, in order to make my case, that interest rates have risen 50 basis points. The receiver doesn't care because he or she still has a positive cashflow; he or she is still only receiving 8.05 percent but now has to pay 6.0 percent on the next reset date. The accountants are not pleased because the 10-year Swap now has 9.5 years to go. The Swap is marked to market by comparing its fixed-rate cashflows with the cashflows of a Swap equal in maturity going in the opposite direction. If the receiver would have to pay 8.55 percent for 9.5 years, the Swap is assumed to have a negative value equal to 50 basis points per year. For every $100 million of 9.5-year Swaps on the books, the accountants are telling him or her to mark the portfolio down $3.2 million. This will not be good for the receiver's bonus! What happened?

Which Is Right?

Unfortunately for the receiver, the mark-to-market approach is the one that all financial institutions must use. Just like a junk bond selling at a deep discount to the original selling price, a Swap is evaluated on its resale price, not its current cashflow. Not only is this the way the accountants will look at the receiver's portfolio, but this is the way any Swap to be sold will be priced. Sophisticated market participants mark their portfolio to market every day. It is not hard to develop a computer model that will do this for you. (This will be explored in much more detail in Chapter 7.) The latter of the two examples we've just looked at shows what can go wrong when these products are not fully understood. In order to avoid this and a myriad or other problems, a comprehensive risk management program should be set up. (See Chapter 13 on risk.)

If you think that the preceding story is far-fetched and couldn't happen, you're wrong. It could and did—at an institution with an excellent credit rating and very stringent credit standards. The problem was that the individual assigned to head up the Swap desk had little or no experience with Swaps, but learned quickly. It's no wonder Mr. Corrigan gets upset.

Cost of Carry

From an accounting and a mark-to-market standpoint, the main concern when evaluating an interest rate Swap is the difference between the fixed rate on the Swap and the market fixed rate. This will be discussed in detail in Chapter 7 on unwinds. The floating rates and the comparison of the current floating rate with the fixed rate on the Swap are irrelevant in these calculations. However, a comparison between the current floating rate and the fixed rate becomes very important when evaluating the cost of carry for the short term. Traditionally, this differential was not that large and was not a concern when deciding on the timing for fixing rates.

In 1991, the yield curve became so steep that this consideration began to play into the decision. With Libor at 5.5 percent, and long-term fixed rates above 8 percent, a company could save over 250 basis points by not fixing. This saving could be amortized over the eventual fixed rate that a company might set, and the company would still be ahead of the game despite ultimately fixing at a higher level. To add insult to injury, not only did this huge differential remain, but rates and spreads slid lower through a good part of the year, doubly rewarding those companies that wanted to fix but held off.

Counterparty Risk

One of the few bright sides to the credit crunch of the early 1990s was that financial institutions started to look at the creditworthiness of their counterparties. Swap availability became subject to the same credit scrutiny that the financial institutions used when doling out other forms of credit—and doling was what they were doing in the early 1990s.

Prior to this period of intense scrutiny and tightening of credit standards, many institutions were quite lax about those with whom they did business. If there was any credit review, it was quite cursory—not everywhere, but at more institutions than will readily admit to such practices. Is it possible that in the beginning these institutions didn't fully understand the risks?

As the credit crunch worsened and the recession dragged on, transactions done with institutions battered by the recession could be vulnerable. This could be further exacerbated by the next problem.

Cash-Starved Companies

When credit availability dries up for a company, that company may be forced to take steps that it would never have contemplated in better times. A company desperate for cash will sell whatever liquid assets it has just to stay afloat. This will include any Swaps (and other derivative products) that may be in the money. Although the new bankruptcy codes allow for netting, in cases of corporate bankruptcies (as opposed to bankruptcies of financial institutions that run matched books) it is unlikely that there will be anything with value left to net. A company on the verge of bankruptcy will have sold any derivatives that are in the money, leaving on its books only those out of the money. And who can blame them? This could possibly lead to the next problem. Although financial institutions running matched books theoretically should not run into this problem, they run into the problem of trading liquidity, which will be discussed later.

Trading Risks

Given the current lack of credit for companies or institutions other than those with the very highest credit ratings, this is not as likely to happen today as it was a few years ago. A company needing to generate some cash might be tempted to write some options to generate premiums. This is only of concern when the options written do not fit in with the company's hedging strategy and are being written solely to generate cash. Writing options is certainly a valid hedging technique, but a company in need of cash might be tempted to overdo it.

This same risk could arise at financial institutions that don't run a completely matched (or hedged) book. Those that don't run a matched book and don't mark their portfolios to market on a very frequent basis present a larger risk to the marketplace. Should these trades go against the writer of the option, the buyer may find that he or she has bought protection from an institution that can't deliver.

Again, the very tight credit standards currently in vogue should make this risk very remote today.

Intraday Trading

Very little is written about the unauthorized position taking on Swaps desks. I'm not talking about authorized position taking, but the position taking that may last for as short a time period as a minute or two or most of the day. Certain institutions authorize their traders to take positions within certain limits. Typically, a level of risk is determined and the trader is allowed the discretion to take a position within these limits. This allows the desk to increase its profits. Of course, if the trader is wrong, the profits of the desk are diminished rather than increased. Where the trader is authorized, the positions will typically be kept open for longer than a day.

It is the unauthorized position taking that could present a problem. This can come from either a trader who is authorized to run a matched book but who doesn't quite do that, or a trader who is authorized to take certain sized positions but who exceeds those limits. A sudden sharp move in the market could leave these individuals in a bad way. They could end up with larger loses than authorized and could find that they are not able to close out their positions when they want or at the levels they need. This happened on both the days the stock market crashed, and it happens more than occasionally in the futures markets where contracts can be up or down the limit, locking the trader out of the market.

The unfortunate thing is that management is frequently aware that the unauthorized trader is taking positions that shouldn't be taken. As long as profits are made, everyone looks the other way. When a large loss is incurred, the trader is often fired. So why do traders take the risk? Two reasons. First, the trader typically gets a share of the profits from the desk, and trading profits increase the pot. And second, many traders just can't help themselves; they're gamblers.

Trading Liquidity
Diminished by Downfall
of One

The derivatives market has sprung up from almost nowhere in the last 10 years. True financial futures were around in the late 1970s and were used for hedging; the foreign exchange market has been around for several decades, but it was not until interest rate Swaps hit the ground in the mid-1980s that the market really took off (although some will argue that the foreign exchange market has been long used as a speculative vehicle). Many are concerned about the lack of regulation and worry that because of the interlocking nature of the market, the downfall of one institution could topple the entire market. Whenever this topic comes up, Drexel is mentioned.

We've already discussed the downfall of Drexel in Chapter 2. The thing that stands out is that the professionals employed by Drexel worked incredibly hard to unwind their positions. The trouble that they had resulted from greed within the marketplace. Let's face it, institutions that had either of these counterparties on their books would have been delighted to get them off. Yet in certain cases, the market participants did not cooperate in the unwinding of these positions. Why? Could common greed have been the answer? Did certain traders see a weaker player in trouble and decide to try and take advantage? Yes, in some cases. But in many others traders cooperated.

It is hoped that in the future when such circumstances arise again, market participants will resist the opportunity to make a quick buck at the expense of one of their former competitors. I know, I know, many will point to a few individuals who worked for both these institutions who would have done the same thing given the opportunity.

Broker Problem

There have been allegations made in the foreign exchange markets that some of the alliances between certain brokers and certain traders is less than (or more than) what it should be. Whether this is on a one-shot basis when one helps another out of a jam and then accepts an under-the-table payment for doing so, or an ongoing relationship between the two with many under-the-table payments is open for debate—and investigation. Does the same thing go on in the Swaps market? Possibly, but one hopes to a much lower extent, if at all.

Off Balance Sheet versus On Balance Sheet

One of the beauties of Swaps, and one of the things that make the regulators shudder, is the fact that this activity was treated as an off–balance sheet item for accounting purposes. Although the extent of the activity was revealed in a footnote, it was not part of the balance sheet. This arose in part because of the initial confusion of how to classify this activity when it first became popular. In fact, in the very beginning there were no guidelines. But that is about to change.

Starting in 1993, the Financial Accounting Standards Board (FASB) has ruled that Swap activities will have to be included in the balance sheet. Activity to the same counterparty will only be reflected in its netted form. To give you an idea of the effect that this will have on certain larger players, one big player revealed that if this guideline were in effect in 1991, its assets and liabilities would have increased 200 percent.

Regulators are very concerned that many institutions are carrying large losses in derivatives positions that are not reflected adequately in their balance sheets.

Lack of Understanding of Products

As the Swap market grew, so did the market for related products. As soon as one dealer began offering a product, in an effort to maintain market share, dozens rushed to offer the same. Often this did not allow sufficient time for the dealer offering the product to develop systems or a true understanding of what was being offered. Sometimes this resulted in poor pricing techniques that forced the dealer to take a loss when booking the trade. Many of these products lived a short life and were quickly replaced by the next novelty.

And if you think the dealers had a hard time understanding what they were selling, imagine the poor corporate client who was constantly being bombarded with new products. The corporate client did not always understand what was being sold. In certain instances, the client did not understand the product and did not realize that one risk was being traded for another or did not fully realize what was being given up.

My personal favorite is collars (which are discussed in more detail in Chapter 10). For a premium, which can sometimes be quite expensive, a corporation can purchase a Cap (also discussed in Chapter 10). The Cap limits the level of the corporate's interest expense while allowing the purchaser of the Cap to enjoy the benefit of lower interest rates should rates decline. However, these Caps can sometimes be quite expensive. So the Swaps salesperson will sometimes suggest a collar (the combination of a Cap and a floor), which gives up some of the downside gains while reducing or eliminating the premium. When a collar is purchased, everyone focuses on the low or no cost and nobody focuses on the fact that the downside gains, should rates go lower, are limited. When the floor is hit, further interest savings are eliminated. The corporate has traded the risk of higher interest rates for a fixed rate. Many do not realize this until the floor is hit.

Certain hedging techniques hedge one risk while exposing the hedger to the opposite risk. This is what happened to the S&Ls that hedged against rising interest rates in the mid- to late 1980s only to have interest rates fall and home mortgage holders refinance and trade up in record numbers. The S&Ls had traded the risk of rising rates for the risk of falling rates.

The lack of full understanding of the derivative products runs on both sides of the desk. Unfortunately, it is not only the purchaser who doesn't fully understand the product. Both the purchaser and the seller are sometimes less than perfectly educated. Sometimes the marketer out pushing the "product of the week" would benefit from additional education and training. As we all become educated in these products and learn to think them through, the risks will diminish.

Leverage

It is possible to control large derivative positions for little or no money at all. When Salomon ran into its problems because of the Treasury bidding scandal, it didn't withdraw from the market because it didn't have the capital to play the interest rate markets anymore. It simply changed the markets in which it played. The same bets were moved from the bond market into the derivatives markets—in particular, futures market, OTC options market, and to a lesser extent the Swaps market. Salomon was able to make the same bets—it just cost less. Capital needed for these transactions was much less than capital needed to actually take these positions in the bond market.

In some ways, derivatives trading is analogous to buying stock on margin. You need a lot less money to buy on margin (or in the derivatives market) than you do outright. And for that reason these positions have the potential to be much more profitable—and are all the more risky. Risk is one of the things that concerns regulators. But should they be concerned?

Probably, in some cases. If these positions go south, Salomon, for example, would lose a great deal of money. But, one or more firms losing a lot of money will not necessarily bring down the system. For that matter, it probably wouldn't even bring down the firm. There would be a large charge and maybe no bonuses, but the firm would go on. And so would the system. And remember, Salomon, like many other financial institutions, authorizes certain traders to take these positions on behalf of the firm. That's what they get paid for. And most of them are quite good at it.

At its very worst, in the demise of Drexel, the market survived. It has been rumored that the Fed had to get involved with the Drexel downfall by making sure payments wired to and from Drexel were completed smoothly. However, for systemic reasons having to do with all lines of business, the Fed insisted that banks instructed to wire money to and from Drexel do so. It's not clear that the derivatives business added more than its proportionate share of risk or problems to the whole procedure.

Using Leverage Correctly

Do financial institutions use leverage correctly? Maybe, maybe not. Just as the market and products are new, so, too, are the calculations necessary to allocate capital. Are they correct? Are financial institutions overextending themselves? Certain reporters and regulators have insinuated that perhaps the derivatives market is approaching something similar to the stock market of 1929, when large positions bought on very small (or large depending on your outlook) margins wreaked havoc and helped crash that market.

The current situation is not quite analogous. The large institutions playing successfully in the derivatives market are much better capitalized than individuals in 1929. Capital requirements for these trades are being increased for commercial banks (but not investment banks). The FASB is addressing the ways that these vehicles have been accounted for in the past and continues to study these techniques.

Tax and Accounting Guidelines

This book is not a final reference on how to handle either the tax or accounting treatment of Swaps. The FASB and the IRS are the definitive sources for that information. Because derivative products are relatively new, the regulatory bodies are still in the process of trying to catch up and set definitive guidelines for the respective treatments. The reader is advised to consult the appropriate experts for advice in these matters. Appendix B contains several FASB opinions relating to Swaps. For further information, contact:

Financial Accounting Standards
  Board
401 Merritt 7
P.O. Box 5116
Norwalk, CT 06856

You'll find the FASB very helpful.

Moving Forward

Most market participants recognize many of the phenomena that concern regulators. And many are cleaning up their acts (where needed) to address these concerns. The last thing that the market needs or wants is for the pendulum to swing the other way—that is, for upper management at an organization or outside regulators to tighten their operations to the point where the institution can no longer operate or can operate only in a very limited capacity.

Controls and Monitoring within the System

Much of the finger pointing—most of which is not unreasonable—is at loose controls and at a management that does not know or understand what its traders are doing. As we all become more knowledgeable and sophisticated about the Swap market and derivative products, the controls are and will be put in place. It's not unreasonable to expect that the group monitoring the trading and operations be separate from the trading itself. This is already happening at many institutions—witness Merrill Lynch's "Risk Police" (discussed in Chapter 2).

Greater Understanding

The complaint that management does not understand what the "rocket scientists" hired are doing might be fair. But from that one should not necessarily assume that the "rocket scientists" are endangering the whole system. What needs to be done is some education of upper management. Management needs to take the time to understand the products and the manner in which they are being used at their institution. And that will require upper management to spend a little time learning about this new market. Perhaps the answer is a series of seminars for upper management given by the "rocket scientists"—starting at the beginning!

With financial markets constantly changing, market participants must realize that their education must go on throughout their working life unless they want to be left in the dust. Derivative products will continue to be developed whether or not we like it. Just as professionals in other fields are required to take a certain number of continuing education courses to maintain their accreditation, those who work in the financial markets need to realize that we also must maintain our skills. This means a continuation of the education process or we'll get left behind. So, to those senior managers who complain that they don't understand all this new-fangled mumbo jumbo: Get out a book or go back to school for a class. You'll find it quite interesting, but you'll also be able to figure out whether the "rocket scientists" have been pulling the wool over your eyes or have been making you a premier leader in the marketplace.

Conclusion

As financial institutions begin or continue to set up comprehensive monitoring systems, establish good controls, and educate their senior management about this market, many of the complaints will stop. The few abuses that do exist, whether owing to ignorance or greed, will be weeded out. But everyone has to participate in this process. Otherwise the market could see itself regulated out of existence (that's probably an exaggeration, but you get the point).

7

Unwinds and
Mark to Market

You may wonder why the topics of unwinding, or terminating, a Swap and marking the portfolio to market are handled in the same chapter. The calculations used in both functions are the same. Before getting into the methodology, we'll go through an overview of the topics.

Mark to Market

The theory behind marking a Swap to market will be discussed first because it is the basis for pricing a Swap unwind. Marking a Swap to market can be done in several ways, all resulting in numbers that are close but not exactly the same. *Mark to market* is a technique for valuing the Swap using current market prices to determine its profit or loss as of a particular point in time. It is sometimes referred to as a drop-dead analysis.

The different techniques usually refer to the yield curve that is used to discount the cashflows. The two most common will be discussed toward the end of this chapter. But we're getting ahead of ourselves. In marking the Swap to market, the Swap being evaluated is compared to one with matching characteristics in all ways except that of paying or receiving. If the Swap is one in which the owner is a fixed payor, then the Swap is compared with the rate on a fixed receiver Swap, and vice versa.

Comparison of Cashflows

One of the hardest concepts for many to grasp is that in valuing a
Swap; the floating rates don't matter. Typically, when people not intimately familiar with Swaps begin to talk about the value of a Swap,
they focus on the difference between the fixed rate and the current
floating rate. They'll say something like "Gee that's a bad deal you've
got there. You're paying 7 percent on that seven-year Swap and six-
month Libor is only 5.5 percent. When we mark that thing to market
we're going to have a huge loss." Not necessarily. If fixed rates are 8
percent on the day you are to mark to market, you actually have a winner on your hands. "How can that be?" you ask. Just keep in mind that
the evaluation of any Swap is based on a comparison between the
fixed rate on the Swap and the current fixed rates that could be
achieved in the marketplace should you wish to reverse the Swap.
With the exception of a small adjustment for the current period floating rate, the floating rates are totally irrelevant to the value of the
Swap. Many find this difficult to comprehend. It is a simple point but
vital to the following discussion.

Mark to Market—A Simple Example

Let's look at a simple example. Tallahassee Company entered into a 10-
year Swap on which it is a fixed-rate payor of 9.5 percent against six-
month Libor. Tallahassee is now going to mark its Swap to market. To
what does it compare its Swap? It compares its Swap to a nine-year
Swap on which it would receive the fixed rate. Why nine-year? After
one year the remaining life on the original 10-year Swap will be nine
years. Why does Tallahassee look at the receive side? The answer
should be clear when we look at the cashflows associated with the evaluation. Let's assume that in nine years you can receive at 8.5 percent
against six-month Libor today. Now, lets look at the cashflows:

Original Swap:	pay 9.5%
	receive Libor
Comparison Swap:	receive 8.5%
	pay Libor
	pay 1%

When all the cashflows from the original Swap and the comparison
Swap are added, you'll note that the Libor payments cancel each other
out. If Tallahassee were to receive 8.5 percent, it would cover most but

not all of the 9.5 percent that Tallahassee must pay on its original Swap. There would be a shortfall of 1 percent per year for nine years.

If it's still not clear why we look at a Swap going in the other direction, let's look at what would happen if we compared it to one going in the same direction. Our cashflows would look like this:

Original Swap:	pay 9.5%
	receive Libor
Comparison Swap:	pay 8.5%
	receive Libor
	pay 18% + receive 2 × Libor

We need the Libors to cancel each other out and the fixed payments to net.

Evaluation of Cashflows

In order to determine Tallahassee's Swap value, we would have to compute the value of 1 percent per year for nine years. If the Swap had a notional amount of $100 million, this would result in a net cashflow of $1 million per year for nine years. In this case, Tallahassee would have to pay the $1 million per year so that the Swap is in a loss position (i.e., *out of the money*). This will result in a negative mark to market and value. In this simple example we've assumed that the mark to market took place on the first day of the second year and that there need be no adjustment for the first period cashflow or accrued interest.

To complete the valuation of the Swap, we'd need to compute the present value of the cashflows today using standard present valuing techniques, which will be discussed later. The cashflows would be discounted using today's interest rates, not the interest rates in effect when the Swap was first put on the books.

Discounting

Those familiar with present value techniques can skip or skim this section. If you're not familiar with the technique, read closely because this is the basis for much of the remaining discussion in the chapter.

If someone offered you a choice of receiving $100 today or $100 a year from now, your choice would be simple. You'd take the $100 today and earn interest on it for the year and at the end of the year have the $100 plus some interest. Now, if you were offered $95 today or $100 a year from now, your choice would not be so simple. The answer would depend on how much interest you could earn on that $95. At

some point, based on current interest rates, you'd be indifferent to receiving a lower amount today instead of a slightly higher amount a
year from now.

Present value takes the amount in the future and brings (*discounts*) it
to the present based on current rates. In this simple example, if one-year
rates were 5 percent, the $100 a year from now would have a present
value of $95.24 (i.e., you could earn $4.76 interest on your $95.24 for one
year resulting in $100 a year from now). The discount rate used is very
important because it can result in big changes in the present value (the
same $100 discounted at 10 percent instead of 5 percent for one year
would have a present value of $90.91).

Discounting Cashflows

Method 1

Let's go back to our example about the negative cashflow of $1 million per
year for nine years. In order to value that Swap, it is necessary to calculate
the present value of the series of cashflows. This is typically done using
one of two discounting techniques. In the beginning days of Swaps, the
cashflows were discounted using the Treasury rate that corresponded to
the maturity of the Swap. In our example, the nine-year Treasury rate
would have been used. (Remember, to get the nine-year Treasury rate,
you'd interpolate between the 7- and 10-year Treasury.) If the nine-year
Treasury rate had been 7.75 percent, the present value of that stream of
cashflows would have been $6,312,355 using simple present value valua-
tions. [On your HP12C, $n = 9$, $i = 7.75$, $pmt = -1,000,000$, and $fv = 0$; solve
for pv (present value).] This does not take into account any further pricing
refinements, which will be discussed later.

Method 2

As Swap valuations became more sophisticated, it became apparent that
this technique was a simplification of the actual process. There are nine
separate payments, and discounting them all at the nine-year rate was
not quite correct. Each cashflow should be discounted using a discount
rate appropriate for the time period (i.e., the first cashflow using a one-
year rate, the second using a two-year rate, etc.). This is how the technique of using a zero coupon yield curve evolved. Each cashflow is valued using its own discount rate. This is a good deal more work, but with
a computer to create the curve, it's not that difficult. The calculations
can still be done on the HP12C; it just takes a little longer.

Semiannual Payments

The pros reading this chapter are probably getting ready to point out that I've used semiannual rates to calculate annual cashflows, and they're right. One of the first refinements that needs to be made is to calculate payments on a semiannual basis. Treasury notes (like most bonds) pay interest twice a year. And plain vanilla Swaps follow this pattern, although many variations exist. As discussed in Chapter 1, the fixed rate in a plain vanilla Swap is swapped for six-month Libor. In the example discussed in the last section, the cashflows would not have been $1,000,000 per year but $500,000 twice a year. The same amount of money, but worth more if it is received earlier and less if received later.

Because all Swap payments are accrued and paid in arrears, the $500,000 twice a year is worth more than the $1,000,000 once a year. Now, redoing our calculations using instead 18 payments of $500,000, we find that the present value (*pv*) is $6,394,445 (on the HP12C $n = 18$, $i = 7.75 \div 2$, *pmt* $= -500,000$, and $fv = 0$). This simple adjustment results in additional value of $82,090 (the difference between the $6,312,355 using 9 annual payments and the $6,394,445 using 18 semiannual payments). Swap payments are assumed to be on a semiannual basis, always paid in arrears, unless otherwise specified.

Further adjustments can be made and will be explored in detail in Chapter 8 as will adjustments for a short first period or short end period. These short periods are referred to as stub periods.

Discount Rate

Many will argue that when discounting, the all-in Swap rate should be used rather than the interpolated Treasury rate. Using the all-in rate will give you either a smaller profit if the Swap is in the money or a smaller loss if it is out of the money. Swap dealers should be consistent in the discounting rate used. They shouldn't try and use the all-in rate when the Swap is in a profit position for you and then the Treasury rate when you're in a loss position. In the example from the previous section, the Swap had a value of $6,394,445 using a Treasury rate of 7.75 percent. If we had used an all-in Swap rate of 8.25 percent, suggesting a spread of 50, the value would have been $6,265,822, or a difference of $46,532. Not a huge difference but enough to discuss.

Unwinding a Swap

When someone *unwinds* a Swap, he or she terminates the Swap. Unwinding is typically done by marking the Swap to market, and involves calculating the value of the Swap and then making or receiving that cash payment. Because no two institutions use the exact same methods, Swap spreads, and yield curves, unwinding is not an exact science. Typically you will not only calculate the value of the Swap, you will also ask several institutions to bid on it.

Nine times out of ten you will get the best price on an unwind of a Swap from the institution that wrote the Swap in the first place. However, some institutions will try and increase their profits on an unwind thinking that they have a captive audience. Or, your unwind might go against an institution's book and, therefore, on the particular day that you want to unwind your Swap you may be able to get a better price at another institution.

The first thing you'll need to do is to see at what levels other institutions are paying or receiving. (Remember, if you're paying on the Swap you want to unwind, then you'll look at the receiving spreads and vice versa.) If the level that the second institution gives you is good, you'll want to ask about assignments, which will be discussed later in this chapter.

Preparing to Unwind

Before you can unwind a Swap, you will need to value it yourself. Your model for valuing might not be as sophisticated as your counterparty's (especially if you're a corporate), but you should have a good idea of its value before asking for prices. This will put you in a much better negotiating position. Even if you only have a financial calculator and no model, you should be able to do the calculations. (And if you're playing in the Swap market, a $70 calculator and a $1500 computer are something you can afford.)

After doing your calculations to estimate your Swap's value, list out the details of the Swap. Or better yet, get out the original confirmation and highlight the important details. You will also need to know the current floating rate on the floating side.

Review the Details

When you call your counterparty to unwind, review the details of the transaction with them. This is especially important if you have more than one Swap. It certainly helps if you're both talking about the same Swap. If you are looking to do an assignment, it is doubly important. Mistakes happen all the time. On one occasion, when trying to unwind a $50 million Swap on a particularly active day, one of the counterparties bidding on the Swap was pricing a $25 million Swap. Because it was a rapidly moving market, there was no time to review the details a second time with the counterparty and he lost the deal. It turned out later that the counterparty was using a model he'd used earlier in the day for a similar transaction and forgot to change the notional amount. Mistakes like that happen all the time.

If you are getting prices from several dealers at the same time, you might be tempted to gloss over some of the details—don't. Good counterparties will insist on reading back the details of the transaction to you before pricing it. If you are getting live prices from three dealers on the same transaction, this can mean reviewing the details six times!

Negotiations

If you've received several prices, or even if you've only received one, there is usually a little room for negotiation. And to a very small extent you may be able to play one counterparty off against another without telling who each one's competition is. However, if you have a highly specialized transaction, don't be surprised if dealers not involved in the trade but aware of it come back and ask you whether you did the trade and if it was with the counterparty you eventually used (or didn't use).

Dealers talk, brag, exaggerate, and in some instances lie. A friend of mine who works for a financial institution, but not in the Swaps group, was at a company party where one of the Swap dealers was bragging about the large Swap he had done with my company. My friend happened to mention it in conversation several months later. We were both surprised—I because my company had never done any Swaps with that dealer's institution, and my friend because he couldn't believe the dealer would lie. And even if dealers don't talk, it sometimes becomes apparent to the rest of the market when the counterparty who did the trade goes into the marketplace to lay it off.

Including or Excluding
Accrued Interest

When reviewing the details of the proposed transaction with your counterparties, it is important to specify whether or not you wish to include accrued interest in your price. I think it's simpler not to include it and then calculate it after you've agreed on a price. But you don't have to do it that way, and there is no agreed upon market convention. The important thing is that everyone is bidding on the same thing—either with or without accrued interest. There are times when this will make little difference, but there are times when it can make a huge difference.

Breaking Your Transaction into Several Pieces

If you have a large piece to unwind—say $100 million or more—you might want to break it into several pieces (tranches) either to be done simultaneously or at different times. If you don't want to put all your eggs in one basket, you might choose to "average in" and unwind on several different days. This is similar to the averaging in theory when buying stocks or mutual funds. Or you might wish to divide your transaction among several different counterparties.

Assignments

Assignments, which are unwinds done with a third party, can be a touchy subject among financial institutions. Many do not like to be assigned and will improve their prices if they know you're considering it (so let them know). Once you've ascertained that the second bank will take assignments (and most if not all do), you'll have to ask them if they'll take your counterparty. There are several legitimate reasons for them to refuse your counterparty. The counterparty may not have a relationship with the bank and therefore no line of credit. Or an institution may be difficult to deal with and the second institution may prefer to avoid acrimonious dealings.

Finally, if your counterparty is of a lower credit quality (i.e., your company is rated AA and your counterparty A), the second bank may pass or revise its pricing in order to accept your proposed counterparty. It is not uncommon for a financial institution to offer a better price to a corporate customer than to a competitor.

Back to your original counterparty. When you tell the counterparty that you're considering an assignment, you'll have to mention who you are considering for the assignment. This is where the relationship you have with this particular counterparty will come into play. If the relationship is very good, you may just name the party you are considering. However, in most instances this is not the best approach. Give the financial institutions several names, including your potential assignee, and let them tell you which names are acceptable to them. They will have the same concerns as the institution considering the assignment.

Most master Swap agreements contain a reasonability clause regarding assignments. Your counterparty cannot reasonably withhold its consent to the assignment. You'll know if the counterparty is being unreasonable if you supply four names of equal or better quality than your own and all of them are refused. Don't be surprised if a financial institution of lower credit quality than themselves is refused or one that is rumored to be downgraded in the near future.

Once you've narrowed your list and have received concurrence from both parties you will be able to proceed with the assignment.

Assignments Defined

In an assignment, a second institution (usually a bank or other financial institution) steps into the shoes of one of the counterparties. If Company A had a Swap with Company B and wished to assign it to Company C, the end result would be a Swap between Company B and Company C based exactly on the terms of the original Swap between Company A and Company B. If the Swap were in a profit position (sometimes referred to as *in the money*) for Company A, Company C would pay Company A for that. If it is out of the money for Company A, then Company A would pay Company C to step into its shoes. The amount paid need never be revealed to Company B. In actual practice it rarely is.

A simple assignment agreement (usually only one page in length) is drawn up and all three parties sign it. Because Company C is stepping into Company A's shoes, Company C will be responsible for the entire next payment. Thus, payments for assignments are usually adjusted for accrued interest for the current period of the Swap. When getting bids for the assignment, you should make sure all parties are on the same basis (i.e., whether including or excluding accrued interest).

It's usually easier to look at the bids without accrued interest. The calculation for accrued interest can be done and confirmed after the trade is completed. It is what it is and should not be subject to negotiation.

Not only should you be sure that the bids either all contain or exclude accrued interest, you should also make sure that all the terms of the Swap are verified both before asking for a bid and before accepting a final bid.

Getting Bids on an Assignment

It is not a bad idea to have a copy of the confirmation of the original Swap in front of you when getting bids on an assignment. You can then read the terms from the confirm to the party you are asking to take the assignment. This is important because even a minor difference in the underlying terms can affect the price on the unwind. Obviously a Swap with quarterly payments will be priced differently than one with semi-annual payments. In Chapter 8 on other pricing refinements you'll get a look at some of the minor differences that can and do exist in the Swap market.

If you want to be ultra safe, you might consider faxing a copy of the confirm to the party from whom you are asking a bid. (If you haven't told the second party who the proposed counterparty is, you can white out the name. However, you take the chance that the person you're asking for the bid will recognize the form.)

Keeping Two Swaps Alive

Sometimes, despite your best efforts, you cannot get the two counterparties to accept each other on assignment. Why not keep both Swaps alive you ask, letting the new counterparty pay you for putting a Swap on the books that is in the money (or pay the counterparty if it will be out of the money). This is sometimes the best solution available although it is far from ideal for the institution looking to unwind the Swap. In fact, many corporate customers refuse to do this. It forces them to stand between two institutions and use up double credit instead of reducing their credit exposure. And as we've discussed earlier, Swap credit can be difficult to come by for certain companies. It also is an additional administrative burden.

Moreover, the company may find itself in an unfavorable position if the credit of one of its counterparties deteriorates in time. This is not the business most companies want to be in and, so, should be avoided.

Another Example

Let's say that on the books you have a Swap for which you are receiving a fixed rate of 9 percent against six-month Libor. The Swap matures on December 1, 1998, and today is December 1, 1991. You look at your Treasury screen (or you call one of your Swap dealers or look in the newspaper) and you see:

7.125	10/98	100.18 − 22
7.500	11/01	100.21 − 25

for your Treasury quotes. You'll note that these two notes are on-the-run issues. If you're looking on a screen, it will be readily obvious. If you're using quotes from a newspaper, make sure you use the most recently issued notes. If there is a wi note trading, use that.

In addition to the preceding Treasury quotes, you've determined (either from a screen or from calling several Swap dealers) that the Swap spreads are as follows:

7-year	44–50
10-year	46–52

We know from earlier discussions that *10/98* refers to a maturity date of October 15, 1998, and that *11/01* to a maturity of November 15, 2001. Because our Swap matures on December 1, 1998, it has seven years to go and will fall between the two dates indicated, 10/98 and 11/01. Although December 1, 1998, is much closer to October 15, 1998, we can't just use the rate on that date. We must interpolate.

Interpolation

Because we are receiving on our original Swap, we will need to compare with a Swap that is paying. Therefore, we'll use the bid side of the Treasury quotes (i.e., the 100.18 on the 1998 note and the par 21 (100.21) on the 2001 note). Using your financial calculator or computer, you now compute the yield to maturity (ytm) on each note. On the 1998 note, we find a yield of 7.018 percent (on an HP12C, $pv = 100^{18}\!/_{32}$, $pmt = 7.125$; 12.011991 enter, 10.151998 $f\,ytm$), and on the note of 2001, a yield of 7.405 percent. You'll note that even though the prices are close, the yields to maturity are quite different, reflecting the different coupon rates. Having arrived at the yields we can interpolate. We set up our interpolation as follows:

$$1127 \quad \begin{bmatrix} 10/15/98 \\ 12/01/98 \\ 11/15/01 \end{bmatrix} \quad 47 \quad \begin{bmatrix} 7.018 \\ x \\ 7.405 \end{bmatrix} \quad .387$$

We find that there are 1127 days between October 15, 1988, and November 15, 2001 (on HP12C, 10.151998 enter, 11.152001 g $^\wedge dys$). However between October 15, 1998, and December 01, 1998, there are only 47 days. (*Note:* If you are using an HP12C to calculate the number of days, make sure to enter December 1, 1998, as 12.011998. If you leave the 0 out, you will get an error message.)

The differential is 4.17 percent (47 ÷ 1127) of the .387 difference. Now we find that we need to add .016 (.0417 × .387) to the October 15, 1998, rate to get our new Treasury level of 7.024 percent (7.018 + .016). You might point out that this is a lot of work to go through for one and a half basis points, and you'd be right. But that one and a half basis points on a $100 million transaction is worth $15,000 per year or somewhere around $80,000 on a present value basis on our seven-year transaction. In my book, and that of most other professionals, that's worth a few minutes of extra work.

To get our spread, we could interpolate, but most people don't break the spreads down into decimal places other than halves (although occasionally on large deals a quarter of a point may be negotiated). In our case we have exactly seven years to go so we'd use 50 (not 44 because we're making a comparison with a Swap where we'd be paying). There is one other thing to note. The Swap spreads don't correspond exactly to the Treasury note maturities—except on four days each year on the first day of issuance of each note. Our Swap has seven years to go, and we're able to get a clean quote for that time period despite the fact that we had to interpolate the Treasury yield.

Interpolating Spreads

You will also find out that the interpolation of spreads is not always as clean as it is on notes. For example, if you have eight and a half years to go on a Swap, you might think you'd use the average of the seven- and ten-year spreads. In the numbers presented so far, you'd pay 51 (the average or midpoint between 50 and 52). This may not always be the case.

The dealer may try and tell you that the spread curve is steep (or flat) and that the spread is actually closer to the ten-year spread (seven-year). You can be sure that if this story is used, it will rarely, if ever, go in your favor. There is a very simple way to check this out. Call several other Swap dealers and ask them for their seven- and ten-year spreads. Then ask them what they'd quote on an eight-and-a-half-year deal. The answers you get will guide you in evaluating whether your original Swap dealer is telling the truth or just trying to get an extra basis point. In our example, however, the ultimate maturity of the Swap under discussion is exactly seven years, so we use the seven-year quote. Even if the maturity had been a few months longer or a few months shorter, we would have used the seven-year level.

Valuing the Swap

After you've arrived at the yield you are going to use on your comparison Swap, you are ready to do your calculations. You will note that we have not yet discussed whether we are marking our Swap to market or pricing an unwind. This is because, as indicated earlier, the calculations are the same. To our interpolated yield of 7.024 percent we add the spread of 50 to arrive at an all-in rate on our Swap of 7.524 percent (7.024 + .50). This figure is then compared to the rate on our original Swap of 9 percent. The difference between the two rates, 1.476 percent (9.00 − 7.524), is used in the calculation of the cashflow.

The floating portions cancel each other out, so it is only necessary to compare the fixed rates. If we are valuing a $100 million Swap, we would multiply .01476 by 100,000,000 to come up with an annual cashflow of $1,476,000 per year. Because we are receiving the higher rate in this example, the cashflow would be in our favor and we would have a profit. Most Swaps are on a semiannual basis, so we'd be looking at a cashflow of $738,000 every six months for seven years. (*Note:* If the Swap had been on a quarterly basis, we'd convert our rates to quarterly rates and then look at quarterly cashflows.)

Using the simpler net present value method, we'd come up with a value of $8,052,860 on our Swap (using an HP12C, $n = 14$, $i = 7.024 \div 2$, $pmt = 738{,}000$, and $fv = 0$; then solve for pv). Using a *zero coupon yield curve*, we'd come up with a number that is a bit higher.

If this Swap had been done in the middle of a Swap period, there would be an additional calculation. You would need to add any outstanding accrued interest. However, in an attempt to keep this example simple, the Swap has started on the first day of a period.

Diagramming the Transaction

Sometimes the transaction becomes much clearer if you draw a diagram. Look at Figure 7-1, which shows the four steps in this transaction. The original transaction—the company's receiving the 9 percent from its counterparty and paying Libor—is shown in (*a*). The unwind Swap—the company's paying 7.524 percent and receiving Libor—is shown in (*b*). Both transactions on one diagram are shown in (*c*). It's easy to see the Libor payments canceling each other out and the two fixed payments netting against each other on this diagram. And finally, (*d*) shows the final result of the two transactions netted.

Looking at the Cashflows

Figure 7-2 shows the same transaction on a cashflow basis. Again, looking at the simple diagram, it's easy to see whether your Swap is in or out of the money.

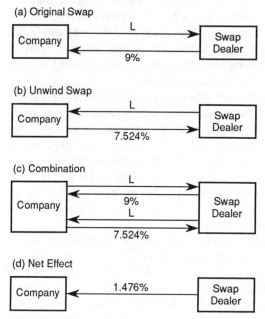

(a) Original Swap

(b) Unwind Swap

(c) Combination

(d) Net Effect

Figure 7-1. Swap and Swap unwind diagram.

Original Swap	9.000%
	(Libor)
Unwind Swap	(7.524%)
	Libor
	1.476%

Figure 7-2. Cashflow diagram of a Swap unwind.

Differences between Mark to Market and Unwinds

There are several subtle differences between the mark-to-market and unwind functions. Although the calculations are the same, you will probably approach the two tasks differently. If you are marking the portfolio to market, you might take the Treasury levels and spreads from the screen and do your calculations. Or you might take the Treasury levels from the newspaper and call one or two dealers for an indicative level on the spreads.

But if you're doing an unwind, your whole attitude will change. For many corporates dealing in the Swap market, this is one of the few areas where they can actually make money for their company. And one or two have been known to speculate in these markets apart from their hedging activity. When an unwind is being negotiated every quarter of a basis point counts. Instead of calling one or two dealers, you might call five. In many cases corporates will want to stay on the line while their transaction is being executed; some will simultaneously watch the screens to determine when their Swap should have been executed. You'll recall from our earlier discussions that this will not make your Swap dealer happy.

Marking Your Portfolio to Market

With the advent of inexpensive powerful computers, any company can mark its portfolio to market with amazing accuracy in a very short period of time. The larger the portfolio, in terms of number of different transactions not size, the longer it will take each day to value the portfolio. But we're still not talking about a great deal of time. And the larger the portfolio, the more important it is to value the portfolio. Once the program has been set up and saved on the computer, an analyst can enter the current interest rate and spread data to update and run the program in about 20 minutes for a portfolio with 25 or more Swaps. As the portfolio gets larger, the time required does not grow proportionately because the Swaps will all reference the same interest rates and spreads.

What Happens When a Loan That Has Been Swapped Is Paid Off?

It is often difficult to predict with any amount of certainty exactly what will happen in the future to any asset or liability. Assets get sold and liabilities get refinanced. Sometimes this is despite the fact that you have been assured by management that this would not happen. And sometimes this is earlier than planned. Business considerations sometimes take precedence over financing concerns. If the Swap was tied to the underlying loan (or asset), you may be forced to unwind the Swap regardless of its value or lack of value. If management is discussing a possible transaction in which the Swap would have to be unwound, make sure they are aware of the consequences of a Swap unwind. If the Swap must be unwound, the method for the unwind was probably agreed to in the loan document. This could result in a windfall profit or loss. Make sure your accountants and tax people are aware of this so that they can let you know of the appropriate tax and accounting ramifications.

If the Swap is not tied to the transaction, you may have the option of keeping the Swap alive or unwinding it. If the Swap unwind is not tied to the transaction, your decision to unwind may depend on whether or not the Swap is in the money, on your interest rate outlook, and also on your other financing plans.

Penny Wise, Pound Foolish

Let's take a look at another example. Sometimes companies can be very short-sighted, especially when it comes to parting with cash. In 1988 the Grenadine Corporation put on a $100 million Swap paying a fixed rate of 9.0 percent and receiving Libor. It did this because it wanted to convert its floating-rate loan to a fixed-rate loan. The rate on its floating bank loan was Libor + 100; the loan had a 10-year maturity. By entering the Swap market, Grenadine had locked in a rate of 10 percent on its loan.

Now let's take a look at Grenadine's cashflows in Figure 7-3. If Grenadine did nothing, it would effectively pay 10 percent on its loan. In 1990, Grenadine, along with everyone else, became convinced that rates were going down. In a falling rate environment, most borrowers want floating-rate loans and Grenadine was no exception. It priced a Swap unwind to see if its Swap was worth anything. Grenadine had waited too long. A call to several dealers revealed that most banks would pay 8.5 percent to unwind an eight-year Swap.

Looking at the cashflows in Figure 7-4, we see that Grenadine's treasurer quickly realized that his company would have to pay the bank to unwind the Swap. The Swap was out of the money by 50 basis points. With eight years remaining on the Swap, this would cost $2,860,000—the present value of 16 semiannual payments of $250,000 each.

Loan	(L + 100)
Swap	(9.0%)
	L
	10.0%

Figure 7-3. All-in rate calculation.

Original Swap	(9.0%)
	L
Unwind Swap	8.5%
	(L)
	.5%

Figure 7-4. First cashflow Swap unwind.

Grenadine didn't want to pay the cash so it waited despite the fact that it believed rates were headed down. After all, reasoned Grenadine's treasurer, how much lower could rates go? One year later, Grenadine was still sitting with its losing Swap position—only it was a bigger loser. As almost everyone is aware, not only did rates plunge in 1991, but Swap spreads did as well.

When Grenadine's treasurer reviewed his Swap position one year later (see Figure 7-5), he was horrified. The Swap had only seven years till maturity but now could be unwound at 7.25 percent instead of 8.5 percent. His Swap was now out of the money to the tune of $9,475,000 or the present value of 14 semiannual payments of $875,000 each. Worse still, Libor had dropped from 8.25 percent to 4.25 percent. He then looked at his cashflows for the year for both the Swap and the loan. He had effectively paid 10 percent or $10 million interest between his Swap and the loan. If he had unwound his Swap, he would have paid only $2,860,000 to do that. Because Libor averaged 6.5 percent, Grenadine would have had interest expense for the year of $6,500,000. This combined with the the money paid to unwind the Swap would have totaled $9,360,000, or $640,000 less than actually spent. In addition, the losing Swap would have been gone and Grenadine, if it thought rates had bottomed, would have been in a position to lock in a new fixed rate at 8.25 percent (the 7.25 percent plus the 100 basis points on the floating loan) or continue to pay about 5 percent on the floating loan (Libor of 4 percent plus the 100 basis points) until it felt like locking in a fixed rate.

Original Swap	(9.00%)
	L
Unwind Swap	7.25%
	(L)
	1.75%

Figure 7-5. Second cashflow Swap unwind.

This, of course, is an extreme example. And the exact opposite could have happened. Grenadine could have spent the $2,860,000 to unwind the Swap and, had interest rates risen, seen its interest expense rise. However, Grenadine had a view on rates, so it was in a position to act. And like many other corporates, Grenadine let a little cash get in the way of what it thought was the right thing to do.

Other Terminology
Reverse Swap

Occasionally you'll hear some market participants talking about doing a reverse Swap. A *reverse Swap* is a new Swap that is executed to unwind an existing position. The new Swap will be at current market levels and will have a tenor that equals the remaining life on the first Swap. The fixed-rate payor of a reverse Swap becomes the floating-rate payor, and vice versa.

Novation

The other term you might hear is novation. *Novation* refers to the creation of a new Swap agreement, thereby simultaneously canceling the old one. This is sometimes done if the terms of one contract are changed—perhaps through the purchase or sale of an option or the rolling of a profit (or loss) from one transaction into an existing Swap.

Portfolio Management through Unwinds

When a Swap is unwound, there are a number of ways to handle the profit or loss. Let's look at the simple portfolio of the Vineland Company. Over a period of time, Vineland put on two $100 million Swaps to hedge a floating-rate loan on its books. Although the two Swaps were put on at different times, their remaining life and reset dates matched exactly. On one Swap Vineland paid 8 percent, and on the other 6 percent. Because both Swaps were with the same counterparty, one of the parties might suggest rewriting the two contracts into one 7 percent Swap. This is occasionally done when a large program is put on piecemeal. For example, a company might do a $300 million program in $25 million pieces. Rather than carry 12 separate contracts, both parties might prefer to have one. This would make the record keeping, especially at the reset dates, easier. These are two simple examples of novation.

But Vineland did not want to do that. Instead with fixed rates for the remaining life of its Swaps at 7.5 percent, Vineland chose to unwind the Swap on which it was the fixed-rate payor at 6 percent. Its profit on this transaction would be the present value of 150 basis points (7.5 − 6.0). If it desired to take the profit up front, it could do so. Or Vineland has two other options. The first, as discussed earlier, is not to take the profit up front but to leave it as an annuity. Depending on its outlook for interest rates and its cashflow needs, Vineland might decide to do just that. This would be handled by either leaving two offsetting Swaps on its counterparty's books or netting the two and writing a new contract.

If Vineland is managing its overall interest rate exposure, it might choose a second option—rolling the profit from the unwind into an existing Swap. Thus, Vineland might take the 150 basis points and reduce the rate on its existing 8.0 percent Swap to 6.5 percent (8.0 − 1.5)—another case of novation because new contracts would have to be written. In many instances, leaving the cash with the institution handling the unwind will get you a slightly better price. And there certainly won't be any arguments over the discounting on the unwind.

8

Other Refinements in Swap Pricing

We've talked about pricing Swaps, Swap unwinds, and marking Swaps to market in a very general way. And we've talked about the theory behind these techniques. One of the big advantages of the Swap market is that it allows a good deal of customization to meet the needs of the individual customer. Many Swaps, even plain vanilla ones, are custom tailored. To meet these customization requirements, there are certain refinements that need to be made to the plain vanilla pricing discussed earlier.

This chapter will offer some refinements to those techniques and will discuss in some detail the mechanisms behind the use of the zero coupon yield curves mentioned in Chapter 7. All these techniques can be programmed on a personal computer using some of the popular spreadsheet applications available or in more sophisticated computer languages. With the exception of the zero coupon yield curve, all the calculations can be done on your financial calculator. (The zero coupon yield curve can too, but it would be quite cumbersome.) So let's get started.

Compounding/Decompounding

As you are probably aware, the quoted yields on Treasury notes are semiannual yields. As long as the Swap you are using will pay on a semiannual basis, there is no need to make any adjustments to this yield.

The spreads also assume semiannual receipts. And this is fine for many Swaps because the most common is against six-month Libor. But if you are swapping against three-month Libor and making quarterly payments, you will need to *decompound* the semiannual fixed rate to a quarterly rate; if you are swapping against one-year Libor (very rare), you will need to *compound* the fixed rate. The most frequent payment periods—after semiannual—are quarterly and monthly. The process of compounding a fixed rate is analogous to compounding the interest on a CD.

These formulas are quite simple if you understand them, but we need a few facts before we start. The interest rate is always expressed as a decimal (i.e., 6 percent as .06). When raising to a power that is a fraction, use the decimal form on your financial calculator (i.e., ½ as .5 and ¼ as .25). Your personal computer will recognize either the decimal or the fraction, but you may have to use an extra set of parentheses in your formulas to accommodate a fraction. In the following discussions, we will use the symbol ^ to indicate raising to a power. So a number squared will be indicated as n^2 and the square root of a number will be indicated as n^.5.

Decompounding

You'll probably use the decompounding formula more than the compounding formula. The decompounding formula is:

$$\text{Rate} = [(1 + i)^{\wedge \frac{1}{n}}] - 1$$

where ^ means raise to the power
  i = the interest rate being decompounded
  n = the number of periods the original rate is being decompounded into

So in a calculation where a semiannual rate is being decompounded into a quarterly rate, n would equal 2. In a calculation where a semiannual rate is being decompounded into a monthly rate, n would equal 6.

Let's convert a semiannual rate of 7 percent to a monthly rate. Because it's semiannual into monthly, n will equal 6 and $\frac{1}{n}$ will equal .16667.

$$\text{Monthly rate} = [(1 + .07)^{\wedge}.16667] - 1 \times 6$$

$$= .06804$$

$$= 6.804\%$$

On an HP12C calculator:

1.07 enter

.16667 $y^\wedge x$

1 −

6x ;

where $y^\wedge x$ is the Y to the x power key

You can see from this example that the difference between the semiannual rate and the monthly rate is almost 20 basis points.

Compounding

The formula for compounding is:

$$\text{Rate} = [(1 + \tfrac{i}{n})^\wedge n] - 1$$

where $^\wedge$ means raise to the power
  n = the number of periods by which the initial rate is to be expanded (i.e., quarterly to semiannual, $n = 2$; semiannual to annual, $n = 2$; monthly to semiannual, $n = 6$; and monthly to annual, $n = 12$)

For example, let's convert a quarterly rate of 7 percent to an annual rate.

$$\text{Annual rate} = (.07/4 + 1)^\wedge 4 - 1$$
$$= .071859$$
$$= 7.1859\%$$

Money Market Basis/Bond Basis

The other adjustment that sometimes needs to be made to the fixed rate is to change it from bond basis to money market basis or vice versa. (Most fixed rates are quoted on a bond basis.) The *bond basis*, sometimes referred to as 30/360, assumes 12 months of 30 days each. On a *money market basis* rates are quoted on a 360-day year. This effectively adds five extra days to your interest calculations. A 6 percent money market rate is not the same as a 6 percent bond equivalent rate.

To convert a money market rate to a bond rate, multiply the money market rate by $^{365}\!/_{360}$. To convert the bond basis rate to a money market rate, multiply the bond rate by $^{360}\!/_{365}$. You will note a certain "inequity" in the fixed versus floating calculation of Swap payments. The floating payment is almost always paid on a money market basis (i.e., actual number of days ÷ 360, whereas the fixed side is most frequently quoted as 30/360). In effect, in the course of a full year, the floating-rate payor pays interest for five days more than the fixed payor (six in the case of leap year). This, however, is market convention.

When asking for rates on Swaps and getting quotes, make sure you and all your potential counterparties are quoting on the same basis.

Corporate Start versus Spot Start

As mentioned earlier, in a large part of the Swap market the floating index is Libor. A Libor rate is usually set two business days before the rate actually goes into effect. Although some banks will sometimes ask for the rate to be set three days in advance, two days is the market convention. This convention also applies to the Libor setting on Swaps. Therefore, most Swaps will start two days after the fixed rate is set. This allows for the floating side to be set in the Libor market. If the Swap is executed very late in the afternoon, a case may be made for starting the Swap three days forward as it is too late to set the Libor rate. This should present no problems but should be discussed beforehand. Sometimes it won't be mentioned until after the Swap has been executed, especially if the execution has taken a bit of time. Again, there usually is no problem with this. The terminology for this type of start, taken from the foreign exchange market, is *spot start*.

A very few Swap dealers (and their numbers are diminishing) may request that you use a corporate start instead of a spot start. The dealers tend to be the players active in the bond market. *Corporate starts* require that the Swap begin not two business days hence but five. This type of start mimics the bond market where trades settle five business days after the trade. This type of start seems to be falling from favor in the market. Still, make sure and say spot start so that everyone is quoting apples and apples.

Up-Front Payments

In the beginning days of Swaps, it was not uncommon to find a financial institution charging its corporate customer an up-front fee for the transaction. Most of these up-front fees were charged in the pre-ISDA days (i.e., before the partial standardization of documentation). This fee was supposed to partially compensate the institution for the legal expenses it would have in setting up the necessary documentation. With the standard ISDA schedule, this is no longer the factor that it once was. Although it is true that the Swap schedule still must be negotiated, it is not an overwhelming expense and is typically not passed on to the customer. In fact, I'd question any institution that tried to do this.

There is another possible reason that an up-front fee might be included. If the paying institution wished to write down the rate over the life of the Swap, it is possible to pay an up-front fee to do this. The up-front fee would be spread over the life of the Swap, and a corresponding lower rate would be charged. This is rarely done.

Although it is possible to do the reverse (i.e., have the receiving institution pay an up-front fee to the payor and write up the rate), this is unlikely to happen. The receiver, in effect, would be lending money to the payor at the Swap rate.

Swap Annuities

When a Swap is unwound, typically the party with the profit receives a cash payment from the party with the loss. There can be some interesting "discussions" over the up-front value of the payments. But this is not always the case. Rather than take those payments in a lump payment, an institution that does not have an immediate need for the cash may choose to leave the cash with the counterparty and take an *annuity* (i.e., receive a series of periodic payments over the remaining life of the Swap). An institution that does this will not have to concern itself with the rate at which the cashflows were discounted. That's because no discounting is necessary.

But there's a second reason you might wish to do this. Let's say you have just unwound a Swap because you believe that rates have peaked. You expect rates to fall and, therefore, wish to be in a floating mode. So you unwind your Swap for which you were a fixed-rate payor. Let's also say that you are right in your forecast and that rates drop. A year later, you think that rates have fallen as far as they are going to go and so you choose to take your lump sum at this point. Why would you do this?

Think a minute about the present valuing techniques used to value these streams of payments. One thing should stand out in your mind. The lower the rate used in the discounting, the higher your payment will be. Therefore, if you wait until rates bottom out, you'll maximize your payments. Let's look at a simple example. You've just unwound your Swap in which you were paying 8 percent at 10 percent. The Swap was for $100 million and had eight years' remaining life. To keep this simple, we're going to make this an annual pay/receive Swap. You've just earned for your firm eight annual payments of $2 million each or, on a present value basis, almost $10.7 million.

But instead of taking that $10 million, you decide to leave it and take an annuity stream. One year goes by and on the day you receive your first $2 million payment, you decide that rates have bottomed out and you'd like to take the remaining seven payments at that point. Rates have dropped back to 8 percent. The present value of the remaining seven payments is $10.4 million. By waiting a year and with rates falling, your company would earn $12.4 million instead of $10.7 million. Even if you had invested the $10.7 million at 10 percent, you'd have only earned interest of a little over a million dollars, bringing your total cash to $11.77 million—and it is unlikely that you'd get 10 percent on a short-term investment if eight-year Swap rates were 10 percent. Keep in mind, however, that if your interest rate forecast is wrong, you could end up costing your company a similar amount of money.

Stub Periods

So far in our discussions we have assumed all even periods. In other words, if we're talking about a 10-year Swap with semiannual settlements, we're always talking about 20 equal periods. But the real world does not always work this way. Things are not always this neat. You may decide to fix the rate on your loan (which had an original term of five years) three months after the loan was put on the books. Or you may decide to unwind a Swap that has a remaining life of seven years, three months, and four days.

In either event, you are left with an odd period—a partial period. This is referred to as a *stub period*. It can be handled in a number of ways, none of which are difficult.

Setting Up a Swap

If you enter into a Swap with a stub period, you have two options for handling it. You have the choice of putting it at the beginning or the end. I strongly recommend the beginning. Let's say you're doing a Swap against six-month Libor and you'll end up with a stub period of two months. If you put the stub at the beginning, you will be very aware of it and handle it correctly. The two-month floating setting will be against two-month Libor for the first period only, and the rate will be set correctly. Both you and your counterparty will have discussed this and there should be no problem. If you leave it to the end, you'll have to hope that you (or someone) remembers it.

In addition, should you choose to unwind or assign the Swap before maturity, this fact will have to be disclosed and worked into the calculations. No big deal; just one more detail and one more place to add confusion to an already complicated calculation.

Assignments

When relating the details to a potential counterparty for assignment, make sure that the stub period, should there be one at the end, is relayed. This will slightly change the way the counterparty evaluates the Swap.

Unwinds

Unwinds are a little more difficult to handle but again no real problem. If the stub period is at the beginning (and in most unwinds it will be), handle the stub period separately. Let's say that you have a Swap with a remaining life of four years and nine months against six-month Libor. This will give you nine full periods and one partial. Calculate the value of the partial—if we've got a 9 percent $100 million Swap being unwound against 7 percent, the partial period value will be $500,000 (.02 × $100,000,000 × $\frac{3}{12}$). Some institutions will not bring this forward (i.e., present value) for the three months, but most will. In a 7 percent rate environment, the value for three months of $500,000 is $491,400. (On your HP12C, $n = 1$, $i = \frac{7}{4}$, $pmt = 0$, $fv = 500,000$; solve for pv.)

Then look at the present value of your nine full period cashflows brought back to the end of your stub period. In other words, pretend the stub doesn't exist. The value of those cashflows would be $7.608 million if there were no stub. (On an HP12C, use $n = 9$, $i = \frac{7}{2}$, $pmt = 500,000$, $fv = 0$; solve for pv.) Then bring this amount forward for three months just as you did on the stub calculation, only this time the $7.608 million goes in the future value slot. You'll find that value to be $7.477 million. Add that to the present value of your stub payment.

If you're unwinding a Swap with the stub at the end, you'll do almost the opposite. Let's assume a Swap with a remaining life of four years and nine months against six-month Libor—again, nine full periods and one partial. Calculate the value of the nine payments as though the stub did not exist. You will need to make no further adjustments to this number. As before, calculate the value of the stub and bring it forward and add it to the value of the full periods. Although stub periods rarely make a big difference in the values, every little bit helps.

New Phenomena Affect the Swap Market

Along with the credit crunch, 1991 saw several other phenomena that affected the Swap market. The yield curve steepened, turning fixed-rate payors into big net payors. Remember that most Swap agreements allow the netting of the fixed and floating payments. New Swaps put on the books with longer maturities would immediately call for large payments on the part of the fixed-rate payor. Although, in most normal times, the differential between the fixed rate and the floating rate usually went in favor of the floating-rate payor, the differentials were never this large. Fixed rates of $8\frac{1}{2}$ percent or 9 percent were being netted against a Libor level of close to 4 percent by year-end. No wonder many corporate payors stayed out of the market.

Potential fixed-rate payors stayed out of the market in droves. They let their loans float and enjoyed floating rates not seen in a lifetime. They paid 4 percent Libor instead of locking in 9 percent, thus saving themselves 5 percent. Many who normally would have fixed didn't, preferring instead to pay much lower Libor levels. They were saving so much money on a current basis that they could afford to lock in a higher rate later on and still come out ahead of the game. It's kind of hard to convince upper management to lock in even 7.5 percent when you can pay 4 percent by continuing to float.

And a funny thing happened. Rates continued to come down, as did spreads. So the lucky ones who hadn't locked in continued to float. Of course, this did not make life real interesting for those Swap dealers restricted to running a matched book. Those authorized to take positions, who guessed correctly, made a bundle of money. This was the year that the cost of carry became a concern in the Swap market—and with good reason. Between the credit crunch, the steep yield curve, and declining spreads and rates, 1991 was a year many Swap market participants would prefer to forget. By the spring of 1992, Libor was still flirting with 4 percent and fixed Swap rates were under 7 percent for five years (and even lower for four years). The big winners were those who didn't fix or those who floated in 1991.

Maximizing the Value of an Unwind

The value of a Swap unwind is the present value of the future cashflows. Present value calculations are affected by the interest rate used to discount the cashflows. The higher the interest rate, the lower the present value; the lower the interest rate, the higher the present value. Those with a Swap in a loss position will prefer to evaluate their position when rates are high, and those with a profit position prefer to evaluate when rates are low. But decisions to unwind Swaps are usually made on a business need or on an outlook for future interest rates.

Quite frequently the outlook for interest rates will be in conflict for the preferred rate to use in discounting. For example, if you are paying a fixed rate on a Swap that is in a gain position, and your outlook for rates tells you that rates are going down, you might decide to unwind your Swap. Although unwinding a Swap when you're a fixed-rate payor and rates are high might be a very smart thing to do, it will not maximize the value of your unwind.

Annuities

Let's assume that you're paying 8 percent on a $100 million Swap with a remaining life of five years. Current Swap rates are 10 percent, but you are expecting a big drop in rates and would like to lock in your profit. You unwind your Swap and earn a differential of 2 percent per year (10% − 8%). On a $100 million transaction this comes to $2 million per year (.02 × $100,000,000). Now most institutions would be happy with the present value of the $2 million per year and take the up-front payment. But who says you have to take the money up front—especially if you expect rates to fall?

Most Swap dealers would be happy to arrange an annuity for you. Rather than take the lesser amount up front (and argue with your Swap dealer about discount rates and methodology), why not arrange to leave the payment with the dealer and take your $2 million per year each year. Most, if not all, dealers will agree to this. Watch the credit rating of any institution holding your funds in this manner.

Rates Decline

If you were correct in your forecast, rates will decline. When you feel they've bottomed out, you might approach your Swap dealer, not only to put on some fixed-rate pay Swaps, but to collect your annuity in a lump sum. True, you'll once again be arguing with the dealer about discounting rates and methods of valuation, but you'll end up with a larger sum of money.

Customized Swaps

One of the things that certain Swap dealers are proudest of is their ability to customize Swaps to the special needs of their customers. They can match Swaps with other products and thus meet the specialized needs of their customers. This customization, of course, comes at a price. The farther from the norm the transaction is, the less likely it is that customers will be able to correctly price the transaction themselves. Of course, if a dealer doesn't know what he or she is doing the dealer may underprice the transaction.

Day Counts

It is not possible to operate efficiently in the interest rate Swap world without understanding the different types of *day counts* used. When calculating payments, comparing prices, or when evaluating prices on unwinds, it is important to specify what type of day count is being used for both the floating side and the fixed side of the Swap. Not everyone uses the same methodology, especially on the fixed side. You need to understand the three main types of day counts in order to calculate payments correctly. By day count we are referring to the calculation done to determine how many days are in a given period. These numbers are then used in calculating interest payments.

Actual/360

The *actual/360* calculation comes from the Libor market where a 360-day year is always used. The actual number of days in the period is counted up and then divided by 360. This figure is then multiplied by the applicable interest rate and the notional amount when calculating payments. It is used for almost all floating-rate payments for U.S. dollar interest rate Swaps.

If you were to add up all the payments made using this methodology for one complete calendar year, you'd quickly discover that you've paid five (six in a leap year) "extra" days' interest.

Actual/365

The *actual/365* methodology is similar to the actual/360 with the substitution of 365 (366 in leap years) for 360. There are no extra days' interest paid. This, along with the next method, is used on the fixed-rate leg of most transactions.

30/360

The *30/360* methodology might be compared to calculating mortgage payments on a fixed-rate mortgage. Each month you make the same payments regardless of the number of days in the month. Your February payment is the same as your July payment. Using 30/360 methodology for day count, the same payment is assumed to be made each month. Very simply, when counting days, each month is assumed to have 30 days.

When calculating the number of days, February gets added in as 30. However, those extra days are not apportioned, they're all added in on the last day of the month. A calculation through February 27 (actually paid on February 28) would only use 27 days. Make the calculation go one day further and February counts as 30 days. Similarly, any month with 31 days gets a "free" day. The thirty-first is not counted.

At the end of a complete calendar year, 360 days of interest will have been paid. Because 30/360 assumes a 360-day year, there are no "extra" or "free" days—no days are really lost or gained.

For those using an HP12C calculator, the conversion from actual/365 to actual/360 is quite simple. To calculate the number of days, enter the earlier date in this form: *mo.da.yr* (remembering that the first nine days of a month must be entered with a zero as a leading integer—that is, February 1, 1991, gets entered as 2.01.1991).

After entering the date, hit the enter key and then enter in the second date—say 3.01.1991—and then hit the *g* key followed by the *EEX* key. In this particular example, the number *28* should show up on your calculator.

Now hit the *x*><*y* key; your calculator should show the correct answer for 30/360 methodology: 30.

30/360 versus Actual/360

At the end of a complete year, the amount of interest paid using either the 30/360 or the actual/365 day count method will be exactly the same.

The only difference will be when the payments were made. Depending on the time of the year, payments will either be larger or smaller but will even out in the end (more or less). Knowing the difference between 30/360 and actual/360 is important when calculating an unwind because the stub period may contain more interest in 30/360 if February falls into the calculation. And as discussed earlier, you always want to compare apples with apples, so when buying or selling, it is important to relay the correct information.

Different Floating Indexes

Although most Swaps are quoted against six-month Libor, it is not uncommon for someone to request a Swap against three-month Libor. When this happens, the rates can be adjusted in one of several ways. The most common is for the semiannual rate on the Swap to be decompounded, using the techniques described earlier, to a quarterly rate. Then the floating payment is reset quarterly instead of-semiannually, and the payments are made quarterly and they are netted.

Very occasionally, the fixed rate is not decompounded and the quarterly payment is either held until the six-month date or it is made at each quarter. If it is held, interest usually accrues to an agreed-upon rate. The agreed-upon rate is usually the floating rate itself. If one payment is made quarterly and the other semiannually, it could be viewed as a loan. This is one of the things that makes regulators look twice. This type of an arrangement is not that common. Although in the beginning days it was not uncommon to see Swaps where one party, usually the fixed-rate payor, paid on an annual basis and the other on a semiannual. In these instances, the party who makes the first payment has some additional credit exposure for the period when it is out of pocket.

Hedging Loans with a Rate
Other Than Libor

Not every loan written is a Libor rate loan. Therefore, a Swap with a floating index of Libor does not provide a perfect hedge for such loans. For example, many commercial paper programs are hedged in the Swap market when the issuer wishes to fix rates. This would be an acceptable hedge if the differential between Libor and commercial paper rates always stayed the same (in terms of commodities, if the basis always stayed the same). But this is not the case. Many are willing to live with this fluctuating differential, believing that over time it will even out. Or they simply may not care to refine their hedging that much.

However, most who are truly hedging are not willing to live with this changing differential. This gave rise to basis Swaps (i.e., the exchange of one floating index for another) and to interest rate Swaps where the floating index rather than Libor is the index desired.

A smart hedger could price out a Swap with Libor as the floating index and a basis Swap and compare it with a Swap that had the desired floating index. In most instances, one Swap should give the same or better results than two Swaps. However, if you're willing to live with the extra work, you may be able to get two Swaps from two different dealers with different biases in their books to give a better all in rate.

And if you're comfortable about calling the direction of the two floating indexes, you might not put your basis Swap on until a later date. If you're right in your outlook, you could save a few basis points.

Mismatch of Dates

Many market participants use the Swap market to adjust the nature of the rates on their loans as they forecast interest rates. Thus, borrowers with five-year floating-rate loans who do not anticipate an increase in rates may leave the loan floating. If two years later they change their outlook, they may then use the Swap market to lock in the rate on their loan for part or all of the remaining life of the loan depending on their outlook for rates and business requirements. (It does them no good to lock in the rate for the remaining three years if they expect to pay the loan off in two—unless they expect rates to be much higher and plan on using the Swap to hedge another loan or plan to take a profit.) The day that such a borrower enters the market will, in all likelihood, not correspond to an interest payment date on the underlying loan. The borrower could either live with this discrepancy or, better yet, arrange for a stub period in the beginning.

Zero Coupon Yield Curve

Many institutions with large portfolios are starting to use zero coupon yield curves to price unwinds. These models, which can be set up on a computer, involve numerous calculations and probably give a more precise valuation for a Swap. Although it is possible to do all the calculations on a hand-held calculator, it would take you quite a while and the market would have moved by the time you completed the calculations (we'll go through those calculations in a moment). The end user who does not have one of these sophisticated models available for pricing unwinds or valuing the company's portfolio will still get a reasonably good result using the present valuing techniques.

Rather than looking at the final maturity of the Swap and discounting the cashflows at that rate, each payment is looked at individually and the cashflows are evaluated for the appropriate time frame. For example, an unwind (or valuation) of a Swap with semiannual payments and a nine-year remaining life would have 18 remaining payments. Each payment would be evaluated separately. There would be 18 separate calculations—not at the applicable Swap rate, but each at its own applicable zero coupon Swap rate. A nine-year Swap with quarterly payments would have 36 separate calculations.

The zero coupon yield curve eliminates payments between the current date and the end date through a simulation. The theory is not as complicated as it sounds, as you'll see when we run through a simple example.

The most sophisticated of these pricing models can be fed right from a Treasury screen. With the proper parameters set up (i.e., the notional amounts, original rate, and maturity), a button can be pushed and a live yield curve is fed computer to computer into the model and the new valuation is spit out.

Zero Coupon Yield Curve Calculation

The concept of zero coupon yield is similar to that of purchasing zero coupon bonds. You invest a sum of money on the first day and then do not receive any interest payments until the bond matures. In this instance, the computer simulates a series of Swaps to eliminate the intervening Swap fixed-rate interest payments for each time horizon. An example will make this a little clearer.

Figure 8-1 shows a five-year Swap yield curve. It is a particularly steep yield curve, like the one we had in 1992. A steep yield curve makes

One-year	3.75%	3.68%
Two-year	4.55%	4.48%
Three-year	5.15%	5.08%
Four-year	5.70%	5.63%
Five-year	6.85%	6.78%

Figure 8-1. Five-year Swap yield curve.

for larger differences when using a zero coupon yield curve, as opposed to a straight present value technique, to discount. In a flatter yield curve environment, the differences are less apparent. For ease of calculations, we are assuming that the rates are annual rates and that there are no stub periods. It is usually assumed that any extra cash balances can be invested or borrowed at Libor. We've also assumed that any interpolations needed to get the appropriate rates have been already done and incorporated in Figure 8-1.

In our simple example, we are trying to unwind a Swap where we are the fixed-rate receiver at 7.78 percent on $100 million. In a plain vanilla present value model, we'd take the difference between 7.78 percent and 6.78 percent to come up with 1 percent (100 basis points), then we'd multiply the 1 percent by $100 million to come up with annual payments of $1 million per year for five years. Discounting those payments at 6.85 percent, we'd come up with a value of $4,116,718.

Figure 8-2 shows the calculations necessary to come up with the zero coupon rate to be used for the fifth year. In these calculations of interest rates, it's always necessary to start with some principal amount. I've chosen $1,000,000. You'd get the same result whether you choose $1 or $100,000,000. So, we show an initial outflow of $1,000,000 and then, looking at our Swap curve, calculate the cashflows on the fixed-rate side. After the initial payment, annual interest payments are calculated using 6.85 percent; the final payment includes a repayment of the initial principal—thus the payment of $1,068,500 rather than just $68,500. (Some will prefer to show the initial amount as a negative number and the signs of all other numbers on the charts the reverse of what we show. It's a matter of personal preference and will not affect your final result.) It is now necessary to eliminate those payments between time period zero and the fifth year. The first payment that is eliminated is the fourth years' interest of $68,500. To eliminate this payment, do a Swap that will result in a fourth-year payment of $68,500. This will entail entering into a Swap that is going in the other direction. So we enter $68,500 as our final fourth-year payment and figure out how much we should have started with so that the final payment will be the required amount.

If the final amount for the fourth year is to be $68,500 and that includes repayment of the original amount and interest at a four-year rate, we divide $68,500 by 1 plus the interest rate to find the original amount. Dividing $68,500 by 1.0563 gives us an original amount of $64,849 (remember to reverse the sign when entering it on your worksheet). Interest on that amount for the intervening years is $3,651 ($64,849 × .0563).

				Cashflow						
Year	5th year	4th year	Total	3rd year	Total	2nd year	Total	1st year	Total	
0	$1,000,000	($64,849)	$ 935,151	($61,714)	$873,437	($59,068)	$ 814,369	($56,971)	$ 757,398	
1	(68,500)	3,651	(64,849)	3,135	(61,714)	(2,646)	(59,068)	59,068	0	
2	(68,500)	3,651	(64,849)	3,135	(61,714)	61,714	0		0	
3	(68,500)	3,651	(64,849)	64,849	0		0		0	
4	(68,500)	68,500	0		0		0		0	
5	(1,068,500)		(1,068,500)		(1,068,500)		(1,068,500)		(1,068,500)	
									7.12%	

Figure 8-2. Zero coupon yield curve, fifth-year calculation.

Cashflow

Year	4th year	3rd year	Total	2nd year	Total	1st year	Total
0	$1,000,000	($54,244)	$ 945,756	($51,918)	$ 893,837	($49,975)	$ 843,862
1	(57,000)	2,756	(54,244)	2,430	(51,814)	51,814	0
2	(57,000)	2,756	(54,244)	54,244	0		0
3	(57,000)	57,000	0		0		0
4	(1,057,000)		(1,057,000)		(1,057,000)		(1,057,000)
							5.79%

Figure 8-3. Zero coupon yield curve, fourth-year calculation.

		Cashflow			
Year	3rd year	2nd year	Total	1st year	Total
0	$1,000,000	($49,292)	$ 950,708	($47,447)	$ 903,262
1	(51,500)	2,307	49,193	49,193	0
2	(51,500)	51,500	0		0
3	(1,051,500)		(1,051,500)		(1,051,500)
					5.20%

Figure 8-4. Zero coupon yield curve, third-year calculation.

Now that the fourth-year payment has been eliminated, let's see where we stand. Column three shows the summation of the first two transactions. In eliminating the fourth-year payment, we've also eliminated part of the third-year payment. You'll also notice that we've reduced our initial amount. This time it is only necessary to eliminate $64,849 for the third year. Using the same technique, we reverse this payment and add the results to the prior summation.

After this technique is used to eliminate the second-year payments and the first, we're left with two numbers: the initial amount after intervening Swaps of $739,985 and the final repayment amount of $1,068,500. Solve for the internal rate of return. (You can also do this calculation on your financial calculator by solving for the interest rate after entering a present value, a future value, and payments of zero and five years.) The rate with which to discount the fifth-year payment is 7.62 percent.

Figures 8-3 through 8-6 show the calculations for the rates to be used to discount the remaining four payments. You can see that the calculations can get quite cumbersome. It helps to have a computer and, even better, one that has the program already set up and is able to get the yield curve fed into it directly.

Figure 8-7 shows the zero coupon yield curve for those wishing to receive (i.e., to reverse) a Swap in which they were already paying a fixed

	Cashflow		
Year	2nd year	1st year	Total
0	$1,000,000	($43,885)	$956,115
1	(45,500)	45,500	0
2	(1,045,500)		(1,045,500)
			4.57%

Figure 8-5. Zero coupon yield curve, second-year calculation.

Year	1st-year cashflow
0	$1,000,000
1	(1,037,500)
	3.75%

Figure 8-6. Zero coupon yield curve, first-year calculation.

Year 1 → 3.75%
Year 2 → 4.57%
Year 3 → 5.20%
Year 4 → 6.12%
Year 5 → 7.62%

Figure 8-7. Zero coupon Swap yield curve.

rate. It would be slightly higher for those wishing to pay (i.e., those wishing to reverse) a Swap in which they were receiving the fixed rate.

Finally, Figure 8-8 shows the value of this unwind using the zero coupon yield curve on each piece. This is compared with the plain vanilla present value technique. You'll note that on this $100,000,000 five-year reversal, there is a difference of almost $110,000. Not a huge sum of money for someone playing with $100,000,000, but enough to focus on. The zero coupon calculations can work for or against you depending on whether you're making or losing money. In either case, the use of the curve tends to slightly magnify the results—the steeper the yield curve, the greater the magnification.

Year 1	3.75%	$929,017
Year 2	4.57%	874,539
Year 3	5.20%	816,593
Year 4	5.79%	754,650
Year 5	7.12%	661,698
Total		$4,036,497
Plain vanilla		
methodology		4,116,718
Difference		($80,221)

Figure 8-8. Zero coupon Swap yield curve comparison.

9
Swaptions

Technically speaking, Swaptions should be included in Chapter 10 on other derivative products. However, the topic is important, and given the amount of material related to it, a separate chapter seems to make sense. After Swaps, it is probably the most used derivative product. Many custom-tailored transactions have Swaptions built in. Many of the new strategies being developed revolve around Swaptions. And a good understanding of this vehicle will help you devise your own.

When I began this book, I asked several friends who were in the business for amusing anecdotes to use. When I asked Deborah Orlando, Director, Barclays Bank PLC, she thought for about two seconds before responding. "Remember the first time you did a Swaption?" she said. "You were trying to figure out whether you were buying a put or a call." Although I was not amused with her choice of stories, it does point out one of the reasons no one bothers to differentiate a put from a call in the Swap market.

Options on Swaps are powerful tools and are used for many different reasons. The word *Swaption* is used collectively to cover both puts and calls. Very few people discuss whether the instrument being bought or sold is a put or a call. Rather, they discuss who bought or sold what rights. For example, I want to buy a Swaption that will give me the right to pay fixed for seven years in six months at 7 percent. Or I'd like to sell an option which will give you the right to pay fixed (or make me receive fixed) at 7 percent for seven years in six months. Very simply put, a *Swaption* is an option on a Swap.

For those who insist, a *payor's Swaption* gives the purchaser the right to pay fixed and would be analogous to a bond put. Conversely, a *receiver's Swaption* gives the purchaser the right to receive fixed and is analogous to a bond call.

Characteristics of a Swaption

As with other types of options, Swaptions are defined by certain characteristics: the underlying, the expiration date, the exercise date, the strike, and the style. All of these characteristics need to be spelled out when pricing a Swaption. If you are buying the option (i.e., taking a long position), you will have purchased the right, but not the obligation, to enter into a Swap whereby you will pay (or receive) the fixed rate on the underlying Swap. A payor's Swaption is one where you have the right to pay the fixed rate, and a receiver's Swaption gives you the right to receive the fixed rate. Conversely, if you are selling or writing the option (i.e., taking a short position), you will have sold the right, but not the obligation, to be required to enter into a Swap whereby you will pay (or receive) the fixed rate on the underlying Swap. Before discussing Swaptions in any detail, we need to define some terms.

The Underlying

The *underlying* is the Swap as defined in the Swaption agreement.

Expiration Date

The *expiration date* is the last date of the option period. Typically, with a spot start Swap, it is two business days after the exercise date; with a corporate start Swap, it would be five business days after the exercise date or a specific date that would be spelled out in the agreement. This date is of little importance because the exercise date is the main focus.

Exercise Date

The *exercise date* is the date when the buyer of the Swaption invokes the right to require the seller of the Swaption to enter into the agreed-on Swap. If this date passes and the option is not exercised, the option expires.

The Strike Price

In a stock option, the strike is the level at which the stock must be bought or sold if the option is to be exercised regardless of where the market is. The strike on a Swaption is similar. The *strike* is the fixed rate that will be paid/received if the Swaption is exercised.

Swaption Premium

As in any other type of option, the *premium* is the price of the option. The premium is typically quoted in basis points. Thus, a price of 50 basis points is $500,000 on $100,000,000 or $50,000 on $10,000,000. Premiums are also usually paid up front, although other arrangements can be made.

Swaption Styles
American-Style Options

Most people who are familiar with stock options or exchange traded options are used to dealing with *American-style options*. These options can be exercised any time the option holder (purchaser) desires. Once the option goes in the money, the seller of the option is at risk that the option will be exercised. And once it is in the money, it is almost guaranteed that at some point it will be exercised. In the Swap market, the option can be exercised at any time that the buyer of the option desires *only* if it is an American-style option. At the time the option is purchased the style is specified. If it can be exercised at any point during the life of the option, it is an American-style option.

European-Style Options

European-style options, on the other hand, can only be exercised on one day at the end of the option period. This is typically two days for a spot start Swap to allow for a Libor setting (if it were a corporate start Swap, it would be five days prior). A European-style Swaption can be in the money for the entire option period and then go out of the money on the exercise date. If that happens the buyer of the Swaption is out of luck. A buyer of a European-style Swaption that is in the money does have another choice.

Swaptions can be sold prior to their expiration. As with Swaps, they can be sold to the original writer of the option or to a third party. If sold to a third party, the option can either be assigned or the two positions can be held open—again using double credit.

Swaption Pricing: European-Style versus American-Style

Most Swaptions are written European-style. If you get quotes for an American-style option and a European-style Swaption with identical parameters other than the style, you'll find that the quotes will not be what you expect.

One would expect an American-style Swaption to be much more expensive than one that is European-style. The two options will either be identical in cost or the American will only be slightly more expensive. Quite frequently there will be no difference in price. The best explanation the experts can come up with is that the pricing models don't price this feature correctly.

Given these facts, one would be better off buying American-style options and selling European-style ones, all other things being equal.

Bermuda-Style Options

Occasionally you will find reference to a *Bermuda-style option*. Such an option is exercisable on several days rather than one day as in European-style. Bermuda-style Swaptions, also referred to as modified American, are rather uncommon.

OTC

Swaptions are traded over the counter (*OTC*) rather than on established exchanges the way stock and futures options are. Two Swaps futures contracts were introduced in 1992. It is not believed that either will survive. If they do, then it will only be a matter of time before we see *exchange-traded* Swaptions.

The over-the-counter feature allows for unlimited customization and financial innovation—two features that have been a boon to this market. Rather than trying to force a solution from tools that don't quite match (i.e., futures contracts), trades can be custom-tailored to the needs of the customer. Most of the trades are large by exchange standards and often combine several products. Options are quite frequently embedded in transactions; in those instances, they are usually paid for not in cash but by an adjustment to the rate.

Value Components

As with any other type of option, a Swaption's value has two components: its time value and its intrinsic value. The time value decays over time and can even increase if volatility in the market increases. The intrinsic value of the Swaption changes from day to day as the market price of the underlying changes. An out-of-the-money Swaption will have no intrinsic value. Usually the difference in prices from two different institutions reflects the volatility figures used by each firm. When getting prices from more than one firm, it will sometimes help to get the volatility figures each is using. This will help you negotiate a better price. However, most traders are reluctant to give out this information no matter how willing the marketing person. Still, it can't hurt to ask.

Delta

There's one more term that needs to be discussed in relation to Swaptions. A stock option that is in the money fluctuates in value dollar for dollar with the value of the underlying. It is said to have a *delta* of 1. An option that goes up or down 50 cents for every dollar movement in the price of the underlying is said to have a delta of .5. Delta measures the relationship between the price movement of the underlying and the price movement of the option. This changes every day and is extremely important to those hedging with options.

Although the same calculations can and are done on Swaptions, they do not have the same importance in the Swaps market owing to the nature of the hedging activity. Still for those few individuals who actively trade Swaptions, delta can be an important calculation. As with any other option, the further out of the money an option, the lower the delta. A delta of a negative number implies an inverse movement in price, and a delta of zero implies no correlation whatsoever.

Pricing Models

Swaption pricing is done by sophisticated computer pricing models. Some of the models used today are variations of the Black-Scholes (option pricing) model developed in the early 1970s to price stock options. Interestingly enough, Mr. Black now works for Goldman Sachs, and Mr. Scholes for Salomon Brothers. Others use Monte Carlo simulation models. Most trading outfits have added their own bells and whistles to their in-house system. As such, many consider (and rightly so) these models proprietary information that is not shared with the outside world. However, if you are a good customer, there's a small chance you'll be able to get your favorite Swap dealer to give you a copy of the trader's model—or a simplified version of it.

It is also possible to develop your own pricing model on a personal computer. This is not easy and requires time as well as an intricate knowledge of the mechanisms of option pricing. (This topic is beyond the scope of this book. You can obtain more detailed information on this subject in the third edition of *The Options Manual* by Gary L. Gastineau, published by McGraw-Hill.)

In any event, despite the differences in the models, the prices computed should be very close. And you as the customer don't really care how the Swaption is priced—you just want the best price. The last statement is almost true. A mispriced option may be from a trading outfit that doesn't really know what it is doing. As discussed in many other places in this book, if the credit rating of this firm is not good, you may have a difficult time assigning the Swaption to someone else. And you may not like the unwind price quoted by this institution. Then you're stuck. A sightly better price may simply reflect the bias in the book of one particular firm at the time you wish to trade. As long as that bias is not a long-term bias, you should not be affected.

Lottery Tickets

Options of any kind that are very much out of the money cost very little money. That's because the odds of their actual exercise are slim. Derivatives dealers refer to such instruments as *lottery tickets*—low price but big returns should they go into the money. Most dealers are also very reluctant to write such options. They gain very little in the way of premium, but if they have to pay off, their losses can be big. To many, the small premium is not worth the risk. You'll also see the term *lottery ticket* in reference to other types of options such as Caps and floors.

Why Swaptions?

As with any other type of option, the reasons for using Swaptions are many. Complicated Swaption strategies were developed to take advantage of pricing discrepancies in different markets. These strategies typically do not have a long life because market participants are quick to jump on the bandwagon and either arbitrage the differences away or improve their pricing. Option strategies not only in the Swap market but in other financial markets as well have become big business.

We'll look at a few strategies, and I'm sure you'll be able to come up with a few more yourself. Once you become familiar and comfortable with this tool, you'll find market inefficiencies yourself. And then there are times when Swaptions fill a legitimate need. For example, a Swaption can be used to cancel a Swap. Finally, some use the Swaptions market either as a trading vehicle (not that frequently because there are other easier and cheaper ways to trade the interest rate market) or as a means for generating some income.

Using Swaptions to Generate Income

A few corporates will sell Swaptions to generate income. Most are reluctant to do so purely to generate income separate from their interest rate management. But there are a few who do it, and there are probably a few more who do it under the guise of interest rate management.

Cyontike's interest rate projections called for interest rates to bottom out within three months and then to rise dramatically. After much deliberation, Cyontike decided to sell a receiver's option to generate some income. It sold a one-year option that would allow the purchaser of the option to receive at current rates. If its forecast is correct, when the exercise date comes around, the purchaser will be able to receive at a higher rate and won't exercise the option. Cyontike will then get to keep the premium. In this particular instance, it is extremely important that the Swaption be European-style because the Swaption may be in the money for the first few months of the life of the Swaption. Cyontike could have generated more income by writing the Swaption for a longer period of time, but it did not want to take that risk—remember, the longer the time horizon for such a transaction, the greater the risk.

If Cyontike had expected rates to continue falling, it would have sold a payor's Swaption giving the purchaser the right to pay at current levels. Again, if rates had fallen as expected, the purchaser would not have exercised the Swaption but would choose to go into the marketplace and pay at the lower rate.

A Few Guidelines When Writing Swaptions for Income

Swaptions for generating income should always be European-style simply because they are easier to manage. As we are all too aware, the interest rate market can respond instantaneously to events overseas. The coup in the Soviet Union caused the bond market to move several points overnight. By the time we arrived at work in the morning, it was back down again. You don't want to come to work one morning and find out that your Swaption had been exercised the night before. Remember, many Swap dealers having operations in several parts of the world effectively never close.

Portfolios should be monitored on a regular basis, and if the market has gone against you and you are not ready to take delivery (perform) under the agreement, consider getting out. This will cost you something. In all probability, you may have to pay more to reverse the position than you earned by putting it on. This is another reason why many are reluctant to enter into this kind of activity.

If you are going to sell a Swaption, I'd recommend a shorter-term life rather than a longer-term one. This will, of course, reduce your income, but it should also reduce your risk. It is much easier (but by no means easy) to project interest rates for a shorter period. The longer the time frame, the less accurate your forecast is likely to be.

One last point. If you are going to engage in using Swaptions as a means of income generation, make sure that you not only have the approval of upper management, but that they truly understand the risks associated with this type of activity. The world is filled with Monday morning quarterbacks—especially when something goes wrong. Writing Swaptions is a legitimate way to generate income for your firm, just as long as everyone understands what you're doing and the risks associated with earning this income.

Trading Swaptions

Trading Swaptions is in many ways similar to writing Swaptions. When it is done, and it is not done with any frequency, it should be done with Swaptions that ideally are in the money. If they are out of the money, you are buying time value, which is very, very expensive. If they are in the money, you may be better off buying or selling a Treasury note or entering into a Swap. Both of these activities have certain disadvantages: The Treasury must be paid for, and the Swap requires periodic payments that the trader does not want to make. Moreover, the trader may not have the credit rating necessary to enter into the Swap or to sell the Treasury note should that be required (instead of buying the note). As with other options, a Swaption may give the trader the most bang for the buck.

Using a Swaption
to Cancel a Swap

A Swaption is sold to cancel a Swap. Indobarc had a Swap in which it was paying 8 percent. The Swap had a remaining life of five years. The 8 percent rate was also where the market was for five-year fixed-rate Swaps. Indobarc could have unwound its Swap for no cost, but it wouldn't have generated any income this way. Because Indobarc did not expect interest rates to do much of anything during the next year, it expected interest rates and Swap rates to trade up and down in a narrow trading range. Yet Indobarc found a way to generate a profit from its Swap.

Indobarc sold a Swaption to the Swap dealer who had the original Swap. It got 75 basis points for a one-year Swaption. On a $100 million Swap, this represented $750,000 or a reduction of almost 19 basis points per year for the five remaining years on the Swap. Indobarc also sold a European-style payor's Swaption struck at 8 percent. At the end of the period, if the Swaption were exercised, Indobarc would receive 8 percent from the same Swap dealer they were paying 8 percent. The two Swaps would cancel each other out. Instead of keeping the two Swaps alive, the original Swap would be canceled. Ideally these Swaptions are struck so that the exercise date coincides with the date of the new floating rate setting on the Swap. If not, adjustments will need to be made for the floating-rate breakage and accrued interest.

If Indobarc had sold the Swaption to someone other than the original counterparty, it would have two options. The first, and cleanest, would be to arrange before selling the Swaption, to deliver the original Swap should the Swaption be exercised. This requires the approval of both institutions prior to the sale, which is not always easy to do.

The second option, always an unattractive solution, would be to keep the two Swaps on the books and to act as the middleman. In this instance, not only would double credit be used, but you'd be using credit where none was needed. This solution is not really attractive.

Problems with Unwinds
Done via a Swaption

If Indobarc is correct in its interest rate forecast, doing an unwind via a Swaption works great. If, at the exercise date, fixed rates are below 8 percent, the Swaption won't be exercised. For example, if rates are at 7.99 percent, the Swaption won't be exercised and Indobarc will keep the premium. And Indobarc will have reduced its interest expense to

7.81 percent. No matter how low rates go, Indobarc will be no worse off and it will have reduced its rate to 7.81 percent. The only disadvantage is that during the life of the Swaption Indobarc would not have been able to unwind its Swap.

If rates go way up, the Swaption will be exercised and Indobarc will have to replace this Swap with one that has a much higher rate. Compensation will be the $750,000. Thus, Indobarc will be indifferent if the Swaption is exercised and the Swap that they enter into to replace it has a rate of 8.19 percent (8.0 + .19) or less. However, if the Swaption has to be replaced with a 9 percent or 10 percent Swap, Indobarc will not be pleased. As with those who write Swaptions to generate income, Indobarc would stand ready to buy its way out of the Swaption, if it went against Indobarc or looked like it would.

Lowering Your Rate Using a Swaption

A Swaption can be used to lower the rate on an existing Swap. Lyerell's loan agreement required that the rate on the loan be fixed. Lyerell had done this by swapping the floating rate granted by the bank to a fixed rate through a Swap. Lyerell became less than enchanted with this situation when it became strongly convinced that the Fed intended to ease in a major league way in order to get the country out of the recession it had fallen into. Lyerell would have liked to unwind its 9 percent Swap with a four-year remaining life when it became convinced of this and let the rate float. But the loan agreement prevented Lyerell from doing this.

Lyerell sold a one-year payor's Swaption that would have required the purchaser to pay Lyerell 8.5 percent if it were exercised. Because Lyerell expected rates to fall, and fall in a big way, it did not think it was taking a big risk. It sold the Swaption for 125 basis points, netting $1,250,000 against a $100 million Swap—this when Swaps for a similar period were at 8.8 percent. Thus, the Swaption was in the money on day one for the purchaser. It was in the money 30 basis points (8.8 − 8.5). A little less than $800,000 of that premium reflected the intrinsic value of the Swaption, with the remaining premium attributable to the time value. When rates fell to 7.5 percent, the Swaption wasn't exercised. Lyerell was able to use that 125 basis points to reduce the rate on its Swap by approximately 38 basis points. Thus, its 9 percent Swap effectively became 8.62 percent.

If Lyerell had been wrong, it would have found itself with a 50 basis point increase over whatever rate it could arrange in the Swap market

Original Swap	(9.0)
Swaption Swap	8.5
	(.5)
New Swap	(x)
New rate	($x + .50$)

Figure 9-1. Swaption Swap.

at the time the Swaption was exercised (see Figure 9-1). This is definitely a Swaption portfolio worth monitoring on a regular basis.

Swaption Strike Rates

One thing to remember when talking about rates on Swaptions is that the strike, and thus our focus, is not only on the direction of interest rates but, more important, on the direction of Swap rates—the summation of the Treasury component and the Swap spread. Thus, it is possible to be right about the direction of interest rates and have that negated or partially negated by the movement of the spreads.

Putting on a Swap Using a Swaption

Frizon Corporation decided that it liked the level of interest rates and wished to fix the rate on a floating-rate loan that had six years to go. However, it didn't expect rates to do much of anything for the next year. Rather than enter into a six-year fixed-rate Swap, Frizon sold a one-year payor's Swaption for 100 basis points. At the end of the one year if the Swaption was exercised, Frizon would be required to pay 8 percent for the remaining five years on the Swap. The 100 basis points reduced the effective rate on its Swap by 25 basis points.

When the year was up if rates fell, the Swaption would be exercised and Frizon would have to pay 8 percent (effectively 7.75 percent). If rates rose, the Swaption would not be exercised and Frizon would get to keep the premium. At that time, Frizon would go into the marketplace and enter into a plain vanilla Swap. Whatever rate it got, the rate would be reduced by 25 basis points. As long as the rate on the new Swap was less than 8.25 percent, Frizon would have been better off selling the Swaption than just entering into a Swap.

Benefits of Using a Swaption to Enter into or Cancel a Swap

As long as interest rates don't move too much in either direction, Swaptions provide an excellent vehicle for earning premiums to enhance the yield on a Swap transaction. Normally traders hate markets where there is little volatility and the underlying trades in a very narrow trading range. However, markets with little volatility and small trading ranges provide excellent opportunities for the smart market participant to pick up "almost free" premiums.

Arbitrage Opportunities

The Swaption market has been used by some to arbitrage pricing inefficiencies between different debt markets. These inefficiencies typically involve options embedded in debt offerings. For example, callable bonds have a call option embedded in them. Several years ago the Swaption market helped savvy borrowers take advantage of the inaccurate way the bond market priced the call features into callable bonds. The borrower issued debt with a call feature. Because the borrower did not have to pay the true cost of the call (i.e., the debt was issued at a lower rate than it should have been to reflect this call feature), the borrower was then able to use the Swaption market to take this value by selling a receiver's Swaption in the Swap market. Borrowers thus reduced their funding costs and monetized the difference between the implied price they paid for the call feature embedded in the debt issue and the premium they received by selling the Swaption.

Needless to say, this only worked for a short period of time, because investors soon figured out what was going on and quickly learned to correctly value the bonds with these features.

This is just one example of how Swaptions can be used in arbitrage situations. Others exist and will pop up occasionally. A good understanding of Swaptions will make it easier for you to recognize them when they do.

Manage Interest Rate Exposure

Asrilon International was bidding on a textile plant in Mexico. If it won the bidding, it intended to immediately modernize the factory and use it as the primary location for the shirts it manufactured. Two other firms were bidding and Asrilon was not sure that it would win the bidding. If it won, it estimated it would need $100 million in order to purchase the factory and modernize it. All the money would be spent very quickly. If it couldn't get the factory for the price it wanted, Asrilon intended to walk away because it couldn't make a financial go of it at a higher price. Asrilon's projections included paying no more than 8 percent on the money it borrowed to finance this venture.

The problem facing the president of Asrilon was that interest rates were rising and he needed to lock in rates at or close to the current levels in order to make the project work. It would do no good to win the bidding and then have to finance the project at 9 percent. The bank had committed to loan the company money at Libor + 60 but would not make a fixed-rate loan. The president of Asrilon asked Sue Spada, the treasurer, for suggestions. Sue asked him if he'd be willing to pay 50 basis points to ensure that Asrilon could lock in current rates even if it didn't win the bidding. The 50 basis points, or $500,000, was what it would cost to ensure that should it win the bidding the interest expense would be affordable. Unfortunately, Sue pointed out, if Asrilon didn't win the bidding and interest rates went down, it would still be out the $500,000. The president thought about it and finally agreed. He didn't like the idea of possibly losing the $500,000 but was willing to pay that in order to continue bidding.

Once the president agreed and understood all the risks, Sue went out and bought a three-month payor's Swaption. This Swaption gave Asrilon the right, but not the obligation, to enter into a five-year Swap paying 7.15 percent. It cost Asrilon 50 basis points or approximately 12 basis points per year. The effective rate on the Swap would be 7.27 percent. Add to this the 60 basis point spread on the loan, and you get the effective cost of borrowing this money: 7.87 percent [the Swap rate plus the amortized cost of the Swaption plus the spread on the loan (7.15 + .12 + .60)]. Not much room for error and certainly very little room for rates to go up.

Asrilon Wins the Bidding

If Asrilon wins the bidding, it has set a Cap on what will be its interest expense. And it has the potential to lock in a lower rate. If rates rise the way it expects, Asrilon's solution is simple. It would exercise the Swaption into a Swap and begin paying 7.15 percent on the Swap. As discussed already, Asrilon would lock in an all-in rate of 7.87 percent.

If Asrilon is wrong and rates fall rather than rise, the company is still okay. It doesn't exercise the Swaption and enters into a new Swap at wherever the market happens to be. The effective cost will be 12 basis points higher than if Asrilon had done nothing. But this is a small price to pay to ensure the success of the project.

Asrilon Doesn't Win the Bidding

If rates go up the way Asrilon expects and it doesn't win the bidding, it will have the opportunity to make a little money. It can either sell the Swaption prior to maturity or exercise it into a Swap and unwind it using standard Swap unwind practices. If rates go up more than a little, Asrilon will stand to make a nice sum of money. For example, if rates go up 50 basis points, Asrilon could make 200 basis points on the unwind—a nice profit for taking a little insurance.

And if rates go down and Asrilon doesn't win the bidding, it walks away only a few dollars poorer.

10

Other Derivative Products: Sounds Complicated but It's Not

Interest rate Swaps are just one tool that today's financial managers have to fine-tune their interest rate exposure. A number of new products hit the market in the mid- to late 1980s as our understanding of financial engineering grew. Although at first glance the topic might seem intimidating, it's not. Many of the products introduced in this chapter (and in the next) are variations on existing products or the combination of two. A basic understanding will help you evaluate them and decide what's right for you. A simple example: In this chapter we'll talk about Caps and floors. An *interest rate Swap* is actually the combination of these two products, a Cap and a floor struck at the same rate. (However, Swaps came first; Caps and floors were devised by breaking the Swap into two components.) It's a little more complicated than that, but you get the picture.

Futures

The oldest derivative products are financial *futures*. As mentioned earlier, they've been around for close to 20 years. As a result, many books have been written about them, their uses, innovative strategies using them, and related products (i.e., options on futures). Anyone interested in learning about the fine points of financial futures should read some of these books.

Caps

Companies that expect interest rates to decline should be perfectly happy with a floating-rate loan (or a fixed-rate swapped to floating). However, they may wish to buy a little insurance in case they are wrong. They may wish to protect themselves from some external factors that could cause rates to shoot up—for example, a war, the threat of war, or a political upheaval either at home or abroad.

By purchasing a Cap, companies can buy such protection. A *Cap* sets a limit on the level of interest rates and, consequently, the amount of interest that will be paid. Caps are typically purchased on Libor and commercial paper, but can be arranged on other floating instruments if desired (for a price, of course).

Premiums are quoted in basis points and usually are paid in a lump sum up front at the beginning of the period. However, arrangements can be made to pay the premium over the life of the Cap period. The seller of the Cap pays the purchaser whenever interest rates go above the agreed-on level. If the rates stay below the agreed-on level, no payment is made.

The lower the strike on the Cap, the higher the premium. Also, the longer the period for which the Cap will be in effect, the higher the premium. Caps can become very expensive if you're not careful. For example, in May 1992, with three-month Libor hovering around 4 percent, a Cap of 5.5 percent on three-month Libor for two years would cost 114 basis points, and a 5.5 percent Cap for seven years would cost 1187 basis points. At 6.5 percent, it would cost 61 basis points and 836 basis points for two and seven years, respectively.

Let's look at the 114 basis point two-year 5.5 percent Cap. The 114 basis points spread over two years (at 5 percent) is equivalent to 61 basis points per year. In order for the purchaser of the Cap to come out ahead of the game, three-month Libor would have to be higher than 6.11 percent (5.5 + .61) on average for the entire period. If the three-month Libor is lower than 6.11 percent, the purchaser would have been better off doing nothing and letting the interest rate float. Let's see why.

If three-month Libor was 5.49 percent (or less) for any period, the purchaser of the Cap would receive nothing. If three-month Libor for the period was 5.75 percent, the purchaser would receive 25 basis points (5.75 − 5.5), which would still be less than the 61 basis points paid for the Cap. It's only when Libor exceeds 6.11 percent that the purchaser of the Cap comes out ahead of the game. The scenario gets worse using higher strikes and longer periods.

Why Buy Caps?

Why are Caps purchased? They are quite frequently bought as insurance. A company can cap its interest expense rather than locking it in (with a Swap or fixed-rate loan) and still participate and gain in any drop in interest rates. Some companies are willing to pay a premium for this protection.

Others buy Caps in anticipation of rising interest rates (and/or increased volatility). These traders are not hedging their loans but are buying the Cap as a trading vehicle, intending to sell it when rates rise. This can be risky if you're wrong. You can lose most, if not all, of your premium, as you would with any other type of long option position that went against you.

Selling Caps

A Cap is an option whose value diminishes with time. Most corporates who use Caps buy them for hedging purposes. However, a small number sell (write) them when they think rates are headed down. This enhances their income and lowers interest expenses. The further out of the money and the shorter the life of the Cap, the lower the chance that the Cap seller will have to perform. Of course, lower risk translates into lower premiums.

Money managers, with divergent objectives from corporate borrowers, also write Caps. The Caps enhance their interest income and increase their returns. Not surprising, in view of floors, Caps are sometimes called ceilings.

Amortizing Caps

The need for a Cap might be to set the limit on the interest expense for an amortizing loan—either one with several paydowns or a floating-rate mortgage that amortizes monthly. In either case, if you've decided to use a Cap, you'll need one that amortizes (or reduces) on the same schedule as your loan.

In the first case where there are only a few large paydowns, it would be fairly easy for you to construct your amortizing Cap yourself. As with the amortizing Swap, an *amortizing Cap* is only a series of smaller Caps with maturities matching the maturities on your loan. In this instance, you might want to get quotes from several dealers on each of the maturities along with one quote on the whole Cap. You might be able to take advantage of different biases in different books in this manner. And then again, you may get a better quote from a dealer if you give the whole trade to one institution. There's only one way to find out. And just because one way works better one time, it doesn't necessarily follow that the same way will work better the next time.

Although a loan that amortizes monthly theoretically could be handled in the same manner, it would be cumbersome and each piece is likely to be quite small. It's better just to get quotes on the whole thing. But still get quotes from several dealers.

If your need was for a Cap that accretes (i.e., increases), you should theoretically be able to buy such a Cap. However, this is very rarely done.

Captions

The right to buy or sell a Cap, or an option on a Cap is referred to as a *Caption*. There is not a huge amount of activity in this product.

Floors

The opposite of a Cap is a floor. Just as a Cap sets a maximum rate, a *floor* sets a minimum rate. This product is more attractive to money managers than it is to corporate borrowers because investors have an obvious interest in limiting on the downside the level of interest income they receive. However, a corporate borrower might sell a floor in order to generate some income or to offset the cost of something else—usually a Cap.

Income from Floors

The income generated from selling floors is usually small when compared to the cost of a Cap. This is one of the reasons that few sell them. As with Caps, the premium increases with the life of the floor. And directly the opposite of Caps, it decreases the higher the level of the strike. When three-month Libor was hovering around 4 percent, floors sold would either have an incredibly low (3 percent?) level or would cost more than most would want to spend (they'd be in the money from day one). But to put it in perspective, in a higher interest rate environment, out-of-the money floors generate little income.

Using a Floor

Rylon Inc. had a floating-rate loan of Libor + 50 with a 7 percent floor. When Rylon put the loan on its books, Libor was over 10 percent and it agreed to the floor never thinking it would be hit. After all, Libor would have to fall below 6.5 percent (7.0 − .5) before that feature was activated. "We should be so lucky," Rylon joked.

Several years later, with Libor approaching 8 percent, the treasurer of Rylon predicted that rates had bottomed out and decided to lock in the rate for the remaining five years of the loan. He was able to do a Swap at 8.5 percent for the five years, locking in a 9 percent (8.5 percent Swap + .5 spread on the original loan) for the remaining life. Because Libor had never come remotely near 6.5 percent in his lifetime, he completely forgot about the floor in the original loan. Although he turned out to be wrong in his interest rate outlook, he was content to pay 9 percent. What he hadn't counted on was paying 10.5 percent. This turned out to be the case despite the fact that he had the Swap. How did this happen? Let's look at Rylon's cashflows for the five years.

Libor averaged 5 percent for those years (see Figure 10-1). As you can see, in this instance, the two Libors didn't cancel each other out. Once Libor fell below 6.5 percent, Rylon was locked in at 7 percent on the loan. At the time that the Swap was put on the books, a 6.5 percent Libor floor would have cost 25 basis points up front or 6.5 basis points per year. If Rylon had taken insurance and bought the floor, it would have truly locked in a rate—9.065 percent instead of 9 percent. True, this rate was higher than 9 percent, but it was certainly much better than 10.5

	Projected	Actual
Loan	(L + 50)	(7.0)
Swap	L	5.0
	(8.5)	(8.5)
	9.0	10.5

Figure 10-1. Rylon's cashflow.

percent. And the treasurer had some pretty fast explaining to do to the CEO when his sure 9 percent interest rate turned out to be 10.5 percent in a falling interest rate environment!

Floortion

An option on a floor is known as a *floortion*. As with Swaptions, no attempt is made with floortions to give puts and calls separate names. The activity in floortions is smaller than Captions, especially because the activity in floors is not great.

Collars

One way of looking at a Swap is to view it as a Cap and a floor struck at the same level. An institution with expectations of lower interest rates would probably want to let the rate on its debt float to take advantage of the lower rates expected. However, wanting a little insurance, the company might decide to purchase a Cap to give some protection should its forecast be wrong.

As mentioned earlier, many corporates experience sticker shock when they first see the cost of this protection. And then certain corporates are quite reluctant to part with cash—especially for something as nebulous as a Cap. There's no way around it. But the ever clever Swap dealer has come up with an answer. The purchaser can give up some of his or her downside gains by selling a floor back to the seller of the Cap. This reduces the cost of the Cap. The amount of the reduction depends on the amount of the potential gain given up. Effectively, this will set up a range (or *collar*, a combination of a Cap and a floor) in which your interest rate will fluctuate. If a Cap is purchased with an 8 percent strike and a floor is sold with a 6 percent strike, the interest rate will be no higher than 8 percent and no lower than 6 percent. This theory of collars led to the development of the zero cost collars.

Zero Cost Collars

Remember those corporates who wish to part with as little cash as possible? Well what if they don't have to part with any cash at all? What could be better? The *zero cost collar* combines a Cap and a floor with strikes set at levels so that no premium needs to be paid. The strikes on each set the range between which the interest rates will float.

In mid-1990, with three-year fixed Swap rates just below 9 percent and Libor a little above 8.25 percent, it would have been possible to "buy" a zero cost collar that would allow interest rates to float between 8 percent and 9.75 percent. With Libor around 4 percent in the spring of 1992, this does not look like such a great deal. Of course, it looks better than a 9 percent Swap. Conversely, if rates had risen significantly, you'd have locked in at 9.75 percent instead of 9 percent—not nearly as unattractive a proposition as being locked in at 8 percent in a 4 percent rate environment.

Keep this in mind as you look at zero cost collar levels. With Libor under 4 percent and fixed Swap rates at 6.2 percent for three years, you can float between 5.25 percent and 8 percent for three years for no cost. Only time will tell if this is a smart move.

Zero cost collars can come back and hit you in the face if interest rates move in a big way against you. Your "free" collar can turn out to be quite expensive. On the other hand, if interest rates stay in a narrowish range, zero cost collars can be a good deal.

Using Collars with Assets

Most of the strategies involving derivative products have to do with managing liabilities. However, those strategies can also be used with assets. It's just not done as frequently. Given the low absolute level of interest rates in 1992, smart financial engineers began to look at derivative products as a means of increasing investment returns. Not only were yields incredibly low by historical comparisons for the last 20 or more years, but the yield curve itself was incredibly steep. This provided the opportunity to sell a zero cost collar to improve yields. The strategy for this is the same as for using a zero cost collar to lock in your interest rate exposure on your debt, except that instead of buying a Cap and selling a floor, you buy a floor and sell a Cap.

An investor, concerned not about rising rates but about falling rates, wants to limit his or her downside exposure. Under simpler circumstances, the investor would purchase a floor. Rather than come out of pocket for the premium, he or she could sell a Cap. This would work if the premiums required and generated could be done with reasonable strikes. In a less steep yield curve environment, this is not always possible to do.

Consider Joan Kreser, a money manager for a large short-term bond fund. With short-term yields below 4 percent, she looked around for ways to improve her yield. With one-year Treasuries around 3.65 percent, she was able to buy a four-year floor with a strike at 4.75

percent for 150 basis points up front. This immediately would improve her returns by 110 basis points. However, with returns already pitiful, she was reluctant to pay for this out of her investor's funds. To her surprise, her derivatives dealer was able to offer her a collar (also called an *investor collar*) for nothing by buying from her a Cap struck at 6.75 percent. Joan benefits from this strategy immediately because her returns on the amount of the Cap purchased jumped to 4.75 percent. She continues to benefit as long as rates stay below 4.75 percent. Joan is no better or worse if rates stay between 4.75 percent and 6.75 percent (in fact, we know she'll be ahead of the game for at least the first period), but she loses when rates rise above 6.75 percent because she's given up the upside above this level. Many would not be comfortable with this strategy for as long a period of time. Some would do it for a shorter time frame. Investors can look to this strategy in steep yield curve environments.

Participating Cap

A *participating Cap* is an option strategy involving the purchase of a Cap with a strike much higher than current market rates and the simultaneous sale of a floor that is in the money (i.e., the rate on this is also higher than current rates). Because the floor is in the money and the Cap is out of the money, the notional amount on the floor is less than the notional amount on the Cap. This is a type of zero cost collar because the notional amounts and strikes are set so that there is no out-of-pocket premium. The purchaser of the Cap benefits when rates fall on that portion of the notional amount that is the differential between the Cap and the floor. And, of course, the protection afforded by the Cap is still there should rates rise. The product most often used instead of a participating Cap is a participating Swap, which is very similar. That product is explained in more detail in Chapter 11, "Other Types of Interest Rate Swaps."

Spreadlocks

As was discussed in the beginning chapters of this book, traditionally spreads and rates have moved in opposite directions. As one went up, the other went down. Thus, a person who liked Treasury levels might not be pleased with the level of spreads, and vice versa. Typically a fixed-rate payor might like the level of spreads but not the Treasury level when expecting rates to fall.

Ever-accommodating Swap dealers developed a product to meet this need—the spreadlock. The *spreadlock* is a vehicle that locks in an agreed-upon spread for a period of time, usually three months. By the end of the period, the spreadlock must be exercised. If the party who has the right and the obligation to exercise doesn't, the spreadlock is automatically exercised at the close of business on the last day of the period.

Spreadlocks can be used to either fix or float rates. And they are written American-style (i.e., they can be exercised at any time during the spreadlock period).

Extending a Spreadlock

Sometimes rates won't do exactly what you think they should do, when you think they should do it. Rates might be heading down as you predicted, but not as quickly as you expected. Or you might now expect them to drop a little more than your original projections. Or worse still, if you are the fixed-rate payor, they may have increased; if you are the fixed-rate receiver, they may have decreased.

Whatever the reason, when the end of your spreadlock period rolls around, you'd prefer to wait to lock in your rate. The Swap dealer who entered into the spreadlock agreement with you will probably agree to extend it—for a cost. The cost should reflect the dealer's cost of carrying the hedge of the spreadlock. Entering into a spreadlock is almost the same as entering into a Swap. True, no periodic payments are made, but the dealer hedges the spreadlock in a similar manner to hedging a Swap.

Typically it will cost a basis point to extend a spreadlock for a month or two. The steeper the yield curve, the more expensive the cost of carry and therefore the addition of extension costs. Some will argue that in an inverted yield curve environment, the dealer makes money on the carry. I've yet to see a dealer who agrees with this or one who will reduce your spreadlock to reflect this.

Execution of a Spreadlock

The execution of the spreadlock is almost exactly the same as the execution of a plain vanilla Swap. Because the spread has been agreed on up front (it was locked in at the time that the spreadlock agreement was entered into), the only thing to watch is the level of the Treasuries. As discussed earlier, your Swap dealer will much prefer that you leave an order, but you might want to monitor the execution.

Unfortunately, if you were a fixed-rate payor and used spreadlocks during most of 1991 and parts of 1992, you didn't do as well as just waiting until Treasuries were at a level you liked. For example, on a seven-year transaction, spreads fell from 75 to 45 while Treasury yields fell from 8.15 to 6.7. This was not supposed to happen. Let's look at what happened to a number of corporates.

With almost everyone expecting rates to fall, spreadlocks looked like a sure thing. A spreadlock put on in January 1991 and extended 11 times (yes, they sometimes are extended that many times) until the end of the year turned a spread of 75 into a spread of 86. Meanwhile rates fell. If this spreadlock was exercised toward the end of the year, the resulting Swap would have had a rate of 7.56 percent (6.70 + .86). Compare this with a plain vanilla Swap done at year end. The rate on that Swap would have been 7.15 percent (6.7 + .45) or 41 basis points less than the spreadlock Swap. But it could have been worse. The market could have behaved as traditional market theory indicates and rates could have gone up as the spreads fell. That would have been a real disaster.

This is *not* the way spreadlocks are supposed to work. Traditional theory tells us the spread should have gone from 75 to, say, 115. If that had been the case, a year-end Swap with a spreadlock and spreadlock extensions would have been 7.56 percent (6.7 + .75 + .11), versus a plain vanilla execution at the higher spread of 7.85 percent (6.7 + 1.15) for a savings of 29 basis points.

Changing Your Mind about a Spreadlock

When you enter into a spreadlock agreement with a Swap dealer, you not only have the right to enter into a Swap, you have the obligation. Thus, those who entered into spreadlock agreements early in 1991 only to see spreads fall could not simply walk away from their obligations. This is one of the reasons why entering into a spreadlock is analogous to entering into a Swap.

Spreadlocks can be unwound, but the unwind can be an expensive proposition if the market has gone against you. In theory, to unwind a spreadlock means exercising the spreadlock into a Swap and then unwinding the Swap using standard Swap unwind pricing. Not only will you have to pay for the adverse spread move, you'll also have to pay a bid offer spread on the Swap. Spreadlocks are not something to be entered into lightly. The same thought given to entering into a Swap should be given to entering into a spreadlock.

Those marking their portfolio to market should include a mark to market of the spreadlock. How? Assume an exercise of the spreadlock into a Swap at current market conditions and then mark the resulting Swap to market.

It should be noted that fixed-rate receivers who did spreadlocks in the beginning of 1991 benefited from the decline in spreads, although not from the decline in rates.

Spreadlocks and On-the-Run Treasuries

Those familiar with the bond markets know that the on-the-run Treasuries are much more liquid than older issues. Four times a year new auctions are held to sell Treasury securities for each maturity. For example, 10- and 30-year bonds are sold every February, May, August, and November. With each auction, a new Treasury becomes the on-the-run issue and, as such, is used in calculating Swap yields. However, when spreadlocks are written, they are tied to a specific Treasury issue. And when the spreadlock is executed, the execution price is tied to the price of the Treasury against which the spreadlock is written. This can cause potential fixed-rate payors some serious problems.

As soon as the auction details are announced, usually about a week before the auction actually takes place, a wi security starts trading and effectively becomes the on-the-run issue. You'll notice that the old issue starts trading at a slight discount (i.e., a higher yield). If you've got a spreadlock tied to the old issue, your effective rate has just increased. This differential can sometimes run as high as six basis points.

What can you do? First, if at all possible, avoid putting on spreadlocks right before an auction date. Second, if your issue becomes an old issue, try and trade out of it. In most instances this will cost you something. The Swap trader will have to buy and sell two securities, and you'll have an extra bid offer spread to pay. On rare occasions the dealer may be able to do it for nothing. This statement will probably outrage most traders who will claim it can't be done or that if it is, then the person who did it doesn't know what he or she is doing.

That may be so or, more likely, the trade may fit a trader's book and the trader is letting you benefit. Rather than try and continually watch the market yourself, looking for that one opportunity when it is possible to get it done for nothing (even I will admit the chances for that are slim), tell the trader that you'll trade out for some minimal level—say one basis point—and let the trader watch the market and do it for you. The trader just might be able to get it done. The longer after the auction you wait to trade out of an issue, the higher the cost is likely to be. So try and bite the bullet and trade out of it earlier rather than later.

Cost of Carrying a Spreadlock versus Execution

Getting out of a spreadlock can be an expensive proposition. Sometimes it might be cheaper to continue holding the spreadlock and paying the dealer to roll it than to actually execute it. Let's say your Swap dealer charges you one basis point per month to carry your spreadlock. There is no cash going out of your pocket now, but eventually when you do execute your fixed rate will be one basis point higher than it might be if you executed immediately. This is if you are the fixed-rate payor. If you're the floating-rate payor, the rate you received would have gone down a basis point.

In the environment where the yield curve is steep and the difference between the fixed and floating rates are high, you might be better off financially just paying to roll the spreadlock. In an environment where Libor is 4 percent and the fixed rate you would be paying is 7.5 percent, a $100 million Swap costs you $291,666 each month. You'd have to pay the difference between the 7.5 percent and 4 percent [i.e., 3.5 percent (7.5 − 4.0) or 350 basis points]. This comes out to $291,666 (.035 × $100,000,000/12). (Yes, I know I didn't take into account the different types of day counts. The example is just to give you a rough idea of the magnitude of the differential.)

Now, this value has to be compared to the value of that one basis point. If we were talking about a 10-year Swap, the value of one basis point per year would be $10,000 (.0001 × $100,000,000). The present value of the $10,000 per year at 7.5 percent is $68,641. Even without looking at it from a present value standpoint, $10,000 per year for 10 years is $100,000. It doesn't take a rocket scientist to figure out that in these circumstances you might be better off carrying the spreadlock. This of course has to be evaluated against your outlook for interest rates. Even if you expect rates to increase, the heavy up-front cost of carrying the Swap (i.e., the differential between the current floating rate and the fixed rate) might still cause you to wait and execute the spreadlock at a future date.

FSAs

Forward spread agreements (FSAs) are variations of the old spreadlocks that most Swap dealers have been offering almost since the beginning of the interest rate Swap market. The main difference between FSAs and spreadlocks is that the FSAs are cash settled at the end of the period rather than executed into a Swap. For someone interested in speculating in spreads alone, FSAs provide a cheaper way to do it—no paying the bid offer spread on the Treasury component. Other than the cash settlement aspect, FSAs are quite similar to spreadlocks.

Treasury Locks

Sometimes, there will be an expectation that rates will rise rather than fall. Therefore, potential fixed-rate payors might expect Swap spreads to fall. They might desire to lock in the Treasury level and lock in the spread at a later date. These trades, where the Treasury level is locked in—hence the name *Treasury locks*—are done with much less frequency than spreadlocks. There was a short period in the spring of 1991 when a Treasury lock done at the beginning of the year looked great for fixed-rate payors because rates had risen and spreads had fallen. Unfortunately, there were many more spreadlocks than Treasury locks. Bond traders reading this chapter will note that Treasury locks are a way of playing the bond market for little cost—basically the bid offer spread on a Swap.

FRAs

Forward rate agreements (FRAs) are agreements between two parties whereby each agrees to net two payments. The two payments are the fixed agreed-upon payment and the market rate on the underlying at the time the contract matures. Let's be a little more specific. A company that is expecting rates to rise, might wish to lock in the rate on a future borrowing. So it enters into an FRA. The agreed-on rate (i.e., the fixed rate or the contractual rate) will be the forward rate for the period. Thus, if the company desired to lock in a six-month Libor rate three months forward, the forward rate would be calculated on six-month Libor. The reference rate in this instance is six-month Libor. This is also referred to as a three by six (i.e., a six-month rate that will start three months from the date the contract is written).

FRAs are generally written for one period (e.g., a six-month contract or a three-month contract), and the bid offer spread on them is quite small. FRAs are available in most currencies, and they are similar to forward start Swaps (which will be discussed in Chapter 11), but they tend to be for a shorter maturity. Corporates might use an FRA in conjunction with a floating-rate loan. They could lock in the next rate resetting on their floating-rate loan through an FRA. Remember, like interest rate Swaps, FRAs do not have to be written with the same institution that has the underlying loan. A corporate might use an FRA if it expected rates to rise owing to uncertainty over political events or simply in anticipation of rising rates. An FRA can also be used when the corporate desires to lock in a rate rather than live with the vagaries of the marketplace. To a lesser extent, FRAs can be used by managers of assets wishing to lock in better returns.

This product is most like the futures market, but it allows the customer the financial innovation and customization that has made the over-the-counter derivatives market so popular.

Fraptions

Like every other derivative product, there are options available on FRAs called *Fraptions*. These are not nearly as popular as Swaptions and their use has been limited. They could be used in those instances when an option on a futures contract is the tool that is desired because the Fraption will allow for more customization.

OTC Currency Options

Currency options began to be traded on a number of exchanges in the early 1980s. Exchange-traded options have many of the same limitations as futures contracts (e.g., lack of customization and small size), making them not the ideal hedging vehicle for the corporate client. Almost simultaneously with the development of the exchange-traded currency option market, the OTC (over-the-counter) currency option market developed. As with other types of options, the buyer of the currency option has the right but not the obligation to buy (a call) or sell (a put) the underlying.

Currency options can be written European-style or American-style (and very occasionally Bermuda-style), although the majority of these options are written European-style. The options settle spot—that is, the premium is paid two days after the contract is traded and is delivered two days after it is exercised. Currency options also have both intrinsic value (sometimes, when it's in the money) and time value (always).

When buying or selling a currency option, it is important that all the details be spelled out and confirmed in a written confirm just as in any other derivative transaction. Option pricing models are often propitiatory but are usually loosely based on the Black-Scholes model.

Corporates often use options to lock in their costs and thereby lock in profits in business transactions. The option protects them against adverse currency moves while allowing them to benefit from favorable currency moves for a very small price. Some sell options simply to generate the premium.

Option pricing and strategies can be quite complex, and a number of books have been written on this topic. The same types of complicated techniques (e.g., straddles and butterflies) utilized with other types of options can be implemented using currency options. The reader interested in pursuing this in detail is directed to one of these books. To give you a flavor, we'll look at three different types of currency options briefly.

Zero Cost Currency Options

Let me start off this explanation about zero cost currency options by saying that I have a strong bias against this product. Zero cost currency options are sold so that there are no out-of-pocket costs for the purchase of the option. The strategy involves buying a call and selling a put (or vice versa) with strikes so that the premium for one offsets the premium for the other. One of the options becomes worthless (hopefully the one you sold) and the other can be exercised. Because you are buying one option and selling another, you're paying an additional bid offer spread, which accounts for the differences in the strikes. If the exchange rate at the time of exercise is between the two strikes, you benefit by buying your foreign exchange at a better rate while having had the protection afforded by the option.

Your currency option dealer will point out that profits can be locked in for no cost using this option. My basic objection to this strategy is that you give up the ability to profit from favorable currency moves just to save a few dollars (i.e., the cost of the option). And if you are wrong in your outlook, the option that is exercised against you can cost you quite a bit.

Exploding Option

An *exploding option* is an option that is embedded in some long-term forward contracts. It permits the purchaser of the option to walk away from the forward contract should the exchange rate get to a certain level (i.e., the option explodes). Exploding options are an example of how several derivative products can be woven together to produce a new product. A closer look at the pricing will probably make you realize that you might be able to produce the same results yourself cheaper.

Boston Option

A *Boston option* is one in which the premium is paid at maturity. The cost of this option will be the cost of an up-front option plus accrued interest. You should be able to figure out very easily, given your cost of funding, whether this product is for you.

Compound Options

A *compound option* is an option on an option. The underlying in compound is another option. So when exercised, the buyer of the option ends up with another option. Compound options are typically written against options on interest rate instruments. They are quite volatile and are, therefore, very expensive. You've got two sets of volatility to pay for: the volatility on the compound option and the volatility on the underlying option. This makes compound options attractive to speculators.

Difference Options

As implied by its name, a *difference option* is an option on the difference in the price of two underlying assets. Typically the two assets are interest rate related—for example, the T-bill rate and the Eurodollar rate. This popular spread, the *TED spread*, is traded on the futures exchanges and is viewed by many as a quality spread. Other difference options are traded over the counter. The differential between the two prices is compared at maturity to the differential on the day the position was put on to determine who wins and who loses. This is an excellent tool for investors who wish to trade spreads between two vehicles rather than the absolute levels on either instrument.

11

Other Types of Interest Rate Swaps

In this chapter we will discuss a wide variety of interest rate Swaps. It is unlikely that you will ever run into some of them, such as the roller coaster Swap. And I'm sure that by the time this book is published, they'll be a few more. Some will live a short life, never to be heard from again. And others will go on to become standard tools in the world of finance.

Corporates and their Swap dealers continue to find ways to extract value from minute discrepancies between the ways that the bond market and the Swap market price credits. Typically, such mispricing only exists for a short period of time. Then market participants figure out what's going on, and the pricing discrepancies vanish, making a particular strategy less profitable and therefore less used. Also, as more dealers offer a new product, margins narrow because pricing becomes more competitive. But after more study, participants find other market opportunities and develop new strategies to take advantage of these opportunities.

In analyzing them, you'll see that each meets a specific business need. You'll also see that if you stop and analyze the business need and the tools available, you'll soon be developing these structures without the help of your Swap dealer—you'll be giving your dealer ideas.

Some of the techniques have more than one name (e.g., a puttable Swap is the same as an extendable Swap), and wherever possible all known names are given.

Financial Innovation

When the credit crunch hit in the early 1990s, many lower-rated companies suddenly found themselves cut off from Swap availability. Institutions that barely looked at credit ratings in the past were cutting Swap availability to customers with whom they had done business for years. As a result, many arguments were had between the Swap desks and the credit departments of their respective institutions.

In an effort to do business with former customers, while satisfying the demands of their credit departments, Swap dealers came up with two innovative approaches: the mark-to-market Swap and the collateralized Swap. It should be noted that as a matter of principle many companies refused to do business on these terms.

The Risk

Financial institutions were concerned that if Swaps were written with lower-quality counterparties, the financial institutions would be at risk should the counterparty default on the Swap or go bankrupt. To be perfectly honest, these were legitimate concerns, although some institutions were more concerned than they needed to be. The magnitude of the risk, should the counterparty default or go bankrupt, could be quantified by the mark-to-market value of the Swap. Thus, if a $100 million Swap had a mark-to-market profit of $2 million, the financial institution was only at risk for $2 million, not $100 million. As this $2 million number went up or down, so did the institution's potential loss. If the Swap went into a loss position, the financial institution had no potential loss. Remember, most dealers run a matched book. So, if one side of the book goes away, the dealers are left with a mismatch and a potential for loss.

The Heart of the Problem

It is this mark-to-market value that Swap dealers focused on. And it is this potential loss that the dealers had to guard against. It should be noted that credit departments and regulators look not only at this risk, but also at the risk of any Swap going bad regardless of its current status. Swap dealers are being forced to allocate capital to these transactions based on the tenor and notional amount of the underlying Swap. This underlying risk and capital allocation has led to much of the current brouhaha.

One of the beauties of the futures market (at least from the dealer's standpoint) is the daily marking to market and settling up of positions.

Because initial margins put up on most contracts usually cover one day's maximum daily losses, the exchanges have much less risk. If a particular customer fails to settle up one day, the broker can sell out the position. This, of course, is an oversimplification, but it gets to the heart of the matter.

Mark-to-Market Swaps

It was this daily marking to market and settling up concept that produced market innovation in the area of mail-to-market Swaps. Under this mechanism, Swaps are marked to market using some previously agreed-on methodology on a periodic basis. The settling up might not be done daily, but weekly or monthly or whenever the gain or loss exceeds a certain minimum amount, say $100,000 or $500,000. Usually the settling up practice goes both ways (i.e., Party A pays Party B and Party B pays Party A depending on who has the loss). Rarely does it go only one way. If there is a wide disparity in the credit rating of the two counterparties, however, the party with the lower rating may be forced to put the proceeds into an escrow account.

The methodology should be agreed on in the Swap master. And all the details related to the procedure—including the source of the data and the time of day that the rates are set—should be agreed on in advance. This can be extremely important on days when figures, such as unemployment data, are released. It is also important on days when the Treasury holds its bond and note auctions. And it can be important if something happens to move the bond market in a big way—for example, a big drop in the stock market, a war, or a coup. Markets can move significantly in the course of a very short period of time. It might not be a bad idea to include a sample example showing how the calculations work in your master.

It is the periodic marking to market that makes certain regulators think that Swaps resemble futures very closely and that futures regulators should regulate Swap markets as well.

Collateralized Swaps

Many find the periodic settling up on a mark-to-market Swap cumbersome. This is one of the reasons that market participants choose to use the Swap market instead of the futures market to hedge in the first place. Rather than settle periodically, they prefer to transact a *collateralized Swap*. This collateralization is more apt to go one way, although it can go two ways.

It can work in a variety of ways. Let's say a company owns some acceptable collateral (Treasuries, high-grade corporate bonds or stocks, and so on). What is acceptable collateral should be spelled out in the master. Also spelled out should be the haircut (i.e., the percentage of overcollateralization required) that will be taken. In other words, a stock worth $100 today might only be counted as $97 or $90. The amount of the haircut is usually a reflection of the quality and liquidity of the underlying security used as collateral. Again, a precise mark-to-market mechanism should be spelled out in the Swap master. This mechanism should cover not only the valuation of the Swap but also the valuation of the security serving as collateral. Moveover, the Swap master should note the amount of collateral, when this amount will need to be raised, when this collateral will be returned, and what happens if additional collateral is required but not provided.

A company using a collateralized Swap will want to ensure that the security is held in an escrow account (if possible), that it is still entitled to whatever income the security earns, and that the security is returned should the Swap go into a serious positive position.

Another Use for
Mark-to-Market Swaps

The mark-to-market Swap can be a double-edged sword. Not only does it give corporates access to a market from which they were being shut out, but it also gave certain lower-rated financial institutions a mechanism to a market from which they were being excluded. The mark-to-market Swaps were also marketed by A and Baa institutions to their higher-rated clients.

This theoretically gave these institutions access to clients who were insisting on only using AAA and AA counterparties. Corporates weren't the only ones affected by the credit squeeze. Some of the biggest players in the market saw their franchise slip away as their credit ratings fell and as corporate America started to focus on the credit rating of their counterparties. Neither the fall of Drexel nor the Treasury scandal at Salomon helped.

Because positions could be marked to market as frequently as daily, there would be little, if any, risk. I rather doubt that many AAA and AA corporates bought this logic because the periodic marking to market and settling up can be cumbersome and most would probably prefer to deal with a counterparty with whom this is not necessary.

Generic Swap spreads reflect the credit of a AA counterparty. Corporates, especially those who trade in and out of their Swap position, wanted what they were paying for—a AA credit counterparty.

This put a strain on the Swap desks of the investment banks and some of the U.S. commercial banks that had been big players in the field. Innovative as ever, though, some found a way to deal with this problem.

Credit-Enhanced AAA Swap Facilities

Merrill Lynch was the first to strike back with an innovative solution. It set up a special purpose vehicle (Merrill Lynch Derivative Products), and was capitalized to the point where the rating agencies gave it a AAA rating. The cost of setting up such a subsidiary is not insignificant. In order to obtain the AAA rating, Merrill had to put up a significant amount of capital—some say as much as 5 to 10 times BIS (Bank of International Settlements) requirements. Needless to say, this subsidiary deals only with AAA and AA institutions. Merrill indicates that this vehicle was not easy to set up and that much time was spent with the rating agencies to ensure that it was set up correctly. Given the amount of effort and capital required to set up the Merrill Lynch Derivative Products, it is likely that other dealers will follow Merrill's lead only if the vehicle turns out to be a clear winner. This vehicle of Merrill Lynch will trade not only Swaps, but other derivative products as well. At the time of this writing, only Goldman Sachs appears to be following.

Other Credit-Enhanced Structures

No one really expects A and Baa Swap dealers who previously had a large share of the interest rate Swap market to take the loss of business resulting from the credit crunch lying down. The Merrill facility is the first of what will probably be many innovative solutions to the current credit crunch–induced problem. One bright spot for these dealers is that it is believed that many AAA counterparties are full up on each other's names and are desperate for new creditworthy names with which to do business.

The ironic part is that at the time of this writing, Merrill Lynch has been upgraded to A1. If things continue well for Merrill and it is upgraded again, it'll fall into the magic AA category, thus opening many new doors for future business.

There has been talk about Swap dealers buying insurance (the way some municipal bonds which are insured purchase insurance) to give the Swap a AAA rating. There has also been talk about their getting a guarantee from a AAA counterparty or a company providing financial guarantees. All this costs money, which might make the dealer who has to buy such credit enhancements either less competitive in bidding situations or less profitable.

Others suggest some kind of pooling of risk, similar to the way futures exchanges are run. Two immediate problems come to mind with this solution. First, Swap futures contracts have been created and seem unlikely to succeed in a big way. Second, the Swap market has done everything it can to keep the Commodity Futures Trading Commission (and every other regulatory body that is interested) from regulating its business. Such an arrangement would reopen an issue none of the players desire to reopen.

When Plain Vanilla Doesn't Work

Plain vanilla Swaps don't meet the hedging and financing needs of all of corporate America. Many Swap dealers prefer to handle more exotic types of transactions—structured financings that marry a Swap into a debt (or equity)—offering or nonstandard Swaps. These transactions are more difficult to do, but they are also more interesting.

Many dealers turn their noses up at plain vanilla Swaps asserting that they prefer more exotic transactions. The plain vanilla Swap business has become straightforward with most participants quite able to negotiate a good price for themselves. This has caused spreads to narrow. Now don't feel too sorry for the Swap dealers. Despite all their complaints, Swap dealers, even those dealing primarily in plain vanilla transactions, are still making money. However, the dealers are no longer able to charge spreads that you can drive a truck through.

Most active Swap market participants will shop around and use the techniques previously discussed to get the best price for their institution. In order to make huge spreads, dealers have to get more innovative. The more complicated the transactions, the harder it is for dealers' clients to figure out what they're doing; it's also harder to comparison shop. This allows Swap dealers to increase their spreads. This is part of the reason why many dealers like to do more complicated transactions. If you take apart the transactions, you may find that you can do them cheaper by handling the parts separately.

To be perfectly fair to Swap dealers, many of whom are intelligent, fair-minded individuals who truly are doing their best to help their customers, plain vanilla Swaps don't meet everyone's needs all the time. Quite frequently, the more complicated vehicles are needed to do the job. Let's take a look at a few simple transactions to get the idea.

Forward Start Swaps

Many corporations know their major funding needs well in advance of the date they actually need the funds. This could happen in the case of a large acquisition, seasonal funding, or a refinancing of current debt. John Allen, treasurer of Troyik Ltd., had that problem. John knew that Troyik would be acquiring Abalco, a small shoe manufacturer, in three months. The $100 million price had been agreed to and it only remained for the lawyers to finish the paperwork and for Troyik to line up the financing.

Troyik's bank had agreed to give a $100 million five-year loan at a floating rate of Libor + 100. Troyik preferred a fixed-rate loan, but the bank would not agree to give it one. John Allen wasn't concerned. He planned to arrange an interest rate Swap to effectively convert the loan to a fixed rate. He liked the current levels in the Swap market (he could pay 7.45 percent for a five-year Swap). His only concern was that the presidential election was one month away. He felt that rates might rise immediately following the election, especially if there was an upset. So he wanted to lock in today's rates for a Swap that would not start for three months.

John needed to do a five-year Swap with a three-month forward start. The *forward start Swap*, which can also be referred to as *deferred Swaps* or *deferred start Swaps*, is not as difficult to transact as it might seem. Let's look at Figure 11-1 and see why. The diagram shows the Swap dealer's position. The Swap dealer will put two Swaps on the books. In the first transaction, the Swap dealer will receive 7.5 percent from Troyik for five years and three months. (With a normal yield curve, the rate on a Swap for five years and three months will be slightly higher than one for five years.) In the second transaction, the Swap dealer will pay 5.5 percent to another counterparty for three months.

Now let's look at Figure 11-2 to see the Swap dealer's cashflows for the first three months. Because the dealer didn't receive the 7.5 percent from Troyik for the first three months, the dealer is out of pocket 2

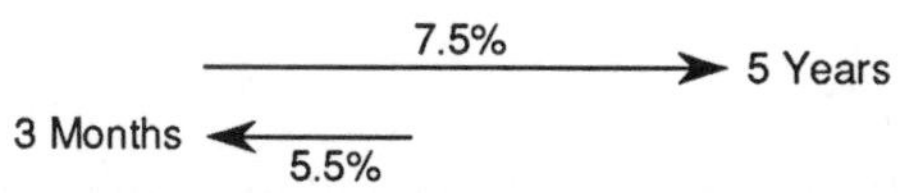

Figure 11-1. Forward start Swap diagram.

5 year 3 month Swap—fixed	7.5
5 year 3 month Swap—floating	(L)
3 month Swap—fixed	(5.5)
3 month Swap—floating	L
	2.0

Figure 11-2. Forward start cashflows.

percent or 200 basis points for that first three months after he or she put the five-year-and-three-month Swap on the books. But Swap dealers are not about to lose that money. They'll change the price on the forward start Swap to make up the money lost during the first three months. A simple present value calculation on the 200 basis points for three months indicates that 12.3 basis points over the life of the Swap will cover the dealer's costs. Troyik's Swap dealer priced the forward start Swap at 7.63 percent. (Other Swap dealers might try and get away with 7.64 percent or 7.65 percent.) John Allen was able to lock in a fixed rate for 8.63 percent for Troyik (remember, you have to add the spread on the underlying loan to get the true effective rate).

You will note that if John Allen had wanted to receive fixed instead of paying fixed, his forward start rate would have been higher.

Amortizing Swaps

Krilco had a different problem. It had a $150 million six-year loan that required principal repayments of $25 million per year. Its bank had offered Krilco a fixed-rate loan at 7.5 percent, but Susan Felts, the financial risk manager for Krilco, was convinced that rates would fall and therefore wanted a floating-rate loan. So she turned to the Swap market to resolve her problem. Instead of doing one six-year Swap for $150 million, she entered into six $25 million Swaps. The first had a tenor of one year, the second a tenor of two years, and so on. She was able to do the six Swaps at the following rates:

$25 million	1 year	6.00%
$25 million	2 years	6.25%
$25 million	3 years	6.50%
$25 million	4 years	6.75%
$25 million	5 years	7.00%
$25 million	6 years	7.25%

At the end of year 1, when Krilco made its first $25 million principal repayment (i.e., when the loan amortized) the first $25 million Swap

	Swap	Loan	Effective Rate
Year 1	6.00	7.5	L + 150
Year 2	6.25	7.5	L + 125
Year 3	6.50	7.5	L + 100
Year 4	6.75	7.5	L + 75
Year 5	7.00	7.5	L + 50
Year 6	7.25	7.5	L + 25

Figure 11-3. Krilco's effective rate schedule.

would expire. By the time the loan matured, the Swap would be gone. The loan and the Swap had the same amortization schedule. Let's look at Figure 11-3 to see the effective rate on the loan.

The effective weighted rate on the Swap would be 6.833 percent, which is the effective rate Krilco received from the Swap counterparty. The Swaps converted Krilco's 7.5 percent fixed-rate loan to a floating rate of Libor + 66.7. Krilco actually went out and did six separate Swaps itself using two different counterparties. It did this because it thought it could get better execution on its own. Krilco could just as easily (actually more easily) have given the amortization schedule to one counterparty and gotten one all-in fixed rate. However, the rate might not have been as good because it's easier for dealers to hide wider spreads in more complicated transactions.

Typical Amortizing Swaps

As you can see from the previous example, it is possible to handle the amortizations on a Swap yourself, especially if there are only a few big annual amortizations. Mortgages, especially mortgages on single-family houses, typically are self-amortizing. Each month a tiny piece of the payment is applied to the principal. At the end of the life of the loan (usually 15 or 30 years), the mortgage has been completely repaid. Forgetting for the moment that people prepay their mortgages (and I admit that this is a pretty big condition to overlook), one can see how an amortizing Swap might be the perfect solution for an S&L that is granting fixed-rate mortgages funded by customer deposits.

Because the amortizations on these loans are frequent and very small, the S&Ls might be just as happy to let the Swap dealer handle the amortizations rather than do it themselves. This might be one of the few instances where you'd be happy to pay someone an extra basis point to handle a messy transaction for you.

When the Swap market was used, the S&L would typically pool a group of fixed-rate mortgages and Swap them to a floating rate. If there were no prepayments, this would have worked quite nicely. However, as we're all aware, it is quite difficult to predict the average life of a mortgage, and although many S&Ls using the Swap market in the mid-1980s tried to work this average life calculation into their hedging and Swap projections, they most often were less than successful.

So although amortizing Swaps are a great idea when the amortization schedule is known, residential mortgages are not a suitable application.

Accreting Swaps

The opposite problem of amortizing debt is faced by companies whose debt accrets up. Typical examples of this are construction loans where additional funds are advanced at various stages of construction, loans that increase to cover interest payments, and loans that increase to cover certain operating expenses or capital improvements. Quite often the exact amount of these draws is known in advance. This is a perfect application for a forward start Swap or, rather, several forward rate Swaps if you wish to lock in current rates.

If a company is comfortable with the amounts of the future draws (or accretions), it can give its Swap dealer the schedule and ask for a rate based on the accretions, or the company can do the *accreting Swap* itself. (Accreting Swaps are also referred to as *staged drawdown Swaps* and *step-up Swaps*.)

Let's look at an example. Simlex Inc. knew it would make the following draws on its construction loan, which would mature in five years on January 1, 1998.

Date	Draw	Total Outstanding
1/1/93	$100 million	$100 million
1/1/94	$50 million	$150 million
1/1/95	$50 million	$200 million

Its bank had agreed to a floating-rate loan of Libor + 75. Because Simlex's management was concerned about rising rates, it wanted to lock the rate. When Pat Hansmith, the company's CFO, decided to fix the rate on the loan, she had several choices. She could fix the rate on each draw with a Swap at the time the company received the money. Because the concern was that rates would rise rapidly in the near term, this would not meet management's objectives. She could also ask her Swap dealer to give her a quote on an accreting Swap, or she could Swap the entire $200 million herself using two $50 million forward start

Swaps and one plain vanilla $100 million Swap. Or she could Swap the entire $200 million to fixed for five years at 7.5 percent and do two $50 million Swaps, receiving a fixed rate of 5.5 percent for one year and 6.5 percent for two years.

Let's look at the diagram in Figure 11-4. Pat has the choice of entering into the separate transactions herself or letting a Swap dealer handle both legs, fixing her one all-in quote. Although there is much to be said for letting a Swap dealer handle both pieces, you may be able to do better yourself. Quite frequently dealers have axes to grind in particular maturities in one direction in their book. Sometimes you can find two different dealers aggressive in two different tenors and will be able to do better yourself by standing in the middle of the transaction.

The downside is that you use up credit with two different Swap dealers rather than have the credit partially offset with one. This is the same problem you run into when unwinding a Swap. You never want to stand in between two counterparties on an unwind. You want to assign. Also some dealers will tell you that they can give you a better price by doing both legs. There's a real easy way to find out if that's true—price the transaction.

U.S. Dollar Interest Rate Swap Market—Standards

Each interest rate Swap market has its own conventions. For example, an interest rate Swap in U.S. dollars typically involves the exchange of a fixed-rate payment paid on an actual/365 day year (or 30/360 year) basis for a floating month Libor payment calculated on an actual/360 day year basis. Most frequently these payments are netted and involve six-month Libor on the floating side. But they can just as easily be quarterly or monthly or against commercial paper—quite frequently are.

In the early years, payments on one side might have been made semiannually and on the other annually. Some might view this as one institution's making a short-term loan to the other. This practice has all

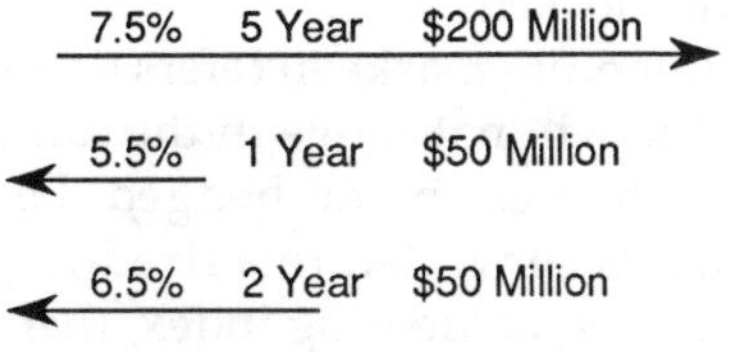

7.5%   5 Year $200 Million →

← 5.5%   1 Year $50 Million

← 6.5%   2 Year $50 Million

Figure 11-4. Simplex's forward start fixed-rate diagram.

but disappeared. Just about anything you want can be priced into an interest rate Swap.

Non–U.S. Dollar Interest Rate Swap Market

Although the largest part of the interest rate Swap market is in the U.S. dollar interest rate market, the market for interest rate Swaps in other currencies is growing. In the U.S. market, Swap quotes are typically quoted as a spread over Treasuries; in other markets, the all-in rate quote is sometimes the way the quote is given. In Great Britain, for example, it's the only way quotes are given. If you're interested in the spreads, you'll have to do the subtraction yourself (i.e., the Swap rate less the appropriate gilt rate).

If you are preparing an interest rate Swap in a currency that you haven't used before, talk with several Swap dealers active in that market beforehand. Get familiar with the way the market is quoted and any other unfamiliar conventions used in that market. Several of these markets (e.g., the ECU market, the German market, and the Spanish market) settle only annually. On the floating side, some use actual/360 day year, some actual/365 day year, and some 30/360 day year. Each floating rate is the appropriate Libor (i.e., a Japanese interest rate Swap is against Japanese Libor, an ECU interest rate Swap is against ECU Libor, and so on).

Basis Risk

As mentioned many times, the most common floating index for the floating component of an interest rate Swap is Libor. When a floating-rate loan is being fixed via an interest rate Swap, the easiest way to do that is through a Swap where the borrower pays a fixed rate and receives a floating Libor rate. However, if the underlying loan has a different floating index, the borrower may face an additional risk—a basis risk. The rate has not been completely locked.

Basis risk (a term borrowed from the commodity markets) refers to the risk that the hedge index used in the hedge will not move in the same direction and at the same magnitude as the item being hedged. For example, if a commercial paper borrowing is converted to a fixed-rate loan using an interest rate Swap with Libor as the floating index, there is the additional risk that Libor rates and commercial paper rates will not go up or down by the same amount each day.

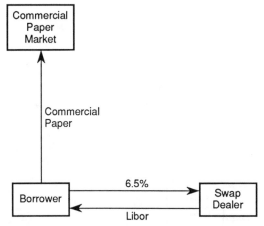

Figure 11-5. Swap diagram with mismatch.

In the example shown in Figure 11-5, a commercial paper borrower has entered into a Swap where the borrower pays the fixed rate of 6.5 percent and receives Libor. If on the day the Swap was executed Libor was five basis points higher than commercial paper, the effective rate might appear to be 6.45 percent. However, that would assume that the differential between the commercial paper and Libor rates stayed at five basis points throughout the life of the transaction. That is unlikely because the differential is constantly changing, and, depending on market conditions, can even turn negative. That differential is not quantifiable in advance and is the basis risk on this transaction. Many might choose to live with this risk, but others do not.

Basis Swaps

This basis risk can be eliminated thorough a *basis Swap,* also called a *floating/floating Swap.* In this instance one floating index is swapped for another floating index. At the time of the transaction we've been discussing, Libor could be swapped for commercial paper + 3 (see Figure 11-6). As in most other Swaps, the payments are netted, resulting in one payment.

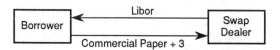

Figure 11-6. Commercial paper/Libor Swap diagram.

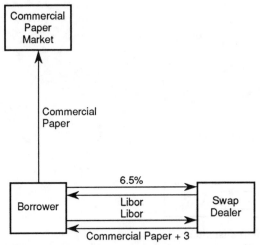

Figure 11-7. Three-transaction diagram.

Now let's look at Figure 11-7 to see all three transactions together (the original borrowing, the fixed/floating Swap, and the floating/floating Swap).

The cashflows in Figure 11-8 show that the two Libor payments cancel each other out and that the effective rate is 6.47 percent. After doing the basis Swap, the rate to the company is locked in no matter what happens to the differential between commercial paper and Libor.

Changing the Basis of a Floating-Rate Loan

Crimlon Company wanted to enter the commercial paper market to finance its new refinery. However, it was turned off by the administrative details associated with running a commercial paper

Commercial paper program	(c.p.)
Fixed/floating Swap	(6.5)
	L
Basis Swap	c.p. + 3
	(L)
	(6.47)

Figure 11-8. Three-transaction cashflows.

program and did not want to go through the ordeal of getting a commercial paper program rated. Crimlon knew that without the coveted short-term rating of A1/P1, a commercial paper program would not be cost-effective.

So Crimlon arranged a loan from its local bank at Libor + 75. Then it did a floating/floating Swap receiving Libor and paying CP + 3. This effectively converted its rate to commercial paper + 78 (see Figure 11-9).

As in our other examples, the Libor components cancel each other out. However, because Crimlon did the Swap with an investment bank and not the bank that lent it the money, interest payments and Swap payments could not be netted. (Even if the Swap had been done with the same lending bank, it still may not have been possible to net the payments. Some institutions keep their interest payments separate from their Swap payments.)

Callable Swaps/Cancelable Swaps

Just as debt can be issued with a call feature, so, too, can a Swap if it is married with an option. This gives the holder of the option the right to call or cancel the Swap. The holder of this option can either be the fixed-rate payor or the fixed-rate receiver. If it is the fixed-rate payor, the rate on the Swap will be higher; if it is the fixed-rate receiver, the fixed rate will be lower. This, of course, assumes that the option is embedded in the Swap and is not paid for up front.

A company that could see conditions whereby it might have to or want to call a particular loan, might use a *callable Swap* or a *cancelable Swap*. A company that wanted to buy a little insurance in case its interest rate predictions were wrong might also pay to incorporate a call feature in its Swap. Although these features can be expensive, they

Loan	(Libor + 75)
Swap	(c.p. + 3)
	Libor
	(c.p. + 78)

Figure 11-9. Crimlon's effective floating rate.

provide protection should things not go the way the company predicted or should the company need to unwind.

A company that believes its outlook on interest rates is correct, might sell one a call or cancel option to enhance its yield. The option premium could either be collected up front or used to buy down the rate for a fixed payor.

Delayed Libor Reset/Libor in Arrears

Let's say you have a very strong idea that rates are going to fall. How can you get the maximum benefit from your predictions? First, you enter into a Swap where you receive the fixed rate and pay floating Libor. But is there anything else you can do? If you could arrange to have the floating rate set at the end of each period instead of at the beginning, your floating payments will be lower (assuming your expectations are correct) as rates decline. You could also try and stretch the payment period—instead of using three-month Libor use six-month Libor or, better yet, one-year Libor. If the fixed rate is annualized using the fixed rate (and it should be), you'll accrue additional savings.

One caveat: Arrange your Swap so that the Libor resettings do not take place as year-end approaches and banks begin to window dress their balance sheets. Libor usually increases and sometimes quite significantly. It immediately drops to normal levels once year-end passes. In fact, if at all possible, it's a good idea if you're a floating-rate payor to avoid resets as year-end approaches. How? Have a stub period at the beginning or end or both if necessary. Of course, if you're a fixed-rate payor, setting the floating index at year-end will suit you fine. (If you're perfectly hedged, you might argue, it should not matter. This is true theoretically. But avoiding year-end Libor resetting on your loans also will save you headaches.) This strategy works particularly well for the floating-rate payor in a steep yield curve environment.

Blended Rate Swaps

We've all heard of the concept of averaging in when buying stock. Well, the same thing is frequently done with Swaps. A corporate with a large-size loan to hedge will generally come to market with several tranches over several days or weeks. By arranging for up-front stub periods of varying lengths, all the other characteristics of the Swap can be held constant. When the corporate has finished its program, it is possible to arrange for all the Swaps with the same counterparty to be rewritten at one blended rate—a *blended rate Swap*. Depending on the size of the trades, the corporate may or may not end up with several counterparties. If one institution is promised the entire deal, it may come up with a better price (or it may not). However, putting a large trade completely with one institution concentrates your credit risk and uses up your credit availability with that institution.

Off-Market Rate Swaps
High Coupon Swaps

The fixed rate on the fixed leg of a Swap transaction can sometimes be altered to achieve certain objectives. In the early days of this business, certain dealers were able to receive an up-front fee for arranging the Swap. This fee (which has all but disappeared) was usually paid up front because, theoretically, it was to help defray the Swap arranger's legal costs for documenting the transaction. In certain instances, rather than be paid up front, the fee was built into the rate. If the corporate was the fixed-rate payor, the rate was slightly higher (and if the corporate was the fixed-rate receiver, it was slightly lower). With ISDA and the standardization of Swap documentation, the high coupon Swap should have faded away. But it hasn't.

A *high coupon Swap* can be another way of borrowing money. A fixed-rate payor will occasionally agree to a higher Swap rate than market conditions would mandate in exchange for an up-front fee. The fixed-rate payor, in effect, has borrowed money through the Swap market. The fixed-rate receiver has made the loan but, in all probability, has not recorded it as such. This is just one of the features of the Swap market that has the Fed and other regulators concerned.

Low Coupon Swaps

Low coupon Swaps, which are also called *discount Swaps*, are similar to but not exactly like high coupon Swaps. A fixed-rate payor who wishes to show a lower rate on financial statements might make an up-front payment to the Swap dealer to lower the rate. Not many object to this. What they do object to is the fixed-rate receiver who agrees to accept a lower fixed rate in return for up-front cash. The distinction is subtle and not everyone makes it. The low coupon Swap is a loan to the fixed-rate receiver who pays for the loan over time by receiving a lower than market rate.

Escalating Rate Swaps

The step-up mortgages that were available several years ago were designed to make home ownership more affordable to young professionals who expected their income to rise over the following few years. In a 10 percent rate environment, one might pay 7 percent the first year, 8 percent the second, 9 percent the third, 10 percent the fourth, and 11 percent the fifth through thirtieth. Well, a similar structure is available from your Swap dealer, but usually not for 30 years. On a seven-year Swap, the rates in years 1 and 2 might be lower, before rising to an above-market level for the last five years to compensate for the lower rates of the first two years.

This *escalating rate Swap* (or *step-up Swap*) is ideally suited for a borrower who might have a new factory that is not yet producing at full capacity but is expected to do so in a year or two. When the revenue from the factory picks up, the fixed-rate payor will have the additional funds to make the higher payments. This structure gives the factory owner a way of holding down the interest expense in those beginning years before income rises to its full projected levels.

As in other types of Swaps where the exposure builds over time, the credit of the counterparty is extremely important. For the fixed-rate payor, unwinding one of these can be quite expensive unless rates have gone up quite a bit.

Differential Swaps

Another Swap being promoted by certain Swap dealers is a *differential Swap* (also referred to as a *Libor differential Swap*, a *cross-indexed Swap*, a *quanto Swap*, and a *Diff*). This is a floating/floating Swap where the indexes are two different Libors—say yen Libor for U.S. dollar Libor. The payments are denominated in one currency and as in other types of interest rate Swaps, but there is no initial exchange of principal. One could swap yen Libor for ECU Libor and have all the payments made in Canadian dollars based on a notional amount denominated in Canadian dollars.

One of the main attractions of this type of Swap is that there is no currency risk. The fact that the interest paid in the initial period is almost always reduced, and sometimes greatly so, also makes this an attractive vehicle. The differential Swap is the perfect tool for multinationals with sophisticated risk management professionals. Money managers, insurance companies, and global mutual fund managers have also been known to enhance their yields through this vehicle. Using a differential Swap is a particularly effective strategy when one expects one rate to stay constant and the other to fall. Given the steep yield curve in the United States in the spring of 1992, experts expect spreads to narrow between U.S. rates and deutsche mark rates as the curve flattens (and U.S. rates rise).

Huron International's assistant treasurer, Harvey Milter, decided to try this product. The transaction was for $10 million. Huron swapped six-month U.S. dollar Libor for six-month yen Libor + 40 for three years. The transaction is shown in Figure 11-10.

On the day the transaction was done, U.S. Libor was 6.5 percent and yen Libor was 7.5 percent. For the first six months, Huron paid $325,000 (.065 × $10,000/2) and received (.075 + .004 × $10,000,000/2) for a net inflow of $70,000. Every six months a new payment will be calculated. As long as yen Libor is more than U.S. Libor − 40, Huron will continue to receive. Only if yen Libor drops below that level will Huron have to pay.

Although these transactions look good at first glance, they have the potential to turn against you should interest rates in the two countries diverge in a way you had not predicted. To date, most transactions have been with Swiss franc, deutsche mark, and yen Libor. Differential Swaps have been more popular in Europe than in the United States.

Because interest rates are somewhat subject to monetary policy as well as political manipulation, you may not always have the control you'd like.

Zero Coupon Swaps

Zero coupon Swaps are analogous to zero coupon bonds. With a zero coupon bond, no interest is paid until the bond matures. It "accrues" with the value of the bond increasing over time to reflect this. A zero coupon Swap works in a similar manner. Usually only one side (and that is almost always the fixed side) does not pay on a regular basis but accrues until the Swap matures. The floating side typically pays on a regular basis. Counterparty credit is an important feature of such an instrument, especially to the receiver of the accruing leg of the Swap.

The zero coupon Swap might also be viewed by some as a loan in disguise as a Swap because the accruing side receives regular payments but doesn't make any payments until the Swap (loan?) matures.

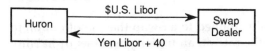

Figure 11-10. Libor differential Swap.

A contractor might be tempted to use such a structure to fund construction. Once the project is completed and sold, the contractor would have the funds to pay off the Swap. This scheme is a little far-fetched because a floating-rate loan would probably be easier to arrange—at least these days.

Issuers of zero coupon bonds might use such a Swap to convert their fixed-rate accruing interest payments to a floating rate on a nonaccruing basis, especially if they expected rates to fall. If rates have risen since the initial debt was issued, there might be an opportunity to lock in additional funds at maturity while benefiting from declining rates (if you believe rates will fall).

Investors who own a zero coupon bond and believe that rates have bottomed out, might do the reverse. They could lock in a positive spread at maturity while benefiting from rising rates. Anne Howe from Gentry Inc. used this strategy to increase the investment return on Gentry's bond portfolio. Gentry owned a zero coupon bond that had been issued with a yield of 9 percent. To simplify this example, we'll assume that Gentry bought the bond when it was issued (that really doesn't matter—the 9 percent could have been the yield to maturity when the bond was purchased by Gentry). Gentry could sell the bond in the open market and take the proceeds and invest them in a floating-rate instrument in order to take advantage of its expectations for rising rates. But the zero coupon bond Gentry had purchased was not particularly liquid and Anne was not pleased by the price being offered in the marketplace.

By entering into a zero coupon Swap as the fixed-rate payor, Gentry was able to achieve two goals. It maximized its gains while converting its investment to a floating-rate instrument. Figure 11-11 shows Gentry's investment after the Swap.

The tenor on the Swap was designed to match the remaining life on the zero coupon bond. Gentry was able to lock in the differential between 9 percent and 7 percent (with the 9 percent investment being grossed up at 9 percent and the 7 percent at 7 percent!), while earning a floating rate. When rates rose as Anne expected, Gentry's investment returns increased and once again beat all the market averages.

Naked Swaps

The term *naked Swap* is usually applied to a Swap that is not put on to hedge a liability or convert the rate on an underlying asset or liability but rather as a play on interest rates or Swap spreads. The term, which is taken from the options market, usually refers to a short option

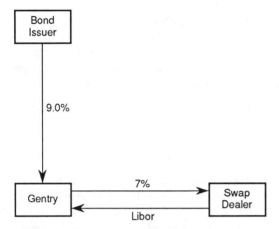

Figure 11-11. Zero coupon Swap.

position where the option writer does not own the underlying security. It is synonymous with position taking, which is discussed in other parts of this book. People rarely admit to taking naked positions despite the fact that it's done all the time.

Roller Coaster Swaps

In *roller coaster Swaps*, the fixed and floating positions go back and forth between the two counterparties. For example, for the first six months you might be the fixed-rate payor and then the next six months the fixed-rate receiver and then back again. And you thought you had to go to Las Vegas to gamble!

Participating Swaps

When a company Swaps its floating debt payments for a fixed-rate payment via the Swap market, it gives up any additional benefits that might accrue to the company resulting from the lower rates. If rates go higher the company is protected, but if they go lower it has forsaken those savings.

Although the idea of locking in a rate appeals to many, not everyone is pleased to give up the potential on the downside. Ever-diligent financial engineers found a solution to this dilemma. In the *participating Swap*, the fixed-rate payor gets some of the downside gain while locking in a maximum rate. The fixed rate on a participating Swap should be higher than the rate on a plain vanilla Swap of equal characteristics. How much higher depends on how much participation in the downward fall of rates will accrue to the fixed-rate payor. A participating Swap is actually the combination of a plain vanilla Swap with a Cap. The price of the Cap is embedded in the fixed rate of the participating Swap.

Puttable Swaps

Sincoln Company owned a factory whose purchase had been financed with a $100 million floating-rate loan at Libor + 100. The original loan had five remaining years. Sincoln leased the factory to Dryden Corporation. In exchange for an above-market rent, Sincoln granted Dryden an option to buy the factory for $120 million in two years. If Dryden exercised its option, Sincoln could pay off its bank loan and pocket $20 million. There was only one problem.

Sincoln could only cover its interest expense on the floating-rate loan if rates remained below 8 percent. Should Libor rise above 7 percent (the interest rate on the Libor + 100 loan would then rise above 8 percent), Sincoln would not have sufficient cashflow to cover the interest payments. It did not wish to dip into its own pockets to cover the shortfall, and it expected rates to rise. Sincoln could enter into a five-year Swap at 6.5 percent. Then, if rates rose and Dryden exercised its option, Sincoln would be left with a naked Swap. This would have a positive value and Sincoln would be able to unwind it at a profit. However, if rates fell and the option was exercised, Sincoln would be left with an option in a loss position. Unwinding the Swap in this instance would eat into some of Sincoln's profits.

Sincoln could do a two-year Swap at 5.75 percent. Again, if rates rose and the option was not exercised, Sincoln would not have adequate cashflow to cover the interest expense for the last three years.

The solution to Sincoln's problem was a *puttable Swap*. Sincoln entered into a two-year 6.75 percent Swap with the right to extend for another three years at the original rate (or the right to "put" a Swap to the original counterparty). Puttable Swaps, also called extendable Swaps, are the combination of a Swap and an option. The price of the option is embedded in the higher fixed rate paid. (If the option holder was the fixed-rate receiver, the price would be embedded in a lower fixed rate.)

The strategy Sincoln applied could also be achieved with a five-year Swap cancelable after two years. You might want to compare prices and see which is cheaper. (They should be almost identical.)

Reversible Swaps

During the 1992 presidential race, you believe that rates will go lower if Bush wins (and you expect him to win). So you decide to enter into a Swap where you are the fixed-rate receiver. However, you think there's a small chance that Clinton (or Perot) will win. And if that happens, you expect the bond market to take a hit.

What can you do to protect yourself while still taking advantage of the expected lower rates? Enter into a reversible Swap. A *reversible Swap* is the marriage of a Swap with a Swaption for twice the notional amount of the original Swap. Once you decide to reverse, the first Swaption unwinds the original Swap and the second puts you in a Swap point in the other direction. Of course, you now know that Clinton won the election, which means this strategy would have backfired had you reversed immediately after the election.

Contingent Swaps

A *contingent Swap* becomes effective once a certain preagreed-on price (rate) level is reached. The most common types of contingent Swaps are Swaptions, for which the option is only exercised when the strike is reached. If the strike is not reached, the Swaption is not exercised and the Swap is never started. Contingent Swaps are also written to be activated by an event rather than a price move. Some exotic contingent Swaps have been tied to things like earthquakes. When the contingent Swap is written to include an earthquake, the agreement will state that the earthquake must be of a certain magnitude and specify the mechanism for measuring this magnitude.

Yield Curve Swaps

The Swap market is occasionally used to play the yield curve (i.e., to speculate in a flattening or steepening of the yield curve). In *yield curve Swaps*, one party might pay a one-year rate while the other pays a two-year rate.

Conclusion

Not only are there many different ways to look at Swaps, the same transaction can have more than one name. Most of the transactions discussed in this chapter are variations of the plain vanilla Swap—just looked at from a different angle. As you've probably noticed, the same concept is often called different things by different people. Many of these concepts are novelties that are written in great numbers when first introduced but then quickly fade away as it becomes apparent that they aren't a real improvement on what's already available. Others, however, remain because they are truly innovative and do add something to our financial bag of tools.

12

Other Types of Swaps: Commodity, Equity, and Currency

Commodity Swaps

Traditionally, anyone who needed to hedge (or wanted to speculate on) commodity prices had only one hedging vehicle—the futures market. The futures market for physical commodities was developed and operational long before financial futures were developed. In fact, farm products (wheat, corn, soybeans, cattle, and so on) were the first products traded on futures exchanges. This is probably why the first futures exchanges were located in the farm belt rather than the financial district.

Futures markets, although opening up a whole new avenue for those who wished to protect themselves against fluctuations in the prices of physical commodities, had some limitations and disadvantages. Several smart financial engineers realized that by marrying some of the characteristics of Swaps with commodities instead of interest rates or foreign exchange, they could develop a new and improved hedging vehicle for commodities. And so *commodity Swaps* were developed. This new product eliminated the features that made futures less than a perfect hedging tool.

Futures provided the first tool for those who needed to hedge commodity prices. Both commodity producers and commodity consumers use the futures market, as do numerous speculators. In fact, the commodity futures probably could not operate without the speculators. But futures markets aren't perfect.

Basis Risk

Hedgers using commodity markets are often exposed to basis risk. This *Basis risk* evolves when a hedger is forced to use a commodity to hedge and the commodity used for the hedging does not move in perfect tandem with the underlying product being hedged. We saw this in our discussion about interest rate basis Swaps (i.e., Libor for commercial paper) in Chapter 11. For example, there are many different types of oil. However, there are only a few different types of oil futures traded and even fewer where there is sufficient volume for a large hedger to execute trades. So, the hedger using the futures market may be forced to hedge using a different type of oil.

So what's the problem you ask? All oil prices usually go in the same direction. And that's true—*usually*. But just because they go in the same direction, doesn't mean they'll go in the same magnitude. So, the futures hedge may not be a perfect hedge; it may overprotect or underprotect you.

With an over-the-counter commodity Swap, your Swap dealer will be able to Swap the same exact product as your underlying commodity, thus eliminating your basis risk. Basis risk, which has long plagued users of the futures markets, is eliminated if the commodity Swap is structured correctly.

Customization

The futures market allows for no customization. Not only are you limited on the basis, but you are also limited on the contract size and the maturity of your contract. If you need an odd size, you'll need to use the nearest number of contracts and take the delivery dates indicated by the exchange.

A commodity Swap allows you to customize your transaction. Of course, you can only customize it to the degree that your Swap dealer allows, and you of course pay for this privilege in the form of a higher bid offer spread.

Cash Settle versus Delivery

If you don't watch your futures positions closely, you may find yourself in the position where you have to take or make delivery of the underlying physical commodity.

Commodity Swaps, however, are *cash settled*; only cash changes hands. There is never any worry about holding positions during the delivery period.

Maturity of Hedge and Market Liquidity

Although nearby futures contracts are fairly liquid, longer-term contracts get liquid fairly quickly. And by long-term in the futures markets we can mean six months. In any event, it is difficult to hedge more than 18 months using futures.

However commodity Swaps can be written for five years or longer. This eliminates the need to roll your futures positions, which can be risky as well as expensive.

Trade Size

Depending on the maturity of the trade desired (remember, the longer the desired trade, the less liquid the futures market), it may be difficult to execute a large trade without disrupting the market. Should you disrupt the market, you'll pay in terms of higher execution costs. You are also limited to doing trades in multiples of the contract size on the exchange. You may have a "stub piece" using the futures market.

Day-to-Day Maintenance

Not only do futures require an initial margin to set up the position, but they also necessitate a daily mark to market of the position to determine daily margin requirements (payments). Although I recommend frequent mark to market of all Swap positions, no daily settlement is required on Swap contracts (except the few that are specifically set up that way).

Fees

All brokers charge a fee to execute a futures contract. A small part of the fee is paid to the exchange, but most of the fee is retained by the brokerage house executing your trades. Every time positions are rolled, more fees are incurred.

There are typically no fees associated with Swaps. The Swap dealer's profits come (as in all Swaps) in the bid offer spreads charged—and in some instance huge bid offer spreads. The newer the business, the larger the spreads.

Adaptation of Commodity Swaps

The adaptation of the interest rate Swap concept to the commodity markets was quite simple and natural. Just as a borrower might be concerned about rising interest rates, a commodity end user might be worried about rising commodity prices. Because most commodity Swaps written at this time are related to energy products, most of our discussion will focus on these products. This is not to say that commodity Swaps couldn't and aren't written with other commodities as underlyings. In fact, contracts with various metals are starting to be written in numbers.

In order to be able to write a Swap for a particular commodity, there must be an agreed-on (published) price index for the given commodity. Without this index there would be no "floating" leg to the transaction. This makes many energy products perfect for Swaps transactions.

A Simple Commodity Swap Example

Let's look at a simple example. An oil producer plans on pumping 100,000 barrels a month for the next year. Calculating all costs (including borrowings whose rates may have been locked in via an interest rate Swap), the oil producer needs $19.50 a barrel to cover all costs. Anything over that is profit; if the oil sells for less than $19.50 a barrel there will be a loss. The oil producer goes to several commodity Swap dealers and asks for fixed-rate commodity Swap prices.

The oil producer is willing to pay a little above the market rate in exchange for the security of knowing that the profits are locked in. Three dealers give quotes: $19.95 per barrel, $19.98 per barrel, and $20.00, per barrel. Because the oil producer wants to receive the fixed price, the highest—$20 a barrel—is selected. The profit is locked in (see Figure 12-1).

The oil producer has locked in a profit of $50,000 per month for the next 12 months. For these calculations, see Figure 12-2.

Figure 12-1. Oil producer's commodity Swap diagram.

The Other Side of the Coin

At the same time that the oil producer is worried that prices will fall, the oil refiner is concerned that prices will rise and previous commitments will force the refiner to take a loss. The refiner is concerned not that prices will fall (in fact, that would help if the refiner were unhedged) but that they will rise. In order to stay competitive, the refiner needs to keep its prices as low as possible, thus allowing the refiner to offer prices as low as the rest of the market. The refiner knows what all its other expenses are and will be able to make a reasonable profit if it can lock in its oil costs below $20.35 a barrel. It, too, has commitments for 100,000 barrels a month for the next year.

Although oil prices are currently running around $20 per barrel, the refiner has seen prices move quickly in the past and, therefore, is willing to give up the downside (i.e., if prices fall or even rise only a little) to lock in a profit. The refiner also approaches its commodity Swap dealers and gets three quotes: $20.10 per barrel, $20.12 per barrel, and $20.14 per barrel. Because the refiner is going to be the fixed-rate payor, it picks the lowest price: $20.10 (see Figure 12-3). Now the refiner is indifferent to the fluctuations in oil prices for the next year.

Total expenses	($19.50/barrel)
Swap	$20.00/barrel
	(Market price)
Income	Market price
Net profit	$.50/barrel

Figure 12-2. Oil producer's profit and loss calculations.

Figure 12-3. Refiner's commodity Swap diagram.

Figure 12-4. Commodity Swap dealer's matched position.

The Commodity Swap Dealers' Profits

Commodity Swap dealers make their profits from the spread between the price paid and the price received (i.e., the bid offer spread). Figure 12-4 shows the transaction from the dealer's perspective.

You can see in the diagram that the market price which the dealer receives from the oil producer is passed directly on to the refiner. On this transaction the profit comes to 10 cents a barrel for the dealer. These simple examples portray two Swaps in a situation where the dealer is able to set up a complete match. As in other Swap markets, this is easier shown on a piece of paper than done in real life.

The Floating Index

As with any other Swap, the floating index must be specified. With interest rate Swaps, the underlying is most often Libor, but the array of indexes used in commodity Swaps is quite extensive—and the list will only grow. In its 1992 Commodity Derivatives Definitions, ISDA listed the following for cash settled transactions:

Diesel Fuel–No.2 Billings–Platt's Oilgram

Diesel Fuel–No.2 Salt Lake–Platt's Oilgram

Fuel Oil–1 Percent NWE (Cargoes CIF)–Platt's European

Fuel Oil–1 Percent NWE (Cargoes FOB)–Platt's European

Fuel Oil–180 CST Singapore (Cargoes)–Platt's Oilgram

Fuel Oil–2.2 Residual (Barge) Platt's Oilgram

Fuel Oil–2.2 Residual (Cargoes) Platt's Oilgram

Fuel Oil–3.5 Percent NWE (Cargoes CIF) Platt's Oilgram

Fuel Oil–3.5 Rotterdam (Barge FOB) Platt's Oilgram

Fuel Oil–380 CST Singapore (Cargoes) Platt's Oilgram

Fuel Oil–380 CST West Coast (Waterborne) Platt's Oilgram

Fuel Oil–No.6 0.7 Percent U.S. Gulf Coast (Waterborne) Platt's Oilgram

Fuel Oil–No.6 3.0 Percent New York/Boston (Cargoes) Platt's Oilgram

Gas Oil–IPE

Gas Oil–0.2 Percent Rotterdam (Barge FOB) Platt's European

Gas Oil–Singapore–Platt's Asia-Pacific

Gas Oil–Singapore–Platt's European

Gasoline Unleaded–NYMEX

Heating Oil–Gulf Coast–NYMEX

Heating Oil–Gulf Coast (Pipeline)–NYMEX

Heating Oil–New York–NYMEX

Heating Oil–New York (Barge) Platt's Oilgram

Heating Oil–New York (Cargoes) Platt's Oilgram

Jet Fuel–Italy (Cargoes FOB)–Platt's Oilgram

Jet Fuel–New York/Boston (Barge)–Platt's Oilgram

Jet Fuel–NWE (Cargoes CIF) Platt's European

Jet Fuel–NWE (Cargoes CIF) Platt's Oilgram

Jet Fuel–Rotterdam (Barge FOB) Platt's Oilgram

Jet Fuel–U.S. Gulf Coast (Pipeline) Platt's Oilgram

Jet Fuel–U.S. Gulf Coast (Waterborne) Platt's Oilgram

Kerosene–Singapore–Platt's Asia-Pacific

Kerosene–Singapore–Platt's European

Kerosene–Singapore–Platt's Oilgram

Natural Gas–Inside FERC

Natural Gas–Natural Gas Week

Natural Gas–NYMEX

Oil–Brent–Argus

Oil–Brent (DTD)–Argus

Oil–Brent–(DTD)–Platt's Oilgram

Oil–Brent–IPE

Oil–Brent–Platt's Oilgram

Oil–Tapis–APPI

Oil Tapis–Platt's Oilgram

Oil Dubai–Platt's Oilgram

Oil–WTI–Argus

Oil–WTI Midland Platt's Oilgram

Oil–WTI–NYMEX

Oil–WTI–Platt's Oilgram

Aluminum–LME

Aluminum–Metals Bulletin

Copper–LME

Copper–Metal Bulletin

Gold Bullion Financial Times

Gold Comex

Unallocated Gold–Loco London Delivery

Lead–LME

Lead–Metal Bulletin

Nickel–LME

Nickel–Metal Bulletin

Platinum–Metal Bulletin

Platinum NYMEX

Silver–COMEX

Silver–Metal Bulletin

Tin–LME

Tin–Metal Bulletin

Zinc–LME

Zinc–Metal Bulletin

Each of the listed commodities is then defined. For example, "Diesel Fuel–No.2–Platt's Oilgram means that the price for a Determination

Date will be the Specified Price per gallon of No. 2 diesel fuel stated in U.S. dollars published under the heading 'U.S. Tank Car Truck Transport: PAD 4: Billings: Diesel No. 2 Fuel' in the issue of Platt's Oilgram that reports prices effective on that Determination Date."

You'll note that a number of the reference price indexes are for contracts traded on various futures exchanges. You will also note that several terms (in this case, specifically *Determination Date* and *Specified Price*) are capitalized. These are known as defined terms and are defined in the Swap document. This practice of beginning terms in capital letters follows that of most, if not all, legal documents and is not peculiar to this industry.

Commodity Business Days

The commodity Swap mimics the interest rate Swap in many ways, but there are a few concepts unique to commodities. For starters, commodity Swaps, in addition to defining business days, also define something called a *Commodity Business Day*. As already noted, many floating prices are pegged to prices on various futures exchanges around the world, which may or may not be open on a particular end date or reset date. This is a day that there is a published price for a given commodity on the given exchange or published by the given source.

Disruption Events

Although anyone with a calendar going out far enough can figure out what days various exchanges are scheduled to be closed, no one can predict *Disruption Events*. These can result from anything including a flood that causes an exchange to close for one or more days, a national holiday declared either to celebrate or mourn some dignitary (the death of a President or the coronation of a new monarch) or other unforeseen events. Disruption fallbacks are also negotiated.

You probably also noticed that the floating leg of the index was determined in many instances by some published price in a variety of publications. Very occasionally these publications may contain typos or outright errors. Sometimes it's very obvious and immediately corrected. Other times, an error may not be so obvious and will take longer to be noticed and ultimately corrected. Realizing this, ISDA has made provisions so that, very roughly speaking, errors caught within 30 days after publication can be corrected provided one party notifies the other.

Specified Price/Determination Date

In an interest rate Swap, especially a plain vanilla one done against Libor, determining the floating leg reset is a no "brainer." It's not so easy in a commodity Swap. Once you've located the correct publication and the correct index, you must find the Specified Price (which was spelled out in your confirm!). You must also determine whether you wanted the high price of the day, the low price, the average of the high and the low, the closing price, the opening price, the bid, the offer, the average of the bid and offer, the settlement, the morning fixing, the afternoon fixing, or something else. This is the Specified Price.

Commodity Swaps talk about a Determination Date, which is the date that the floating reset is calculated.

This discussion is meant to give an overview of commodity Swaps. Those seriously interested should contact ISDA and obtain a complete copy of their 1992 ISDA Commodity Derivative Definitions. A copy of the ISDA commodity Swap Transaction—Cash Settled is included in Appendix D.

End Users

Who uses commodity Swaps? Well, if you take a quick look at the defined indexes, you will realize that those engaged in any sort of business involving energy and metals could be potential market participants—not only producers and refiners (as was shown in the simple examples), but airlines, metal producers, manufacturers whose products contain oil (e.g., tire manufacturers), breweries (they need to buy aluminum for cans in addition to their fuel costs), consumer products producers, and so on. More businesses have commodity price exposure than would appear at first glance. After a rocky start, the commodity Swap market seems poised to take off in the 1990s.

Applications

One successful oil company was able to use the commodity derivatives market to lock in customer home oil price levels. Customers were offered the opportunity to lock in the cost of their home fuel oil for the following winter at 99 cents a gallon. If they signed up for this program, they were assured of this price. After figuring out their exposure based on the number of customers who signed up and the customers' average use, the company was able to go into the Swaps and OTC options markets and hedge its risk. Then came Desert Storm. This oil company looked great. And as the price of home fuel oil rose, many who hadn't signed up originally tried to get in on the program. The company was able to make a second offering—at a slightly higher cost. Through the use of the derivatives market, this oil company was able to reduce its risk and pass that reduction on to its customers.

MARTA (the Metropolitan Atlanta Rapid Transportation Authority) also used the commodity derivatives market to eliminate the risk of price fluctuations in its budget. As with most other transit authorities around the country, MARTA is not able to pass higher fuel costs on to its customers. Eventually MARTA may be allowed a price increase, but that takes time—sometimes years. Meanwhile the authority must live with whatever losses the system generates.

At the beginning of its 1990/1991 fiscal year, a heating oil Swap was done for the following year for the 9 million gallons of oil they anticipated buying. Because MARTA had locked in its fuel costs, there would be no budget variances (and possible losses) resulting from the "increased" cost of fuel. MARTA's timing was perfect. When Iraq invaded Kuwait in 1990, MARTA was not subject to the wide price fluctuations that accompanied the invasion.

As the comfort level with these products grow, expect to see more innovative deals like these filtering down to Main Street.

Speculators

The preceding examples show covered or hedged positions. The commodity Swap market also provides opportunities, just as the futures markets do, for speculators. Those with a view on market prices and a good credit rating can use the commodity Swap market to speculate or take positions on future commodity prices. And they can do this without some of the inconveniences of the futures market.

Other Commodity Derivatives

Just as there are a variety of products related to interest rate Swaps, their applicability, in most instances, to commodities is easy to see. It's not hard to imagine circumstances where someone might wish to purchase a Cap or a floor on certain commodity prices. And many of the option techniques of Swaptions on interest rate Swaps are applicable to commodity Swaps.

Equity Derivatives Market

One of the key requisites for having a functioning commodity Swap market for a particular commodity was an agreed-on price index. There is probably no market in the world with indexes more famous than the equity market: the S&P 500, the DJIA (Dow Jones Industrial Average), the Wilshire 5000, the Nikkei 225, and so on. Since their introduction in the early 1980s, stock index futures have proved immensely popular. And it wasn't long before options on these futures were introduced.

Not long ago, we had Triple Witching Hours and these "new high-tech products" caused the market to move violently (usually down). Public outcry was great. A number of commentators claimed that, along with program trading (another high-tech innovation), the market was being ruined. A few changes were made (the uptick/downtick rule and modification of triple simultaneous expirations), and the market not only survived but continues to thrive.

Equity Swaps and OTC equity options are the next innovations just now hitting this market. And their potential is enormous. OTC Equity options permit customization not available through exchange-traded options.

Equity Swaps

Equity Swaps, in their simplest form, involve the exchange of some floating interest rate (usually, what else? Libor) and an equity index (possibly plus a spread). See Figure 12-5. These arrangements can involve payments in any currency regardless of the underlying index. Thus, Japanese Libor could be swapped against a return linked to the S&P 500. This flexibility and customization are part of the growing appeal of these new instruments. Expect this market to grow as sophisticated money managers and financial engineers create new applications to solve old problems using these instruments.

Equity Swaps Hit Main Street

With bank certificate of deposit rates at lows never imagined by a generation that grew up with double-digit interest rates, money

Figure 12-5. A simple equity Swap.

poured out of banks in 1991 and 1992. (By 1992, Citibank was paying 2 percent on NOW accounts.) As depositors took their money elsewhere, chiefly to mutual funds, smart bankers looked for ways to hold on to these deposits. A few banks (Bankers Trust, Chase Manhattan, and Swiss Bank, to name a few) began offering *market-linked deposits*. These deposits (in some instances as low as $2000, but usually requiring a minimum of $10,000) are FDIC insured up to $100,000. The rates on these are tied to a variety of things—the most common being the S&P 500, and the most exotic (at least at this point) being Latin American debt.

Not only are the deposits insured, but should the market drop (heaven forbid), investors are guaranteed to get back the original principal. This adds appeal to the investor concerned about preserving capital. In the simplest example, the bank takes an investor's deposit, buys a zero coupon bond, which takes care of the guarantee of principal, and uses some of the remaining funds to buy an option, which will take care of the stock index return.

In more sophisticated terms and for the more exotic linked products, the hedging will consist of zero coupon bonds and options as well as equity Swaps, equity-index futures, and perhaps stocks. These deposits typically have maturities of five or more years. They are being sold by some stock brokers. If interest rates stay low, expect these deposits to become increasingly popular and, as a by-product of this growth, thus giving the equities derivatives markets a big boost.

Implications

Investment bankers and mutual fund managers are not expected to take this lying down. The banks are going after their franchise and are offering FDIC insurance and guaranteed return of principal to boot. Merrill Lynch has already announced its own five-year instrument; it looks like the bank product with two exceptions—no FDIC insurance but a return of 115 percent of the S&P index. Merrill Lynch also guarantees return of principal. Expect more products along these lines.

Currency Swaps

Sometimes it is cheaper for a company to fund itself in a currency different from the currency in which it needs those funds. Without the currency Swap market, the company would either have to use a series of foreign exchange forwards to hedge itself or leave itself exposed to adverse currency moves. In addition, certain countries have stringent regulations when it comes to foreign exchange. Through assignments in the Swap markets, it is sometimes possible to get around these restrictions.

A *currency Swap* (also called a foreign exchange Swap) in its simplest form involves the exchange both at inception and maturity of an agreed-on amount plus periodic interest payments that are usually netted. For the purposes of a simple example, assume an exchange rate of 127 yen per one U.S. dollar. In this currency Swap, there are three parts: the initial exchange of principal, the interim interest payments, and the final exchange of principal at maturity.

In this transaction, US$10 million is swapped for a comparable amount of yen—1.27 billion yen. On day 1 of the Swap, the company sends its Swap dealer US$10 million, and the Swap dealer sends the company 1.27 billion yen. This is the *initial exchange of principal* and is done at the spot rate. Although most contracts call for this exchange, many do not because the value of the two currency amounts is identical.

During the life of the Swap contract, periodic interest payments are made. Just as in an interest rate Swap, they are usually netted in the Contractual Currency. At maturity, the same amounts of currency that were part of the initial exchange are re-exchanged. Thus, the Swap dealer now gives the company back its $10 million and the company gives the Swap dealer back its 1.27 billion yen. This *final exchange of principal* always takes place because the two amounts of money are no longer of equal value. With floating exchange rates, the 1.27 billion yen would be worth $8,466,667 if the yen/$ exchange rate had risen to 150 yen/dollar, or $12,700,000 if the exchange rate had fallen to 100 yen/dollar.

Currency Swap with no Interim Payments

Quite frequently, a company will have a need only for the final payment and not the interim payments (e.g., a company making a major purchase abroad, a company with a debt repayment or investment maturing or large expected receivable in another currency). In these instances, you will need to get quotes on long-dated forwards. The line between currency Swaps and the foreign exchange market can get blurred. As a general rule of thumb, transactions with a life of two years or less are handled by foreign exchange desks, and those with longer lives are handled as currency Swaps. Usually the group handling currency

Swaps is part of the Swaps group rather than the foreign exchange group of any particular institution.

Anyway, a company with a need for a long-dated currency forward (i.e., the need to purchase a currency for a date greater than two years) will find such a transaction to be priced a little better if done as a Swap rather than through traditional foreign exchange channels. In these instances, there are only two legs to the transaction: the first and third. And as before, in many instances, there is no initial exchange of principal. This time, however, the final exchange of principal is not the same as the initial exchange. Depending on the side you're on, a rate is calculated assuming that you're borrowing in one currency and investing in the other.

Thus, a U.S. company needing yen several years from now is assumed to be borrowing at a U.S. dollars rate and investing at a yen rate. Rates in the United States are higher than in Japan. So if the company could buy the 1.27 billion yen for $10 million now, the forward rate might be 120 yen/dollar for yen to be purchased five years from now. The company could enter into an agreement to buy the 1.27 billion yen in five years for $10,583,333 (1,270,000,000/120). The company has locked in its price by entering into this currency Swap. True, it will not benefit if the exchange rate goes in its favor, but the company has completely eliminated the risk of rates going against it.

The currency Swap market is not very liquid once you get into maturities longer than four or five years. Although there are always a number of players willing to step up to the plate for a 10-year interest rate Swap transaction, the same cannot be said about currency Swaps. And the spreads on transactions past five years are huge—assuming you can find someone willing to do the transaction in the first place.

The Future of the Currency Swap Market

The currency Swap market, despite being first and meeting some very important market needs, has not grown to the extent of the interest rate market. Some see the foreign exchange market diminishing somewhat, especially if Europe does actually move to one currency in 1999.

Whether or not the currency Swap market grows, the commodity Swap and derivatives market and the equity Swap and derivatives market should expand in the 1990s.

13

Managing Risk: Setting Up a Risk Management Program

So What's a Company to Do?

Hedging is a relatively new phenomena in the arena of interest rates. Although farmers and others involved in the production of commodities have long had futures markets to help manage risk, it was only during the 1970s that the first interest rate futures contract was developed and began trading on exchanges. And it wasn't until the mid-1980s that the use of Swaps became commonplace. Prior to that there was little interest rate risk management. Companies were more or less stuck with whatever loans they could get from their bankers. Of course, the commercial paper market had developed, insurance companies lent money, and companies could issue debt or equity. So companies weren't completely helpless. But they did not have the flexibility we have today, nor did they have the wide choice of instruments. And this is where the problem lies.

There are so many new products available to help manage interest rate risk that it is not always easy to figure out which is best for the job. The responsibility for choosing the right product, or for deciding to do nothing at all, often falls by default on a person who lacks the time, staff, or knowledge to make informed decisions.

Setting Up a Financial Risk Program

There are three types of financial risks to which a company could possibly be exposed: interest rate risk, foreign exchange risk, and commodity price risk. Not all companies face all risks, but most are exposed to one or more. New products are continually being developed to address these issues; their introduction makes it imperative that a company understand what it is getting into when purchasing these products. If a firm is not careful, it may actually be increasing its risk. Therefore, it is important for the end user to understand these products and all their implications in order to properly evaluate their usefulness and appropriateness in solving a company's problems.

A financial risk management program should be set up. The biggest disasters can occur when the risks associated with these products are not fully understood. Depending on the nature and volume of a company's activity, it may even be appropriate to designate one person whose only responsibility is risk management. For a smaller company, this function can usually be handled by the treasurer or the CFO. The important thing is that someone take responsibility, otherwise you may find two people within the same organization hedging in a manner that offsets each other. Don't laugh; as absurd as this may seem, it happens. And this is even worse at financial institutions where several different desks run separate books in the same vehicle.

One bank was delighted to take a trade with the U.S. branch of a financial institution and then lay it off with that institution's Tokyo desk. It doesn't take a genius to figure out what was wrong with this picture.

Understand the Problem

The first thing that a company needs to do in setting up a financial risk management program is to identify all the problems (i.e., places that have financial risk). A company that does not evaluate its financial risks, and does nothing to manage them, may actually be placing itself in the riskiest position of all—at the mercy of the marketplace, which is not very forgiving.

Interest rates are not the only thing that can rise or fall dramatically. Oil prices can skyrocket overnight, as we saw when Iraq invaded Kuwait in 1990. We've all heard of skyrocketing commodity prices when an early frost hits a particular growing area. And a company with no hedging program, with assets in one currency and liabilities in another, can lose all its profits in adverse currency moves.

The first step is to identify all the potential risk areas. Although it's ideal to have one person or one department handle this function, quite frequently information from several areas is required. Coordination between several different departments is often needed. Once the areas that could pose a potential risk have been identified, a plan of action can be prepared. Sometimes it is necessary to figure out a way for the profits and/or losses from the hedging to be shared between two or more departments.

Understand the Product

There are a myriad of products available that may or may not be appropriate to manage the financial risk of your company. Not only is it important to understand how a product may reduce a company's risk, but it is also important to understand how it might increase risk. Or, even if it doesn't increase the company's risk, it may take away some of the company's profit potential. Let me give you a simple example.

Companies that do not think that interest rates are going up might want to let the interest rate on their debt float so that they can take advantage of the lower rates. This can be done either through the use of floating-rate loans or by converting fixed-rate loans to floating-rate loans through the Swap market. A company may want to buy itself a little insurance just in case it is wrong in its interest rate forecast. The company's Swap dealer might suggest the purchase of a Cap. A Cap limits the amount that the company's interest rates can go up. If the company buys a 9 percent Libor Cap, the financial institution that sells it the Cap would cover the interest expense over 9 percent. However, Caps are very expensive. So, the Swap dealer might suggest that the company purchase a zero cost collar instead. What this will do, for *no* cost, is put both a Cap and a floor on the company's interest rates. If rates go above 9 percent in our simple example, the financial institution would reimburse the company. But if rates went below the floor (let's assume 6 percent), the company would reimburse the financial institution.

The strikes on the Cap and floor are struck so that the premium that would be earned by selling the floor equals the cost of the Cap. In a 7 percent rate environment, this might not look like a bad deal. If interest rates fall below 6 percent, the company would not benefit any further from the lower rates. If the company purchasing the collar did not fully understand its risks (i.e., it would be locked into a fixed rate at 6 percent should rates go below 6 percent), there could be a problem. Many people, when proposing such a purchase to upper management, focus on the zero cost of the collar but not the floor. They assume that the floor will never be hit. Most who bought zero cost collars in the end of 1990 or the beginning of 1991, assuming that rates were close to their lows, learned that floors can and do get hit.

Similarly, zero cost foreign exchange options (buying a put and selling a call at different strikes, or vice versa) can present big problems if your initial outlook was wrong.

Understand Both the Problems and the Products

Not used correctly, certain financial products can increase the interest rate risk of the end user. As cautioned earlier, make sure you understand the products and what you are hedging. Certain S&Ls and thrifts used interest rate Swaps in the mid- and late 1980s to match their assets and liabilities. They converted fixed-rate mortgages given to consumers to floating-rate assets using the Swap market and other sophisticated hedging techniques. They protected themselves against rising interest rates and avoided some of the disasters that led to the downfall of many such institutions in the late 1970s and early 1980s when interest rates skyrocketed. However, they did not protect themselves adequately against falling interest rates. As rates fell, their mortgage holders rushed to refinance their mortgages at lower rates.

Although these institutions had tried to calculate an average life factor into the portfolio, their calculations, which are never precise, proved to be disastrously wrong as Americans refinanced and traded up in record numbers in the mid- and late 1980s. When this happened, these institutions were left with Swaps on their books with no offsetting asset. And these Swaps were in a big loss position. Through a lack of understanding of all the risks associated with the products, the S&Ls and thrifts had replaced the risk of skyrocketing interest rates with that of plummeting interest rates.

Anyone contemplating using a Swap to convert an interest rate on a loan should realize that should the loan be prepaid, the Swap remains.

Occasionally Swaps are tied in to loans, and in these cases the prepayment of the loan usually mandates an immediate mark to market of the Swap with the out-of-the-money counterparty paying the in-the-money counterparty. This can become a major consideration when contemplating a refinancing. Sometimes the cost of unwinding the Swap (or the implied Swap) can make the potential refinancing unattractive.

Formulate a Plan and Implement It

Once the company's financial risks are fully identified and the company understands the products that are available, it is ready to devise a plan or strategy to deal with the exposure. This plan may include the use of interest rate Swaps, currency Swaps, commodity Swaps, Caps, collars, floors, Swaptions, foreign exchange contracts, futures contracts, and options, to name a few. Doing nothing is also an option. Sometimes the cost of a proposed strategy will be greater than the likely savings. As discussed already, CAPS can be very expensive. Sometimes when you figure out the impact of the cost of the product on your rates, you may decide that the risk is something you can live with.

In devising the strategy, a best and worst case scenario should always be included. That way there can be no surprises. The worst case scenario should be made clear to top management who are evaluating the plan. Remember portfolio insurance. This product, popular in the mid-1980s, fell out of grace in one day—the day the stock market fell 500+ points. Always, always, always map out a worst case scenario—the one where everything goes wrong!

In presenting your strategy, it usually will be necessary to take into account the tax and accounting ramifications of your strategy. Make sure and check with the experts in those departments before presenting your plans. Also make sure that they have reviewed the latest IRS and FASB rulings on the subjects before giving you their advice.

Tolerance for Risk versus Tolerance to Part with Cash

There is one other major concern for many institutions, and that is the cashflow affect. Some products are very expensive (then again, some cost nothing). For example, you may believe that interest rates are coming down and, therefore, want to let your borrowing expenses float. But you want to secure a little upside protection by buying a Cap. Caps can be very expensive and are usually paid for up front. As I write this, it would cost approximately 500 basis points to Cap three-month Libor at 7 percent for five years. On a $100 million portfolio, this insurance would cost the firm $5 million. Your company may find this a little expensive, or cash may not be a consideration. Knowing your company's tolerance for risk and its willingness to pay for products up front will help you decide on the right strategy.

Worst Case Scenario

Always make sure everyone fully understands the worst case scenario. You may have looked like a genius when you first fixed the company's five-year loan at 9 percent. However, as interest rates fall and Libor approaches 5 percent, the company will be making huge payments on its out-of-the-money Swaps. And there will be people only too happy to point this out. You want to ensure that they remember not only that you pointed out that this could happen, but that it is necessary in order to maintain the company's desired mix between fixed- and floating-rate debt.

Evaluate Your Results

Once your strategy is up and running, you should periodically evaluate it to see if it continues to meet your needs and expectations. The company may have a new interest rate forecast or a new forecast for commodity prices. Its borrowing needs may have changed. In addition, new products may have come on the market that may better suit your needs. Even the shape of the yield curve and your future expectations of its shape could affect your decisions. Finally, and most tempting, some of the products you purchased may have appreciated in value, and you may be able to generate some cash for the company if the position is sold.

If, for example, a company that fixed rates with a Swap, in anticipation of rising rates, now believes rates have peaked, it may wish to convert its interest rate exposure to floating by selling its Swap. And, if the company was right in its first evaluation, the Swap will have some value. The unwind of the Swap will result in a profit for the company. If, however, it had been wrong in its initial evaluation, the sale of the Swap would result in a loss and the company would have to pay the Swap counterparty in order to get out of the Swap. In this second instance, your knowledge of the company's willingness and ability to pay to get out of a losing position is critical once again. Some hate to do this and will sit and watch a bad position get worse rather than pay up. If the position has a long enough tenor, the company reasons, eventually it will improve. This might be the time for you to do a few calculations and show what it will cost the company while it is waiting for the position to improve! But before making a recommendation, check with the accounting and tax experts.

Periodic Reviews of Risk Management Portfolios

How often should an entity review its risk management portfolio? Some only look at their portfolio at the end of an accounting period, and others look at it every day. Given the simplicity of setting up a program to monitor positions on a personal computer and the low cost of these machines, portfolios can easily be marked to market every day. That way there will be no surprises at the end of a quarter. Sure, spreads and rates might not move very much from day to day in a slow market, but an adverse change of a basis point or two per week will result in an adverse move of 25 basis points over the quarter. Not a pleasant result to report to management.

Obviously, larger portfolios will take longer to mark to market than smaller ones. But it is even more important to mark large portfolios to market because the absolute value of those changes will be all that larger. Although you mark the portfolio to market each day, the results might not be formally reviewed that often. Upper management might only look at the results on a monthly or quarterly basis or when there is something noteworthy to report.

Amend the Plan

Once you have evaluated your results, you can amend your plan to reflect the performance of the products you purchased and your new market expectations. Again, you will need to make sure that everyone fully understands any new products and the risks associated with them. Also, the company must understand the risks of the new program. Whenever I present my worst case scenario and am skeptically asked if I really think that such and such would happen, I ask, "Did you ever think that the stock market would fall 500 points in one day?"

Monitoring Risk within a Derivatives Portfolio

We've talked about setting up a risk management program and we've talked about the different kinds of risk that are endemic to the marketplace. What can a company do to guard itself against some of the risks in the marketplace once it has set up a program to monitor its financial risk? There are several things.

Work with Many Different Counterparties

Spread your Swap business around. Diversify your portfolio just as you would any other portfolio. Limit your exposure to one counterparty to a small portion of your portfolio. The number of counterparties you use will be indicated by the size of your portfolio. A company with $100 million of notional amount of Swaps will probably have four counterparties, whereas one with $1 billion notional amount may have 8 to 10. Sure, it's easier to do all your business with one entity, but you won't get the best prices. And more important, you'll have protection should that entity go under. Think it can't happen—remember how fast Drexel went under?

Be Credit Conscious

Don't pick your counterparties strictly by price. In fact, if one institution consistently offers the lowest prices, be suspicious. See if it is just as good at pricing an unwind of the position. Check the credit ratings of the people with whom you intend to do business. Many institutions prefer to do business with those rated AAA or AA, but it is not always possible to be so selective if your company is not rated that high. If your company is rated that high, you are in a position to be selective about ratings. Privately owned companies or those companies with no long-term debt rating should aim for the highest rated counterparties as possible.

You may have good reason to do business with entities of slightly lower ratings. Make sure that this lower rating reflects a better price.

Monitor the Long-Term Debt Ratings of Your Counterparties

Once a trade is put on the books with a particular entity, you should continue to monitor its credit rating. This need not be done with great frequency, but it would not be unreasonable to check the credit ratings of those entities with which you have positions once a quarter.

What Should You Do if Your Counterparty Is Downgraded?

If you discover that a counterparty with which you have a significant position has been downgraded, you will want to consider your options. The two main factors in this analysis will be the remaining life of the transaction and the outlook for the institution that was downgraded.

The shorter the remaining life of the transaction, the less concerned you will be. A transaction with less than a year to run will probably be difficult to transfer and may not be worth investigating.

The level of the downgrade and the expected future of the entity also will affect your decision. If you expect the entity that was downgraded to be downgraded again in the future, you might want to consider reassigning the position while you can. The lower the credit rating of the entity, the harder it will be to assign to someone else. Also the lower the rating, the more it will cost you to assign. If you wait and the institution is downgraded again, you'll have an even more difficult time. Unfortunately, at the same time that you are reaching these decisions about a particular institution, so is the rest of the market, which further complicates your prospective transaction.

Although it might seem simplest to unwind the original transaction with the original counterparty and put on a new one for the remaining life, this strategy also has problems. The original counterparty will have trouble unwinding your position in the marketplace and, consequently, will charge you a higher price. You will end up paying an extra bid offer spread. And finally, if your original position was out-of-the-money, your company will have to come up with some cash for the unwind.

Often, the market will be full of rumors of an impending downgrade even before the rating agencies downgrade an institution. So even if you are smart enough to anticipate the downgrade and try and act preemptively, you may have some problems.

This discussion has pointed out some of the possible problems you may have with deteriorating credits. Try and anticipate the marketplace and don't always be ready to settle for the absolute lowest price when swapping. Consider all factors.

Using a Downgrade to Your Advantage

It is possible to use a downgrade to your advantage. One Swap dealer who was downgraded used that information to his advantage (I suspect without the knowledge or consent of top management of that institution). What this trader did was to call customers with positions on his books and say to them something like, "You know we've been downgraded and I suspect that you'd like to get our name off your books." If the customer agreed, the dealer would proceed to make an offer that was 20 basis points off the market. He'd negotiate for something less but still end up with a much larger profit or smaller loss than expected. Then he'd try the same technique with the offsetting trade. This trader was picking up large profits for his institution without increasing the company's risk. In fact, he was winding down the company's positions at a time when the institution's capital was needed in other areas. And his bonus was probably tied to the profits he generated. Contrast this with what happened to Bank of New England as reported in *The Wall Street Journal* on June 18, 1991.

When a Downgrade Hurts

First of all, despite the success of the dealer just mentioned, most times when an institution is downgraded, it hurts business. The institution will find it harder to do business, and Swap dealers may see new business vanish.

In late January 1990, Bank of New England had $30 billion in assets on its balance sheet. In addition, the bank also had $36 billion in off–balance sheet transactions, mainly foreign exchange and interest rate transactions. As the bank's credit deteriorated, the bank's traders had to turn these transactions into cash. They had to do this while trying to hold onto as much of their profits as possible. As the bank tried to unwind its portfolio, word of its troubles spread. And many of the bank's counterparties seized the opportunity to take advantage of the situation by charging the bank unreasonable levels to unwind their positions. (This second scenario is more apt to be what happens when an institution is downgraded.)

Confirmations: Two Signatures

Confirmations for derivative product transactions should require two signatures. If it requires only one, it should be the signature of a person in the organization other than the party initiating the transaction. This protects not only the institution but the individuals involved in the trading end of the business. Companies should insist on speedy delivery of all confirmations from counterparties and require employees to have them signed within 48 hours of the initiation of the transaction.

Doing Nothing

On occasion you'll hear some financial geniuses remark that this stuff is too complicated or perhaps too risky, so they will take the safest route—they'll do nothing. What these individuals do not realize is that doing nothing is perhaps the riskiest strategy of all. It leaves you completely at the mercy of the market. The Swap market gives intelligent market participants a tool to limit their interest rate exposure. It gives floating-rate borrowers a way to lock in a fixed rate when they feel that rates are going to increase, and it gives fixed-rate borrowers a way to unlock their interest rate expense and let it float down when they expect interest rates to fall.

And for those who are about to point out that the credit crunch of 1991 has locked many would-be market participants out of the market, let me point out that that is not completely true. Although these organizations are excluded from parts of the derivatives market, there are certain tools available to them: mark-to-market Swaps, collateralized Swaps, in some instances futures, and finally the ability to do business with Swap counterparties of slightly lower quality. For most market participants, these may not be the first choice for how to hedge their debt, but they do offer some alternatives.

Although doing nothing because of a lack of market availability is frustrating, doing nothing because of a lack of knowledge is not very smart. The answer in these instances is to get yourself educated—fast. Call several Swap dealers. You'll be pleasantly surprised when you see the amount of information and the level of sophistication most of them display. But study everything completely before you act. And make sure you understand. If you don't, ask questions until you do.

**Don't get yourself talked into something
you don't understand.**

14

The Future

Much has happened since the start of the 1980s. Product and markets that were nonexistent at the beginning of the decade have grown into a $4 trillion plus business (Interest Rate Swaps and other derivatives). Although at first it was extremely profitable for those who jumped in, the market is now experiencing some growing pains. Some of this is natural to any market, and some of it is a reflection of the unique financial circumstances that afflict all financial markets today. Most who are currently involved in the markets have never dealt with a credit crunch, falling real estate values, unemployment of any extent in the white-collar sector, or razor thin spreads. In the last few years, we've seen the downfall of one of the premier investment houses, a Treasury bidding scandal, and more than a few investment bankers go to jail.

We've adjusted and will continue to adjust. The derivative marketplace will look a little different 10 years from now. What will it look like? You'll get two views here—from two different sides of the desk. First you'll hear from the dealer community—Debbie Orlando, Director at Barclay's Bank PLC. Debbie has over 10 years' experience involved in a variety of different derivative products; she uses this experience to look back a little and then into the future. Then, of course, you'll hear my perspective from the corporate side.

The Evolution of the Swaps Market in the 1990s

by Deborah K. Orlando*

The early 1990s have thus far been trying times for most people, particularly those in the financial services industry. Layoffs, eroding margins, and increased competition threaten not only ways of doing business, but livelihoods as well. The nature of the marketplace has changed so dramatically that, while it presents opportunities for the innovative, it also brings new challenges to all participants. In particular, the market for off–balance sheet instruments (i.e., Swaps and derivative products), previously unaffected by the changing environment, is being confronted now with declining margins, the threat of deregulation, and overcapacity. Never in the history of the Swaps market have the stakes been so high.

Throughout the 1980s, the Swaps market experienced explosive growth as companies became aware that interest rate volatility could impact seriously their debt-swollen balance sheets. A multitude of derivative instruments (Caps, floors, Treasury options, Swaptions, Captions, municipal, commodity, and equity-linked products) were developed to meet the supposedly ravenous appetite of investors and end users. Now, however, in a pattern familiar to other 1980s high-growth industries, we are poised for a substantial reduction in both margins and the number of Swap market participants.

During 1992, the Federal Reserve has allowed short-term interest rates to plunge, with no imminent increase on the horizon. Swap spreads are stuck at historical lows, as the negative cost of carry generated by the steepness of the yield curve dissuades end users from paying fixed to lock in longer-term rates. Companies have restructured to eliminate excessive debt, reducing borrowing needs and, in turn, the need for Swap transactions. Additionally, the future appeal of the market for off–balance sheet products is in question for the first time in its history owing to increased government scrutiny and the threat of either self-imposed or externally mandated reregulation of some sort, probably including increased capital requirements.

Over the past several months, both the Federal Reserve and the Bank of England have spoken out strongly against the apparent naiveté of banking's senior management regarding the risk issues of the derivatives market, including the actual positions their derivatives specialists are taking. In fact, when top management of a bank hires someone to run its derivatives area, it often relies on that

---

*The opinions expressed in this article are those of the writer, and are not necessarily representative of those of Barclay's Bank, PLC.

person's expertise and integrity in setting up *both* the trading and controls of these products. The Fed has expressed concern that large off–balance sheet exposures are perhaps taken without the thorough understanding of top management. Recent Fed proposals would seek to measure interest rate risk in some uniform manner, and require those who have excessive risk to hold additional Tier 1 capital. This could be quite onerous for certain institutions, and would, in the least, substantially raise banks' and, in turn, their clients' costs of doing business. As a result, it is likely that many financial institutions that had made more or less half-hearted entrance into the Swaps market over the last few years will be the first casualties of such decisions. Liquidity in the interbank market will certainly be tighter, as these banks no longer find Swaps and derivatives to be cost-efficient hedging mechanisms for asset/liability mismatches, and arbitrage trading becomes less profitable.

To counteract the negative tide of criticism from the regulators, the ISDA (International Swap Dealers Association) has prepared a new master agreement for Swaps and derivatives transactions. This agreement covers multicurrency, cross-border deals and encourages cross-product netting to reduce counterparties' exposure to one another. In this way, the ISDA hopes to mitigate concerns that undisclosed credit and market exposure in these markets will lead to a "domino effect" of financial failures in the industry. The overall degree of success that ISDA has in promoting the self-policing of the industry will determine whether the Fed eventually steps in to increase capital requirements and requires other restructuring of off–balance sheet products. Any of these changes would certainly serve to raise the cost of doing business in these products and, accordingly, reduce the number of industry participants.

Where, then, are the opportunities for growth and profit as we endure these lean years? Over the years, plain vanilla interest rate Swaps and options have become commoditized to a great extent as end users compete one dealer against the other and more new players enter the pricing game vying for critical mass. Start-up swappers and banks whose credit quality have declined often act as loss leaders to undercut the competition and earn customer business. Cross-currency Swaps, although still the most liquid market for hedging longer-dated currency exposure, should not experience the degree of growth of past years because the effect of heavier capital adequacy requirements on pricing reduces possible arbitrages between the debt and Swap markets. Nevertheless, these Swaps still do provide effective access to foreign-denominated borrowings that might otherwise be unavailable to certain companies via the conventional debt markets.

Certain areas of the Swaps market, particularly equity derivatives, seem to hold special promise over the next several years. Certain financial institutions with equity-trading subsidiaries have exposure to the equities markets and the exchange-traded tools available to hedge equity exposure. These futures and options contracts are generally cash-settled, which eliminates the dealers' need to deal with the physical underlying. Accordingly, as barriers between commercial and investment banks continue to break down, the equities derivatives market should continue to grow in size and liquidity. Eventually, though, as the market matures, margins may suffer.

Commodity-linked Swaps/derivatives, on the other hand, should experience a more restrained, yet profitable, growth pattern for already existing market participants. The commodities market has producers and end users who already have access to, and substantial experience with, liquid hedging tools via the futures and contract (forward) markets. This makes it quite difficult for more than a handful of financial intermediaries to provide a more efficient hedging vehicle than the actual commodity market can itself provide.

For this reason, the market may remain in the hands of a limited group of bankers who know how to effectively utilize these futures markets or, otherwise, handle the underlying physical commodity and its associated risk. Many will attempt to break into this market; few, however, will know how to really hedge the basis risk that arises between the commodity being hedged and the hedging instrument. Hedging this risk more effectively than the actual producers/users of the underlying commodity can is the key to differentiating oneself from the competition in the commodity derivatives market. Therefore, those institutions with already established contacts in commodities trade finance will have the advantage.

For the remainder of this century we can expect, first, a period of higher costs for all involved owing to reregulation. Then, as many of the less successful latecomers drop out, the Swaps and derivatives market should experience a flight to credit quality and an eventual widening of spreads as we move into the 2000s. To the extent that new transactions can be structured, which allow one party to take more of a certain risk in exchange for less of another risk (e.g., equity/interest rate or commodity/foreign exchange Swaps), there may be room for some higher value-added transactions. Thus, the higher-margined Swaps and derivatives business will go to the innovative in the next decade.

The Next 10 Years
for Swaps and
Other Derivatives

I agree with Debbie on just about everything she says. As in any maturing market, there will be some consolidation. Some of the weaker players will get left in the dust and eventually leave the business. Ultimately, this will result in a stronger market with players who know what they are doing.

The credit crunch that started in 1990 will end or, more likely, very gradually disappear. As the U.S. economy improves, we'll see the fortunes of some down-and-out companies improve, and with that improvement will come higher credit ratings and, therefore, access to more markets. All this will happen gradually.

There may or may not be some localized disaster, such as the one involving the municipalities in England several years ago. But should one happen, it will be localized and in no way trigger the kind of systemic meltdown that we sometimes read about. Several things will ensure that.

Education

For starters, as these products mature, they will start—and already are in certain instances—to be taught in our schools. Students coming out of business school will not only know what stocks and bonds are, but also how to use Swaps and futures.

And the senior management of our large corporations and financial institutions will learn more about these products and become more familiar with them. As this happens, and it will, they will institute the proper controls and monitoring in those cases where it is lacking. Senior managers do not need to understand every minute calculation in order to hire the right types of people to handle these tasks. They do, however, need some understanding of what they are talking about. Just as the president of a company may be able to read the financial statements of his or her company without knowing how to make every tiny journal entry, so too will he or she be able to adequately control and monitor derivatives activity.

Limiting Risk

When senior managers better understand what can be done with some of these tools, they will come to realize that the correct use of these tools helps, rather than hinders, the firm. One of the key concepts in derivatives markets is the use of these products to limit risk—to lock in prices or interest rates and, therefore, profits. As this happens, people will become more matter-of-fact about these instruments. Eventually, they will be seen as just another financial tool to be used in managing the company's risk.

The question might be "Should we borrow fixed or floating?" And after that determination is made, a second question will be asked: "Can we get a lower rate going straight to the marketplace, or should we use the Swap market?" If a decision is made to, say, float, then another question can be asked: "Should we buy a Cap to protect us in case rates go through the roof?"

Increased Sophistication

Increased sophistication on the part of some market participants will spread to others. As companies start managing their various (interest rate, foreign exchange, and commodity) risks using the Swap market, they will begin to seek ways to increase their income without substantially increasing their risk. Even though I abhor them, zero cost collars are a simple way to do this. Some institutions write short-term options (as do many stock portfolio managers) to generate income and, thereby, reduce their borrowing costs. This will continue, and others may adopt these techniques as well.

Credit Consciousness

The market will continue to be credit conscious. Gone forever are those beginning days when documentation was not a concern and credit was not a real issue. Although we may get away from the stringent overreaction that currently characterizes the market, credit will continue to be an issue—and rightly so. These products are supposed to reduce risk. You don't reduce your risks by entering into transactions with entities that may not be around when it comes time to deliver. This will allow the best credits to continue to be selective about with whom they do business. Eventually (if there isn't already), there will be tiering in the marketplace.

Capital Requirements/Reporting Requirements

Regulators, both in the United States and abroad, will continue to look at capital requirements for derivative transactions. Transactions that were previously handled as off–balance sheet items eventually may find their way onto the balance sheet itself, at least for commercial banks. If and when this happens, the Financial Accounting Standards Board abstracts may eventually follow these guidelines for all and not just commercial banks.

Increased Regulation

It pains me to say this, but I don't see how a market of this size can expect to go completely unregulated. Somehow, some regulatory body will probably be put in place. Whether or not this regulatory body is an offshoot of ISDA or one of the existing regulatory bodies (CTFC, the Fed, SEC, and so on) or a new body remains to be seen. The CFTC has already taken an unsuccessful crack at overseeing the market, and eventually someone else will also. This will ultimately benefit the market because regulation will relieve those who fear that the market will bring down the whole banking system of the civilized world.

Improved Monitoring and Controls

Market participants as a whole will continue to improve their monitoring and control systems for all their derivatives trading. As much as they didn't like Jerry Corrigan's remarks, many realized that he wasn't completely off-base. If all that comes from his remarks is that many market participants with poor controls take a closer look at their books and implemented some monitoring systems and internal controls, then something important was achieved. And those remarks have made everyone in the business aware of just how important monitoring and controls are.

True Level of Risk within the System

The ISDA released a study on July 28, 1992, in response to those who claimed that the derivatives are the next disaster just waiting to hit the financial system. Arthur Andersen & Company surveyed firms handling approximately 70 percent of the Swaps market to figure out the level of losses. Total losses reported were $358 million. Just under half ($178 million) came from the debacle in London where local authorities were allowed to walk away from losses after it was determined that they did not have the authority to enter into those contracts in the first place. At first glance this may appear to be a huge sum, but you must put it in perspective.

Given a total notional amount of $3.1 trillion, this loss represents a little over one hundredth of one percent. Some will immediately protest that this is not the correct measurement—that the loss should be compared to the value of the portfolio (i.e., the mark-to-market value).

This value at the time the study was done was $77.5 billion. Comparing the $358 million loss to this, we come out with a loss of less than half of one percent—a loss most regulated banks would be happy to take on their real estate portfolio!

This study may help put the systemic risk question in perspective, and it may help hold off the regulation question, at least for a time.

Future Market Growth

The biggest market growth in the next few years should come on both the equity and commodity sides, with equities possibly being the big winner. The aging of baby boomers (and consequently greater savings on their part), low yields currently available in most risk-free fixed-rate investments, the expectation of continued low fixed rates at least for the next few years, increased pension fund contributions, and the continued growth of savings plans such as 401Ks and 403Bs will cause a renewed focus on the equity markets.

As investors from all the groups just mentioned continue to see double-digit returns in equities compared with low single-digit returns in fixed-rate investments, they will pour money into the stock market as they become disgusted with their banks and other fixed-rate returns.

More Main Street Applications

The financial engineers who worked for almost a decade on the debt side will focus some of their energy, not only on the asset side, but on Main Street instead of Wall Street applications. We'll start to see more products aimed at "mom and pop." As these products become more popular, the financial engineers will help educate everyone about these new markets.

The market-linked deposits dreamed up by those bankers are just the beginning. If these products are successful (and I can't see how they won't be), we'll see more products like them. But just remember the building block approach. Most of these products are simply a combination of others, or they require looking at an old product from a different angle. Once again, it'll be a whole new ball game.

Organizations

Chicago Board of Trade
LaSalle at Jackson
Chicago, IL 60604
1-800-The-CBOT

Financial Accounting Standards
  Board
401 Merritt
P.O. Box 5116
Norwalk, CT 06856-5116
203-847-0700

International Swap Dealers
  Association Inc.
1270 Avenue of the Americas
New York, NY 10020-1702
212-332-1200

FASB Abstracts

EITF Abstracts

Issue No. 84-7

Title: Termination of Interest Rate Swaps

Dates Discussed: July 24, 1984; September 25, 1984; October 18, 1984

Reference: FASB Statement No. 80, *Accounting for Futures Contracts*

ISSUE

Interest rate swaps are contractual agreements between two parties to exchange "interest" payments regularly. Generally, one party agrees to make fixed periodic payments and the other party agrees to make variable payments that are based on a market rate (for example, the T-Bill rate) applied to a "notional" (theoretical) principal amount. As interest rates change, the agreement will become favorable for one party and unfavorable for the other. Recently, some enterprises have (1) terminated agreements, (2) sold their position to another enterprise, or (3) achieved the same effect by entering into another swap that offsets the first agreement. Accepted practice for interest rate swap agreements apparently had been to record only the net receivable or payable at each payment date (with accruals when the balance sheet date falls between two payment dates).

The issue is, if an interest rate swap is sold or terminated and cash is received, whether the gain or loss is recognized on sale or termination or is recognized over the life of some financial instrument deemed to have been hedged by the swap agreement.

EITF DISCUSSION

Hedged Transactions

The Task Force reached a consensus that gains and losses on terminated interest rate swaps that were accounted for as hedges should not be recognized immediately in income because the termination of an interest rate swap accounted for as a hedge is closely analogous to a terminated futures hedge described in Statement 80. Under that Statement, the gain or loss on a terminated futures hedge, to the extent it has been an effective hedge, must continue to be deferred and recognized when the offsetting gain or loss is recognized on the hedged transaction. The FASB staff noted that many interest rate swaps are currently accounted for as hedge transactions, with the gain or loss on the swap termination deferred and recognized when the offsetting gain or loss is recognized on the hedged transaction.

Nonhedged Transactions

Several Task Force members raised questions about interest rate swaps that are *not* accounted for as hedges. The FASB staff representative stated that termination of such a swap agreement would not be analogous to the transaction described in Statement 80 and that the accounting treatment might be different depending on the accounting followed in the Swap agreement prior to termination. Some Task Force members stated that banks and brokers have begun entering into swap transactions that are not accounted for as hedges, but Task Force members were uncertain as to the accounting being followed. No consensus was reached on nonhedge transactions.

STATUS

A related issue was subsequently addressed in Issue No. 84-36, "Interest Rate Swap Transactions." For that Issue, the Task Force agreed that, if there is an underlying debt obligation on the balance sheet of the company entering into the swap transaction, the company should account for the swap arrangement like a hedge of the obligation and record interest expense using the revised interest rate, with any fees or other payments amortized as yield adjustments.

The accounting for swaps was subsequently addressed in an article, "Interest Rate Swaps—Your Rate or Mine?" written by two FASB staff members, Keith Wishon and Lorin S. Chevalier. The article was published in the September 1985 issue of the *Journal of Accountancy*.

No further EITF discussion of Issue No. 84-7 is planned.

EITF Abstracts

Issue No. 84-36

Title: Interest Rate Swap Transactions

Dates Discussed: November 15, 1984; February 14, 1985; March 28, 1985

Reference: FASB Statement No. 80, *Accounting for Futures Contracts*

ISSUE

Interest rate swaps are contractual agreements between two parties to exchange "interest" payments regularly. Generally, one party agrees to make fixed periodic payments and the other party agrees to make variable payments that are based on a market rate (for example, the T-Bill rate) applied to a "notional" (theoretical) principal amount.

The issues are:

1. Whether the interest rate swap agreement should be viewed as an investment (similar to an interest rate futures contract) and, if so, whether the hedge criteria of Statement 80 for futures contracts should apply to those transactions

2. Whether the accounting should differ if the participant does not hold the underlying asset or liability

3. How the termination of an interest rate swap is accounted for.

EITF DISCUSSION

The Task Force reiterated its consensus on Issue No. 84-7, "Termination of Interest Rate Swaps," that gains and losses on terminated interest rate swaps that were accounted for as hedges should not be recognized immediately in income. The Task Force discussed the accounting for a swap transaction if the purpose of entering into the transaction is to change the nature of a liability (for example, from a fixed to a variable interest obligation). The Task Force agreed that, if there is an underlying debt obligation on the balance sheet of the company entering into the swap transaction, the company should account for the swap arrangement like a hedge of the obligation and record interest expense using the revised interest rate, with any fees or other payments amortized as yield adjustments.

Task Force members noted diversity in practice when there is no underlying debt liability on the balance sheet of the company entering into the transaction and that those transactions may become more common if interest rate swaps are traded in secondary markets.

STATUS
The accounting for swaps was subsequently addressed in an article, "Interest Rate Swaps—Your Rate or Mine?" written by two FASB staff members, Keith Wishon and Lorin S. Chevalier. The article was published in the September 1985 issue of the *Journal of Accountancy*.

No further EITF discussion is planned.

Appendix C
ISDA Master Agreement

This appendix presents the complete ISDA master agreement for local currency–single jurisdiction.

(Local Currency—Single Jurisdiction)

ISDA®

International Swap Dealers Association, Inc.

MASTER AGREEMENT

dated as of ....

.... and ....

have entered and/or anticipate entering into one or more transactions (each a "Transaction") that are or will be governed by this Master Agreement, which includes the schedule (the "Schedule"), and the documents and other confirming evidence (each a "Confirmation") exchanged between the parties confirming those Transactions.

Accordingly, the parties agree as follows:—

1. Interpretation

(a) *Definitions*. The terms defined in Section 12 and in the Schedule will have the meanings therein specified for the purpose of this Master Agreement.

(b) *Inconsistency*. In the event of any inconsistency between the provisions of the Schedule and the other provisions of this Master Agreement, the Schedule will prevail. In the event of any inconsistency between the provisions of any Confirmation and this Master Agreement (including the Schedule), such Confirmation will prevail for the purpose of the relevant Transaction.

(c) *Single Agreement*. All Transactions are entered into in reliance on the fact that this Master Agreement and all Confirmations form a single agreement between the parties (collectively referred to as this "Agreement"), and the parties would not otherwise enter into any Transactions.

2. Obligations

(a) *General Conditions*.

(i)   Each party will make each payment or delivery specified in each Confirmation to be made by it, subject to the other provisions of this Agreement.

(ii) Payments under this Agreement will be made on the due date for value on that date in the place of the account specified in the relevant Confirmation or otherwise pursuant to this Agreement, in freely transferable funds and in the manner customary for payments in the required currency. Where settlement is by delivery (that is, other than by payment), such delivery will be made for receipt on the due date in the manner customary for the relevant obligation unless otherwise specified in the relevant Confirmation or elsewhere in this Agreement.

(iii) Each obligation of each party under Section 2(a)(i) is subject to (1) the condition precedent that no Event of Default or Potential Event of Default with respect to the other party has occurred and is continuing, (2) the condition precedent that no Early Termination Date in respect of the relevant Transaction has occurred or been effectively designated and (3) each other applicable condition precedent specified in this Agreement.

Copyright ©1992 by International Swap Dealers Association, Inc.

(b)   *Change of Account*. Either party may change its account for receiving a payment or delivery by giving notice to the other party at least five Local Business Days prior to the scheduled date for the payment or delivery to which such change applies unless such other party gives timely notice of a reasonable objection to such change.

(c)   *Netting*. If on any date amounts would otherwise be payable:—

    (i)   in the same currency; and

    (ii)   in respect of the same Transaction,

by each party to the other, then, on such date, each party's obligation to make payment of any such amount will be automatically satisfied and discharged and, if the aggregate amount that would otherwise have been payable by one party exceeds the aggregate amount that would otherwise have been payable by the other party, replaced by an obligation upon the party by whom the larger aggregate amount would have been payable to pay to the other party the excess of the larger aggregate amount over the smaller aggregate amount.

The parties may elect in respect of two or more Transactions that a net amount will be determined in respect of all amounts payable on the same date in the same currency in respect of such Transactions, regardless of whether such amounts are payable in respect of the same Transaction. The election may be made in the Schedule or a Confirmation by specifying that subparagraph (ii) above will not apply to the Transactions identified as being subject to the election, together with the starting date (in which case subparagraph (ii) above will not, or will cease to, apply to such Transactions from such date). This election may be made separately for different groups of Transactions and will apply separately to each pairing of branches or offices through which the parties make and receive payments or deliveries.

(d)   *Default Interest; Other Amounts*. Prior to the occurrence or effective designation of an Early Termination Date in respect of the relevant Transaction, a party that defaults in the performance of any payment obligation will, to the extent permitted by law and subject to Section 6(c), be required to pay interest (before as well as after judgment) on the overdue amount to the other party on demand in the same currency as such overdue amount, for the period from (and including) the original due date for payment to (but excluding) the date of actual payment, at the Default Rate. Such interest will be calculated on the basis of daily compounding and the actual number of days elapsed. If, prior to the occurrence or effective designation of an Early Termination Date in respect of the relevant Transaction, a party defaults in the performance of any obligation required to be settled by delivery, it will compensate the other party on demand if and to the extent provided for in the relevant Confirmation or elsewhere in this Agreement.

3.   Representations

Each party represents to the other party (which representations will be deemed to be repeated by each party on each date on which a Transaction is entered into) that:—

(a)   *Basic Representations*.

    (i)   *Status*. It is duly organised and validly existing under the laws of the jurisdiction of its organisation or incorporation and, if relevant under such laws, in good standing;

    (ii)   *Powers*. It has the power to execute this Agreement and any other documentation relating to this Agreement to which it is a party, to deliver this Agreement and any other documentation relating to this Agreement that it is required by this Agreement to deliver and to perform its obligations under this Agreement and any obligations it has under any Credit Support Document to which it is a party and has taken all necessary action to authorise such execution, delivery and performance;

    (iii) *No Violation or Conflict*. Such execution, delivery and performance do not violate or conflict with any law applicable to it, any provision of its constitutional documents, any order or judgment of any court or other agency of government applicable to it or any of its assets or any contractual restriction binding on or affecting it or any of its assets;

(iv) *Consents*. All governmental and other consents that are required to have been obtained by it with respect to this Agreement or any Credit Support Document to which it is a party have been obtained and are in full force and effect and all conditions of any such consents have been complied with; and

(v) *Obligations Binding*. Its obligations under this Agreement and any Credit Support Document to which it is a party constitute its legal, valid and binding obligations, enforceable in accordance with their respective terms (subject to applicable bankruptcy, reorganisation, insolvency, moratorium or similar laws affecting creditors' rights generally and subject, as to enforceability, to equitable principles of general application (regardless of whether enforcement is sought in a proceeding in equity or at law)).

(b) *Absence of Certain Events*. No Event of Default or Potential Event of Default or, to its knowledge, Termination Event with respect to it has occurred and is continuing and no such event or circumstance would occur as a result of its entering into or performing its obligations under this Agreement or any Credit Support Document to which it is a party.

(c) *Absence of Litigation*. There is not pending or, to its knowledge, threatened against it or any of its Affiliates any action, suit or proceeding at law or in equity or before any court, tribunal, governmental body, agency or official or any arbitrator that is likely to affect the legality, validity or enforceability against it of this Agreement or any Credit Support Document to which it is a party or its ability to perform its obligations under this Agreement or such Credit Support Document.

(d) *Accuracy of Specified Information*. All applicable information that is furnished in writing by or on behalf of it to the other party and is identified for the purpose of this Section 3(d) in the Schedule is, as of the date of the information, true, accurate and complete in every material respect.

4. Agreements

Each party agrees with the other that, so long as either party has or may have any obligation under this Agreement or under any Credit Support Document to which it is a party:—

(a) *Furnish Specified Information*. It will deliver to the other party any forms, documents or certificates specified in the Schedule or any Confirmation by the date specified in the Schedule or such Confirmation or, if none is specified, as soon as reasonably practicable.

(b) *Maintain Authorisations*. It will use all reasonable efforts to maintain in full force and effect all consents of any governmental or other authority that are required to be obtained by it with respect to this Agreement or any Credit Support Document to which it is a party and will use all reasonable efforts to obtain any that may become necessary in the future.

(c) *Comply with Laws*. It will comply in all material respects with all applicable laws and orders to which it may be subject if failure so to comply would materially impair its ability to perform its obligations under this Agreement or any Credit Support Document to which it is a party.

5. Events of Default and Termination Events

(a) *Events of Default*. The occurrence at any time with respect to a party or, if applicable, any Credit Support Provider of such party or any Specified Entity of such party of any of the following events constitutes an event of default (an "Event of Default") with respect to such party:—

(i) *Failure to Pay or Deliver*. Failure by the party to make, when due, any payment under this Agreement or delivery under Section 2(a)(i) or 2(d) required to be made by it if such failure is not remedied on or before the third Local Business Day after notice of such failure is given to the party;

(ii) *Breach of Agreement*. Failure by the party to comply with or perform any agreement or obligation (other than an obligation to make any payment under this Agreement or delivery under Section 2(a)(i) or 2(d) or to give notice of a Termination Event or any agreement or obligation under Section 4(a)) to be complied with or performed by the party in accordance with this Agreement if such failure is not remedied on or before the thirtieth day after notice of such failure is given to the party;

(iii) *Credit Support Default*.

(1) Failure by the party or any Credit Support Provider of such party to comply with or perform any agreement or obligation to be complied with or performed by it in accordance with any Credit Support Document if such failure is continuing after any applicable grace period has elapsed;

(2) the expiration or termination of such Credit Support Document or the failing or ceasing of such Credit Support Document to be in full force and effect for the purpose of this Agreement (in either case other than in accordance with its terms) prior to the satisfaction of all obligations of such party under each Transaction to which such Credit Support Document relates without the written consent of the other party; or

(3) the party or such Credit Support Provider disaffirms, disclaims, repudiates or rejects, in whole or in part, or challenges the validity of, such Credit Support Document;

(iv) *Misrepresentation*. A representation made or repeated or deemed to have been made or repeated by the party or any Credit Support Provider of such party in this Agreement or any Credit Support Document proves to have been incorrect or misleading in any material respect when made or repeated or deemed to have been made or repeated;

(v) *Default under Specified Transaction*. The party, any Credit Support Provider of such party or any applicable Specified Entity of such party (1) defaults under a Specified Transaction and, after giving effect to any applicable notice requirement or grace period, there occurs a liquidation of, an acceleration of obligations under, or an early termination of, that Specified Transaction, (2) defaults, after giving effect to any applicable notice requirement or grace period, in making any payment or delivery due on the last payment, delivery or exchange date of, or any payment on early termination of, a Specified Transaction (or such default continues for at least three Local Business Days if there is no applicable notice requirement or grace period) or (3) disaffirms, disclaims, repudiates or rejects, in whole or in part, a Specified Transaction (or such action is taken by any person or entity appointed or empowered to operate it or act on its behalf);

(vi) *Cross Default*. If "Cross Default" is specified in the Schedule as applying to the party, the occurrence or existence of (1) a default, event of default or other similar condition or event (however described) in respect of such party, any Credit Support Provider of such party or any applicable Specified Entity of such party under one or more agreements or instruments relating to Specified Indebtedness of any of them (individually or collectively) in an aggregate amount of not less than the applicable Threshold Amount (as specified in the Schedule) which has resulted in such Specified Indebtedness becoming, or becoming capable at such time of being declared, due and payable under such agreements or instruments, before it would otherwise have been due and payable or (2) a default by such party, such Credit Support Provider or such Specified Entity (individually or collectively) in making one or more payments on the due date thereof in an aggregate amount of not less than the applicable Threshold Amount under such agreements or instruments (after giving effect to any applicable notice requirement or grace period);

(vii) *Bankruptcy*. The party, any Credit Support Provider of such party or any applicable Specified Entity of such party:—

(1) is dissolved (other than pursuant to a consolidation, amalgamation or merger); (2) becomes insolvent or is unable to pay its debts or fails or admits in writing its inability generally to pay its debts as they become due; (3) makes a general assignment, arrangement or composition with or for the benefit of its creditors; (4) institutes or has instituted against it a proceeding seeking a judgment of insolvency or bankruptcy or any other relief under any bankruptcy or insolvency law or other similar law affecting creditors' rights, or a petition is presented for its

winding-up or liquidation, and, in the case of any such proceeding or petition instituted or presented against it, such proceeding or petition (A) results in a judgment of insolvency or bankruptcy or the entry of an order for relief or the making of an order for its winding-up or liquidation or (B) is not dismissed, discharged, stayed or restrained in each case within 30 days of the institution or presentation thereof; (5) has a resolution passed for its winding-up, official management or liquidation (other than pursuant to a consolidation, amalgamation or merger); (6) seeks or becomes subject to the appointment of an administrator, provisional liquidator, conservator, receiver, trustee, custodian or other similar official for it or for all or substantially all its assets; (7) has a secured party take possession of all or substantially all its assets or has a distress, execution, attachment, sequestration or other legal process levied, enforced or sued on or against all or substantially all its assets and such secured party maintains possession, or any such process is not dismissed, discharged, stayed or restrained, in each case within 30 days thereafter; (8) causes or is subject to any event with respect to it which, under the applicable laws of any jurisdiction, has an analogous effect to any of the events specified in clauses (1) to (7) (inclusive); or (9) takes any action in furtherance of, or indicating its consent to, approval of, or acquiescence in, any of the foregoing acts; or

(viii) *Merger Without Assumption.* The party or any Credit Support Provider of such party consolidates or amalgamates with, or merges with or into, or transfers all or substantially all its assets to, another entity and, at the time of such consolidation, amalgamation, merger or transfer:—

(1) the resulting, surviving or transferee entity fails to assume all the obligations of such party or such Credit Support Provider under this Agreement or any Credit Support Document to which it or its predecessor was a party by operation of law or pursuant to an agreement reasonably satisfactory to the other party to this Agreement; or

(2) the benefits of any Credit Support Document fail to extend (without the consent of the other party) to the performance by such resulting, surviving or transferee entity of its obligations under this Agreement.

(b) *Termination Events.* The occurrence at any time with respect to a party or, if applicable, any Credit Support Provider of such party or any Specified Entity of such party of any event specified below constitutes an Illegality if the event is specified in (i) below, and, if specified to be applicable, a Credit Event Upon Merger if the event is specified pursuant to (ii) below or an Additional Termination Event if the event is specified pursuant to (iii) below:—

(i) *Illegality.* Due to the adoption of, or any change in, any applicable law after the date on which a Transaction is entered into, or due to the promulgation of, or any change in, the interpretation by any court, tribunal or regulatory authority with competent jurisdiction of any applicable law after such date, it becomes unlawful (other than as a result of a breach by the party of Section 4(b)) for such party (which will be the Affected Party):—

(1) to perform any absolute or contingent obligation to make a payment or delivery or to receive a payment or delivery in respect of such Transaction or to comply with any other material provision of this Agreement relating to such Transaction; or

(2) to perform, or for any Credit Support Provider of such party to perform, any contingent or other obligation which the party (or such Credit Support Provider) has under any Credit Support Document relating to such Transaction;

(ii) *Credit Event Upon Merger.* If "Credit Event Upon Merger" is specified in the Schedule as applying to the party, such party ("X"), any Credit Support Provider of X or any applicable Specified Entity of X consolidates or amalgamates with, or merges with or into, or transfers all or substantially all its assets to, another entity and such action does not constitute an event described in Section 5(a)(viii) but the creditworthiness of the resulting, surviving or transferee entity is materially weaker than that of X, such Credit Support Provider or such Specified Entity, as the case may be, immediately prior to such action (and, in such event, X or its successor or transferee, as appropriate, will be the Affected Party); or

(iii) *Additional Termination Event.* If any "Additional Termination Event" is specified in the Schedule or any Confirmation as applying, the occurrence of such event (and, in such event, the Affected Party or Affected Parties shall be as specified for such Additional Termination Event in the Schedule or such Confirmation).

(c)   *Event of Default and Illegality.* If an event or circumstance which would otherwise constitute or give rise to an Event of Default also constitutes an Illegality, it will be treated as an Illegality and will not constitute an Event of Default.

6.   Early Termination

(a)   *Right to Terminate Following Event of Default.* If at any time an Event of Default with respect to a party (the "Defaulting Party") has occurred and is then continuing, the other party (the "Non-defaulting Party") may, by not more than 20 days notice to the Defaulting Party specifying the relevant Event of Default, designate a day not earlier than the day such notice is effective as an Early Termination Date in respect of all outstanding Transactions. If, however, "Automatic Early Termination" is specified in the Schedule as applying to a party, then an Early Termination Date in respect of all outstanding Transactions will occur immediately upon the occurrence with respect to such party of an Event of Default specified in Section 5(a)(vii)(1), (3), (5), (6) or, to the extent analogous thereto, (8), and as of the time immediately preceding the institution of the relevant proceeding or the presentation of the relevant petition upon the occurrence with respect to such party of an Event of Default specified in Section 5(a)(vii)(4) or, to the extent analogous thereto, (8).

(b)   *Right to Terminate Following Termination Event.*

(i)   *Notice.* If a Termination Event occurs, an Affected Party will, promptly upon becoming aware of it, notify the other party, specifying the nature of that Termination Event and each Affected Transaction and will also give such other information about that Termination Event as the other party may reasonably require.

(ii)   *Two Affected Parties.* If an Illegality under Section 5(b)(1) occurs and there are two Affected Parties, each party will use all reasonable efforts to reach agreement within 30 days after notice thereof is given under Section 6(b)(i) on action to avoid that Termination Event.

(iii)   *Right to Terminate.* If:—

(1)   an agreement under Section 6(b)(ii) has not been effected with respect to all Affected Transactions within 30 days after an Affected Party gives notice under Section 6(b)(i); or

(2)   an Illegality other than that referred to in Section 6(b)(ii), a Credit Event Upon Merger or an Additional Termination Event occurs,

either party in the case of an Illegality, any Affected Party in the case of an Additional Termination Event if there is more than one Affected Party, or the party which is not the Affected Party in the case of a Credit Event Upon Merger or an Additional Termination Event if there is only one Affected Party may, by not more than 20 days notice to the other party and provided that the relevant Termination Event is then continuing, designate a day not earlier than the day such notice is effective as an Early Termination Date in respect of all Affected Transactions.

(c)   *Effect of Designation.*

(i)   If notice designating an Early Termination Date is given under Section 6(a) or (b), the Early Termination Date will occur on the date so designated, whether or not the relevant Event of Default or Termination Event is then continuing.

(ii) Upon the occurrence or effective designation of an Early Termination Date, no further payments or deliveries under Section 2(a)(i) or 2(d) in respect of the Terminated Transactions will be required to be made, but without prejudice to the other provisions of this Agreement. The amount, if any, payable in respect of an Early Termination Date shall be determined pursuant to Section 6(e).

(d) *Calculations.*

(i) *Statement.* On or as soon as reasonably practicable following the occurrence of an Early Termination Date, each party will make the calculations on its part, if any, contemplated by Section 6(e) and will provide to the other party a statement (1) showing, in reasonable detail, such calculations (including all relevant quotations and specifying any amount payable under Section 6(e)) and (2) giving details of the relevant account to which any amount payable to it is to be paid. In the absence of written confirmation from the source of a quotation obtained in determining a Market Quotation, the records of the party obtaining such quotation will be conclusive evidence of the existence and accuracy of such quotation.

(ii) *Payment Date.* An amount calculated as being due in respect of any Early Termination Date under Section 6(e) will be payable on the day that notice of the amount payable is effective (in the case of an Early Termination Date which is designated or occurs as a result of an Event of Default) and on the day which is two Local Business Days after the day on which notice of the amount payable is effective (in the case of an Early Termination Date which is designated as a result of a Termination Event). Such amount will be paid together with (to the extent permitted under applicable law) interest thereon (before as well as after judgment), from (and including) the relevant Early Termination Date to (but excluding) the date such amount is paid, at the Applicable Rate. Such interest will be calculated on the basis of daily compounding and the actual number of days elapsed.

(e) *Payments on Early Termination.* If an Early Termination Date occurs, the following provisions shall apply based on the parties' election in the Schedule of a payment measure, either "Market Quotation" or "Loss", and a payment method, either the "First Method" or the "Second Method". If the parties fail to designate a payment measure or payment method in the Schedule, it will be deemed that "Market Quotation" or the "Second Method", as the case may be, shall apply. The amount, if any, payable in respect of an Early Termination Date and determined pursuant to this Section will be subject to any Set-off.

(i) *Events of Default.* If the Early Termination Date results from an Event of Default:—

(1) *First Method and Market Quotation.* If the First Method and Market Quotation apply, the Defaulting Party will pay to the Non-defaulting Party the excess, if a positive number, of (A) the sum of the Settlement Amount (determined by the Non-defaulting Party) in respect of the Terminated Transactions and the Unpaid Amounts owing to the Non-defaulting Party over (B) the Unpaid Amounts owing to the Defaulting Party.

(2) *First Method and Loss.* If the First Method and Loss apply, the Defaulting Party will pay to the Non-defaulting Party, if a positive number, the Non-defaulting Party's Loss in respect of this Agreement.

(3) *Second Method and Market Quotation.* If the Second Method and Market Quotation apply, an amount will be payable equal to (A) the sum of the Settlement Amount (determined by the Non-defaulting Party) in respect of the Terminated Transactions and the Unpaid Amounts owing to the Non-defaulting Party less (B) the Unpaid Amounts owing to the Defaulting Party. If that amount is a positive number, the Defaulting Party will pay it to the Non-defaulting Party; if it is a negative number, the Non-defaulting Party will pay the absolute value of that amount to the Defaulting Party.

(4) *Second Method and Loss.* If the Second Method and Loss apply, an amount will be payable equal to the Non-defaulting Party's Loss in respect of this Agreement. If that amount is a positive number, the Defaulting Party will pay it to the Non-defaulting Party; if it is a negative

number, the Non-defaulting Party will pay the absolute value of that amount to the Defaulting Party.

(ii) *Termination Events.* If the Early Termination Date results from a Termination Event:—

(1) *One Affected Party.* If there is one Affected Party, the amount payable will be determined in accordance with Section 6(e)(i)(3), if Market Quotation applies, or Section 6(e)(i)(4), if Loss applies, except that, in either case, references to the Defaulting Party and to the Non-defaulting Party will be deemed to be references to the Affected Party and the party which is not the Affected Party, respectively, and, if Loss applies and fewer than all the Transactions are being terminated, Loss shall be calculated in respect of all Terminated Transactions.

(2) *Two Affected Parties.* If there are two Affected Parties:—

(A) if Market Quotation applies, each party will determine a Settlement Amount in respect of the Terminated Transactions, and an amount will be payable equal to (I) the sum of (a) one-half of the difference between the Settlement Amount of the party with the higher Settlement Amount ("X") and the Settlement Amount of the party with the lower Settlement Amount ("Y") and (b) the Unpaid Amounts owing to X less (II) the Unpaid Amounts owing to Y; and

(B) if Loss applies, each party will determine its Loss in respect of this Agreement (or, if fewer than all the Transactions are being terminated, in respect of all Terminated Transactions) and an amount will be payable equal to one-half of the difference between the Loss of the party with the higher Loss ("X") and the Loss of the party with the lower Loss ("Y").

If the amount payable is a positive number, Y will pay it to X; if it is a negative number, X will pay the absolute value of that amount to Y.

(iii) *Adjustment for Bankruptcy.* In circumstances where an Early Termination Date occurs because "Automatic Early Termination" applies in respect of a party, the amount determined under this Section 6(e) will be subject to such adjustments as are appropriate and permitted by law to reflect any payments or deliveries made by one party to the other under this Agreement (and retained by such other party) during the period from the relevant Early Termination Date to the date for payment determined under Section 6(d)(ii).

(iv) *Pre-Estimate.* The parties agree that if Market Quotation applies an amount recoverable under this Section 6(e) is a reasonable pre-estimate of loss and not a penalty. Such amount is payable for the loss of bargain and the loss of protection against future risks and except as otherwise provided in this Agreement neither party will be entitled to recover any additional damages as a consequence of such losses.

7. **Transfer**

Neither this Agreement nor any interest or obligation in or under this Agreement may be transferred (whether by way of security or otherwise) by either party without the prior written consent of the other party, except that:—

(a) a party may make such a transfer of this Agreement pursuant to a consolidation or amalgamation with, or merger with or into, or transfer of all or substantially all its assets to, another entity (but without prejudice to any other right or remedy under this Agreement); and

(b) a party may make such a transfer of all or any part of its interest in any amount payable to it from a Defaulting Party under Section 6(e).

Any purported transfer that is not in compliance with this Section will be void.

8.   Miscellaneous

(a)   *Entire Agreement.* This Agreement constitutes the entire agreement and understanding of the parties with respect to its subject matter and supersedes all oral communication and prior writings with respect thereto.

(b)   *Amendments.* No amendment, modification or waiver in respect of this Agreement will be effective unless in writing (including a writing evidenced by a facsimile transmission) and executed by each of the parties or confirmed by an exchange of telexes or electronic messages on an electronic messaging system.

(c)   *Survival of Obligations.* Without prejudice to Sections 2(a)(iii) and 6(c)(ii), the obligations of the parties under this Agreement will survive the termination of any Transaction.

(d)   *Remedies Cumulative.* Except as provided in this Agreement, the rights, powers, remedies and privileges provided in this Agreement are cumulative and not exclusive of any rights, powers, remedies and privileges provided by law.

(e)   *Counterparts and Confirmations.*

(i)   This Agreement (and each amendment, modification and waiver in respect of it) may be executed and delivered in counterparts (including by facsimile transmission), each of which will be deemed an original.

(ii)   The parties intend that they are legally bound by the terms of each Transaction from the moment they agree to those terms (whether orally or otherwise). A Confirmation shall be entered into as soon as practicable and may be executed and delivered in counterparts (including by facsimile transmission) or be created by an exchange of telexes or by an exchange of electronic messages on an electronic messaging system, which in each case will be sufficient for all purposes to evidence a binding supplement to this Agreement. The parties will specify therein or through another effective means that any such counterpart, telex or electronic message constitutes a Confirmation.

(f)   *No Waiver of Rights.* A failure or delay in exercising any right, power or privilege in respect of this Agreement will not be presumed to operate as a waiver, and a single or partial exercise of any right, power or privilege will not be presumed to preclude any subsequent or further exercise, of that right, power or privilege or the exercise of any other right, power or privilege.

(g)   *Headings.* The headings used in this Agreement are for convenience of reference only and are not to affect the construction of or to be taken into consideration in interpreting this Agreement.

9.   Expenses

A Defaulting Party will, on demand, indemnify and hold harmless the other party for and against all reasonable out-of-pocket expenses, including legal fees, incurred by such other party by reason of the enforcement and protection of its rights under this Agreement or any Credit Support Document to which the Defaulting Party is a party or by reason of the early termination of any Transaction, including, but not limited to, costs of collection.

10.   Notices

(a)   *Effectiveness.* Any notice or other communication in respect of this Agreement may be given in any manner set forth below (except that a notice or other communication under Section 5 or 6 may not be given by facsimile transmission or electronic messaging system) to the address or number or in accordance with the electronic messaging system details provided (see the Schedule) and will be deemed effective as indicated:—

(i)   if in writing and delivered in person or by courier, on the date it is delivered;

(ii)   if sent by telex, on the date the recipient's answerback is received;

(iii) if sent by facsimile transmission, on the date that transmission is received by a responsible employee of the recipient in legible form (it being agreed that the burden of proving receipt will be on the sender and will not be met by a transmission report generated by the sender's facsimile machine);

(iv) if sent by certified or registered mail (airmail, if overseas) or the equivalent (return receipt requested), on the date that mail is delivered or its delivery is attempted; or

(v) if sent by electronic messaging system, on the date that electronic message is received,

unless the date of that delivery (or attempted delivery) or that receipt, as applicable, is not a Local Business Day or that communication is delivered (or attempted) or received, as applicable, after the close of business on a Local Business Day, in which case that communication shall be deemed given and effective on the first following day that is a Local Business Day.

(b) *Change of Addresses.* Either party may by notice to the other change the address, telex or facsimile number or electronic messaging system details at which notices or other communications are to be given to it.

11. Governing Law and Jurisdiction

(a) *Governing Law.* This Agreement will be governed by and construed in accordance with the law specified in the Schedule.

(b) *Jurisdiction.* With respect to any suit, action or proceedings relating to this Agreement ("Proceedings"), each party irrevocably:—

(i) submits to the jurisdiction of the English courts, if this Agreement is expressed to be governed by English law, or to the non-exclusive jurisdiction of the courts of the State of New York and the United States District Court located in the Borough of Manhattan in New York City, if this Agreement is expressed to be governed by the laws of the State of New York; and

(ii) waives any objection which it may have at any time to the laying of venue of any Proceedings brought in any such court, waives any claim that such Proceedings have been brought in an inconvenient forum and further waives the right to object, with respect to such Proceedings, that such court does not have any jurisdiction over such party.

Nothing in this Agreement precludes either party from bringing Proceedings in any other jurisdiction (outside, if this Agreement is expressed to be governed by English law, the Contracting States, as defined in Section 1(3) of the Civil Jurisdiction and Judgments Act 1982 or any modification, extension or re-enactment thereof for the time being in force) nor will the bringing of Proceedings in any one or more jurisdictions preclude the bringing of Proceedings in any other jurisdiction.

(c) *Waiver of Immunities.* Each party irrevocably waives, to the fullest extent permitted by applicable law, with respect to itself and its revenues and assets (irrespective of their use or intended use), all immunity on the grounds of sovereignty or other similar grounds from (i) suit, (ii) jurisdiction of any court, (iii) relief by way of injunction, order for specific performance or for recovery of property, (iv) attachment of its assets (whether before or after judgment) and (v) execution or enforcement of any judgment to which it or its revenues or assets might otherwise be entitled in any Proceedings in the courts of any jurisdiction and irrevocably agrees, to the extent permitted by applicable law, that it will not claim any such immunity in any Proceedings.

12. Definitions

As used in this Agreement:—

"Additional Termination Event" has the meaning specified in Section 5(b).

"Affected Party" has the meaning specified in Section 5(b).

"*Affected Transactions*" means (a) with respect to any Termination Event consisting of an Illegality, all Transactions affected by the occurrence of such Termination Event and (b) with respect to any other Termination Event, all Transactions.

"*Affiliate*" means, subject to the Schedule, in relation to any person, any entity controlled, directly or indirectly, by the person, any entity that controls, directly or indirectly, the person or any entity directly or indirectly under common control with the person. For this purpose, "control" of any entity or person means ownership of a majority of the voting power of the entity or person.

"*Applicable Rate*" means:—

(a)   in respect of obligations payable or deliverable (or which would have been but for Section 2(a)(iii)) by a Defaulting Party, the Default Rate;

(b)   in respect of an obligation to pay an amount under Section 6(e) of either party from and after the date (determined in accordance with Section 6(d)(ii)) on which that amount is payable, the Default Rate;

(c)   in respect of all other obligations payable or deliverable (or which would have been but for Section 2(a)(iii)) by a Non-defaulting Party, the Non-default Rate; and

(d)   in all other cases, the Termination Rate.

"*consent*" includes a consent, approval, action, authorisation, exemption, notice, filing, registration or exchange control consent.

"*Credit Event Upon Merger*" has the meaning specified in Section 5(b).

"*Credit Support Document*" means any agreement or instrument that is specified as such in this Agreement.

"*Credit Support Provider*" has the meaning specified in the Schedule.

"*Default Rate*" means a rate per annum equal to the cost (without proof or evidence of any actual cost) to the relevant payee (as certified by it) if it were to fund or of funding the relevant amount plus 1% per annum.

"*Defaulting Party*" has the meaning specified in Section 6(a).

"*Early Termination Date*" means the date determined in accordance with Section 6(a) or 6(b)(iii).

"*Event of Default*" has the meaning specified in Section 5(a) and, if applicable, in the Schedule.

"*Illegality*" has the meaning specified in Section 5(b).

"*law*" includes any treaty, law, rule or regulation and "*lawful*" and "*unlawful*" will be construed accordingly.

"*Local Business Day*" means, subject to the Schedule, a day on which commercial banks are open for business (including dealings in foreign exchange and foreign currency deposits) (a) in relation to any obligation under Section 2(a)(i), in the place(s) specified in the relevant Confirmation or, if not so specified, as otherwise agreed by the parties in writing or determined pursuant to provisions contained, or incorporated by reference, in this Agreement, (b) in relation to any other payment, in the place where the relevant account is located, (c) in relation to any notice or other communication, including notice contemplated under Section 5(a)(i), in the city specified in the address for notice provided by the recipient and, in the case of a notice contemplated by Section 2(b), in the place where the relevant new account is to be located and (d) in relation to Section 5(a)(v)(2), in the relevant locations for performance with respect to such Specified Transaction.

"*Loss*" means, with respect to this Agreement or one or more Terminated Transactions, as the case may be, and a party, an amount that party reasonably determines in good faith to be its total losses and costs (or gain, in which case expressed as a negative number) in connection with this Agreement or that Terminated Transaction or group of Terminated Transactions, as the case may be, including any loss of bargain, cost of funding or, at the election of such party but without duplication, loss or cost incurred as a result of its terminating, liquidating, obtaining or reestablishing any hedge or related trading position (or any gain resulting from any of them). Loss includes losses and costs (or gains) in respect of any payment or delivery required to have been made (assuming satisfaction of each applicable condition precedent) on or before the relevant Early Termination Date and not made, except, so as to avoid duplication, if Section 6(e)(i)(1) or (3) or 6(e)(ii)(2)(A) applies. Loss does not include a party's legal fees and out-of-pocket expenses referred to under Section 9. A party will determine its Loss as of the relevant Early Termination Date, or, if that is not reasonably practicable, as of the earliest date thereafter as is reasonably practicable. A party may (but need not) determine its Loss by reference to quotations of relevant rates or prices from one or more leading dealers in the relevant markets.

"*Market Quotation*" means, with respect to one or more Terminated Transactions and a party making the determination, an amount determined on the basis of quotations from Reference Market-makers. Each quotation will be for an amount, if any, that would be paid to such party (expressed as a negative number) or by such party (expressed as a positive number) in consideration of an agreement between such party (taking into account any existing Credit Support Document with respect to the obligations of such party) and the quoting Reference Market-maker to enter into a transaction (the "Replacement Transaction") that would have the effect of preserving for such party the economic equivalent of any payment or delivery (whether the underlying obligation was absolute or contingent and assuming the satisfaction of each applicable condition precedent) by the parties under Section 2(a)(i) in respect of such Terminated Transaction or group of Terminated Transactions that would, but for the occurrence of the relevant Early Termination Date, have been required after that date. For this purpose, Unpaid Amounts in respect of the Terminated Transaction or group of Terminated Transactions are to be excluded but, without limitation, any payment or delivery that would, but for the relevant Early Termination Date, have been required (assuming satisfaction of each applicable condition precedent) after that Early Termination Date is to be included. The Replacement Transaction would be subject to such documentation as such party and the Reference Market-maker may, in good faith, agree. The party making the determination (or its agent) will request each Reference Market-maker to provide its quotation to the extent reasonably practicable as of the same day and time (without regard to different time zones) on or as soon as reasonably practicable after the relevant Early Termination Date. The day and time as of which those quotations are to be obtained will be selected in good faith by the party obliged to make a determination under Section 6(e), and, if each party is so obliged, after consultation with the other. If more than three quotations are provided, the Market Quotation will be the arithmetic mean of the quotations, without regard to the quotations having the highest and lowest values. If exactly three such quotations are provided, the Market Quotation will be the quotation remaining after disregarding the highest and lowest quotations. For this purpose, if more than one quotation has the same highest value or lowest value, then one of such quotations shall be disregarded. If fewer than three quotations are provided, it will be deemed that the Market Quotation in respect of such Terminated Transaction or group of Terminated Transactions cannot be determined.

"*Non-default Rate*" means a rate per annum equal to the cost (without proof or evidence of any actual cost) to the Non-defaulting Party (as certified by it) if it were to fund the relevant amount.

"*Non-defaulting Party*" has the meaning specified in Section 6(a).

"*Potential Event of Default*" means any event which, with the giving of notice or the lapse of time or both, would constitute an Event of Default.

"*Reference Market-makers*" means four leading dealers in the relevant market selected by the party determining a Market Quotation in good faith (a) from among dealers of the highest credit standing which satisfy all the criteria that such party applies generally at the time in deciding whether to offer or to make an extension of credit and (b) to the extent practicable, from among such dealers having an office in the same city.

"*Scheduled Payment Date*" means a date on which a payment or delivery is to be made under Section 2(a)(i) with respect to a Transaction.

"*Set-off*" means set-off, offset, combination of accounts, right of retention or withholding or similar right or requirement to which the payer of an amount under Section 6 is entitled or subject (whether arising under this Agreement, another contract, applicable law or otherwise) that is exercised by, or imposed on, such payer.

"*Settlement Amount*" means, with respect to a party and any Early Termination Date, the sum of:—

(a)   the Market Quotations (whether positive or negative) for each Terminated Transaction or group of Terminated Transactions for which a Market Quotation is determined; and

(b)   such party's Loss (whether positive or negative and without reference to any Unpaid Amounts) for each Terminated Transaction or group of Terminated Transactions for which a Market Quotation cannot be determined or would not (in the reasonable belief of the party making the determination) produce a commercially reasonable result.

"*Specified Entity*" has the meaning specified in the Schedule.

"*Specified Indebtedness*" means, subject to the Schedule, any obligation (whether present or future, contingent or otherwise, as principal or surety or otherwise) in respect of borrowed money.

"*Specified Transaction*" means, subject to the Schedule, (a) any transaction (including an agreement with respect thereto) now existing or hereafter entered into between one party to this Agreement (or any Credit Support Provider of such party or any applicable Specified Entity of such party) and the other party to this Agreement (or any Credit Support Provider of such other party or any applicable Specified Entity of such other party) which is a rate swap transaction, basis swap, forward rate transaction, commodity swap, commodity option, equity or equity index swap, equity or equity index option, bond option, interest rate option, foreign exchange transaction, cap transaction, floor transaction, collar transaction, currency swap transaction, cross-currency rate swap transaction, currency option or any other similar transaction (including any option with respect to any of these transactions), (b) any combination of these transactions and (c) any other transaction identified as a Specified Transaction in this Agreement or the relevant confirmation.

"*Terminated Transactions*" means with respect to any Early Termination Date (a) if resulting from a Termination Event, all Affected Transactions and (b) if resulting from an Event of Default, all Transactions (in either case) in effect immediately before the effectiveness of the notice designating that Early Termination Date (or, if "Automatic Early Termination" applies, immediately before that Early Termination Date).

"*Termination Event*" means an Illegality or, if specified to be applicable, a Credit Event Upon Merger or an Additional Termination Event.

"*Termination Rate*" means a rate per annum equal to the arithmetic mean of the cost (without proof or evidence of any actual cost) to each party (as certified by such party) if it were to fund or of funding such amounts.

"*Unpaid Amounts*" owing to any party means, with respect to an Early Termination Date, the aggregate of (a) in respect of all Terminated Transactions, the amounts that became payable (or that would have become payable but for Section 2(a)(iii)) to such party under Section 2(a)(i) on or prior to such Early Termination Date and which remain unpaid as at such Early Termination Date and (b) in respect of each Terminated Transaction, for each obligation under Section 2(a)(i) which was (or would have been but for Section 2(a)(iii)) required to be settled by delivery to such party on or prior to such Early Termination Date and which has not been so settled as at such Early Termination Date, an amount equal to the fair market value of that which was (or would have been) required to be delivered as of the originally scheduled date for delivery, in each case together with (to the extent permitted under applicable law) interest, in the currency of such amounts, from (and including) the date such amounts or obligations were or would have been required to have been paid or performed to (but excluding) such Early Termination Date, at the Applicable Rate. Such amounts of interest will be calculated on the basis of daily compounding and the actual number of days elapsed. The fair market value of any obligation referred to in clause (b) above shall be reasonably determined by the party obliged to make the determination under Section 6(e) or, if each party is so obliged, it shall be the average of the fair market values reasonably determined by both parties.

IN WITNESS WHEREOF the parties have executed this document on the respective dates specified below with effect from the date specified on the first page of this document.

....

(Name of Party)   (Name of Party)

By: ....   By: ....
    Name: Name:
    Title: Title:
    Date: Date:

(Local Currency—Single Jurisdiction)

ISDA®

International Swap Dealers Association, Inc.

SCHEDULE
to the
Master Agreement

dated as of . . . .

between . . . . and . . . .
("Party A")   ("Party B")

Part 1. Termination Provisions.

(a)   *"Specified Entity"* means in relation to Party A for the purpose of:—

Section 5(a)(v), ...

Section 5(a)(vi), ...

Section 5(a)(vii), ...

Section 5(b)(ii), ...

and in relation to Party B for the purpose of:—

Section 5(a)(v), ...

Section 5(a)(vi), ...

Section 5(a)(vii), ...

Section 5(b)(ii), ...

(b)   *"Specified Transaction"* will have the meaning specified in Section 12 of this Agreement unless

another meaning is specified here . . . .

. . . .

. . . .

(c)   The *"Cross Default"* provisions of Section 5(a)(vi) will/will not * apply to Party A
                                                                       will/will not * apply to Party B

If such provisions apply:—

"Specified Indebtedness" will have the meaning specified in Section 12 of this Agreement unless

another meaning is specified here . . . .

. . . .

---

* Delete as applicable.

"Threshold Amount" means ....

....

d) The *"Credit Event Upon Merger"* provisions of Section 5(b)(ii) will/will not * apply to Party A

will/will not * apply to Party B

e) The *"Automatic Early Termination"* provision of Section 6(a) will/will not * apply to Party A

will/will not * apply to Party B

f) *Payments on Early Termination.* For the purpose of Section 6(e) of this Agreement:—

(i) Market Quotation/Loss * will apply.

(ii) The First Method/The Second Method * will apply.

g) *Additional Termination Event* will/will not apply*. The following shall constitute an Additional

Termination Event:— ....

....

....

....

....

....

For the purpose of the foregoing Termination Event, the Affected Party or Affected Parties shall be:— ..

....

Part 2. Agreement to Deliver Documents.

For the purpose of Section 4(a) of this Agreement, each party agrees to deliver the following documents, as applicable:—

Party required to deliver document	Form/Document/ Certificate	Date by which to be delivered	Covered by Section 3(d) Representation
....	....	....	Yes/No*
....	....	....	Yes/No*
....	....	....	Yes/No*
....	....	....	Yes/No*
....	....	....	Yes/No*

---

* Delete as applicable.

Part 3. **Miscellaneous.**

(a)   *Addresses for Notices.* For the purpose of Section 10(a) of this Agreement:—

Address for notices or communications to Party A:—

Address: ....

Attention: ....

Telex No.: .... Answerback: ....

Facsimile No.: .... Telephone No.: ....

Electronic Messaging System Details: ....

Address for notices or communications to Party B:—

Address: ....

Attention: ....

Telex No.: .... Answerback: ....

Facsimile No.: .... Telephone No.: ....

Electronic Messaging System Details: ....

(b)   *Calculation Agent.* The Calculation Agent is ...., unless otherwise specified in a Confirmation in relation to the relevant Transaction.

(c)   *Credit Support Document.* Details of any Credit Support Document:— ....

....

....

....

(d)   *Credit Support Provider.* Credit Support Provider means in relation to Party A, ...

....

....

Credit Support Provider means in relation to Party B, ...

....

....

(e)   *Governing Law.* This Agreement will be governed by and construed in accordance with English law/the laws of the State of New York (without reference to choice of law doctrine)*.

(f)   *Netting of Payments.* Subparagraph (ii) of Section 2(c) of this Agreement will not apply to the

following Transactions or groups of Transactions (in each case starting from the date of this

Agreement/in each case starting from ....*) ....

....

....

---

* Delete as applicable.

"Affiliate" will have the meaning specified in Section 12 of this Agreement unless another meaning is

specified here ....

....

4. **Other Provisions.**

ISDA Definitions

This appendix presents the complete 1991 ISDA Definitions except for Section 7.1 on rate options.

1991 ISDA DEFINITIONS

Any or all of the following definitions and provisions may be incorporated into a document by wording in the document indicating that, or the extent to which, the document is subject to the 1991 ISDA Definitions (as published by the International Swap Dealers Association, Inc.). All definitions and provisions so incorporated in a document will be applicable to that document unless otherwise provided in that document, and all terms defined in these Definitions and used in any definition or provision that is incorporated by reference in a document will have the respective meanings set forth in these Definitions unless otherwise provided in that document. Any term used in a document will, when combined with the name of a party, have meaning in respect of the named party only.

ARTICLE 1

CERTAIN GENERAL DEFINITIONS

Section 1.1. Swap Transaction. "Swap Transaction" means (a) any transaction which is a rate swap transaction, basis swap, forward rate transaction, commodity swap, interest rate option, forward foreign exchange transaction, cap transaction, floor transaction, collar transaction, currency swap transaction, cross-currency rate swap transaction, currency option or any other similar transaction (including any Option with respect to any of these transactions), (b) any combination of these transactions and (c) any other transaction identified as a Swap Transaction in the related Confirmation.

Section 1.2. Confirmation. "Confirmation" means, with respect to a Swap Transaction, one or more documents exchanged between the parties which, taken together, confirm all of the terms of a Swap Transaction.

Section 1.3. Banking Day. "Banking Day" means, in respect of any city, any day on which commercial banks are open for business (including dealings in foreign exchange and foreign currency deposits) in that city.

Section 1.4. Business Day. "Business Day" means (a) in respect of any date that is specified in these Definitions or in a Confirmation to be subject to adjustment in accordance with any applicable Business Day Convention, a day on which commercial banks and foreign exchange markets settle payments in the

§ 1.4(a)

place(s) and on the days specified for that purpose in the relevant Confirmation and, if place(s) and days are not so specified, a day:

(i) on which commercial banks and foreign exchange markets settle payments in the same currency as the payment obligation that is payable on or calculated by reference to that date in:

(A) the financial center indicated for each of the following currencies:

Currency	Financial Center(s)
Australian Dollar	Sydney
Belgian Franc	Brussels
Canadian Dollar	Toronto
Danish Krone	Copenhagen
Deutsche Mark	Frankfurt
Dutch Guilder	Amsterdam
Finnish Markka	Helsinki
French Franc	Paris
Hong Kong Dollar	Hong Kong
Italian Lira	Milan
Luxembourg Franc	Brussels and Luxembourg
New Zealand Dollar	Wellington and Auckland
Norwegian Krone	Oslo
Spanish Peseta	Madrid
Sterling	London
Swedish Krona	Stockholm
Swiss Franc	Zurich
Yen	Tokyo

(B) New York and London, if the currency is the U.S. Dollar and either (x) the payment obligation is calculated by reference to any "LIBOR" Floating Rate Option or (y) the payment obligations of the other party to the Swap Transaction are payable in the U.S. Dollar and are calculated by reference to any "LIBOR" Floating Rate Option;

(C) New York, if the currency is the U.S. Dollar and neither clause (B)(x) nor (B)(y) above is applicable; and

(D) the principal financial center of a currency, if the currency is other than those currencies specified in Section 1.5 of these Definitions; and

(ii) that is an ECU Settlement Day, if the payment obligation that is payable on or calculated by reference to that date is to be made in the European Currency Unit; and

§ 1.5(l)

(iii) that is a Business Day or ECU Settlement Day, as the case may be, in respect of each relevant currency where the payment obligations that are payable on a Payment Date are denominated in different currencies; and

(b) in respect of a Reset Date for the determination of a Relevant Rate by reference to a Price Option and notwithstanding that the Reset Date may be a day other than a Business Day under the terms of subsection (a), any day scheduled as a trading day on each Exchange in respect of that Price Option or the Swap Transaction.

Section 1.5. Currencies.

(a) **Australian Dollar.** "Australian Dollar", "A$" and "AUD" each means the lawful currency of Australia.

(b) **Belgian Franc.** "Belgian Franc", "Bfr" and "BEF" each means the lawful currency of the Kingdom of Belgium.

(c) **Canadian Dollar.** "Canadian Dollar", "C$" and "CAD" each means the lawful currency of Canada.

(d) **Danish Krone.** "Danish Krone", "DKr" and "DKK" each means the lawful currency of the Kingdom of Denmark.

(e) **Deutsche Mark.** "Deutsche Mark", "DM" and "DEM" each means the lawful currency of the Federal Republic of Germany.

(f) **Dutch Guilder.** "Dutch Guilder", "DFl" and "NLG" each means the lawful currency of The Kingdom of The Netherlands.

(g) **European Currency Unit.** "European Currency Unit", "ECU" and "XEU" each means a currency, one unit of which is equal in value to the European Currency Unit that is used in the European Monetary System.

(h) **Finnish Markka.** "Finnish Markka" and "FIM" each means the lawful currency of the Republic of Finland.

(i) **French Franc.** "French Franc", "Ffr" and "FRF" each means the lawful currency of the Republic of France.

(j) **Hong Kong Dollar.** "Hong Kong Dollar", "HK$" and "HKD" each means the lawful currency of Hong Kong.

(k) **Italian Lira.** "Italian Lira", "Lira" and "ITL" each means the lawful currency of the Republic of Italy.

(l) **Luxembourg Franc.** "Luxembourg Franc", "Lfr" and "LUF" each means the lawful currency of the Grand Duchy of Luxembourg, including the Commercial Luxembourg Franc and the Financial Luxembourg Franc.

(i) "Commercial Luxembourg Franc", "Commercial Lfr" and "Commercial LUF" each means the Luxembourg Franc that is used for transactions in foreign currencies that are required by the

1.5(l)

Belgian-Luxembourg Exchange Institute to be settled on the regulated exchange market of the Belgian-Luxembourg Economic Union.

(ii) "Financial Luxembourg Franc", "Financial Lfr" and "Financial LUF" each means the Luxembourg Franc that is used for transactions in foreign currencies that may be settled on the exchange market of the Belgian-Luxembourg Economic Union without restriction.

(m) **New Zealand Dollar.** "New Zealand Dollar", "NZ$" and "NZD" each ?ans the lawful currency of New Zealand.

(n) **Norwegian Krone.** "Norwegian Krone", "NKr" and "NKR" each means e lawful currency of the Kingdom of Norway.

(o) **Spanish Peseta.** "Spanish Peseta", "Pta", "SPp", "SPP" and "ESP" each ?ans the lawful currency of Spain.

(p) **Sterling.** "Sterling", "£", "GBP" and "STG" each means the lawful currency the United Kingdom.

(q) **Swedish Krona.** "Swedish Krona", "SKr" and "SEK" each means the lawful rrency of the Kingdom of Sweden.

(r) **Swiss Franc.** "Swiss Franc", "Sfr", "CHF" and "SWF" each means the vful currency of Switzerland.

(s) **U.S. Dollar.** "U.S. Dollar", "Dollar", "U.S.$", "$" and "USD" each means e lawful currency of the United States of America.

(t) **Yen.** "Yen", "¥" and "JPY" each means the lawful currency of Japan.

Section 1.6. ECU Settlement Day. "ECU Settlement Day" means any day that ▸ is not either (i) a Saturday or a Sunday or (ii) a day which appears as an ECU ▸n-Settlement Day on the display designated as page "ISDE" on the Reuter ɔnitor Money Rates Service (or a day so designated by the ECU Banking sociation, if ECU Non-Settlement Days do not appear on that page) and, if ECU ▸n-Settlement Days do not appear on that page (and are not so designated), a y on which payments in the European Currency Unit cannot be settled in the ernational interbank market and (b) is a day on which payments in the European rrency Unit can be settled by commercial banks and in foreign exchange markets the place in which the relevant account for payment is located.

ARTICLE 2

PARTIES

Section 2.1. Fixed Rate Payer; Fixed Amount Payer; Fixed Price Payer. "Fixed te Payer", "Fixed Amount Payer" or "Fixed Price Payer" means, in respect of wap Transaction, a party obligated to make payments from time to time during ? Term of the Swap Transaction of amounts calculated by reference to a fixed

§ 3.6

per annum rate or a fixed price or to make one or more payments of a Fixe Amount.

Section 2.2. Floating Rate Payer; Floating Amount Payer; Floating Pri Payer. "Floating Rate Payer", "Floating Amount Payer" or "Floating Price Paye means, in respect of a Swap Transaction, a party obligated to make payments fro time to time during the Term of the Swap Transaction of amounts calculated l reference to a floating per annum rate or a floating price or to make one or mo payments of a Floating Amount.

ARTICLE 3

TERM AND DATES

Section 3.1. Term. "Term" means the period commencing on the Effectiv Date of a Swap Transaction and ending on the Termination Date of the Swa Transaction.

Section 3.2. Effective Date. "Effective Date" means the date specified as suc for a Swap Transaction, which date is the first day of the Term of the Swa Transaction.

Section 3.3. Termination Date. "Termination Date" means the date specifie as such for a Swap Transaction, which date is the last day of the Term of the Swa Transaction. The Termination Date shall not be subject to adjustment i accordance with any Business Day Convention unless the parties specify in Confirmation that the Termination Date will be adjusted in accordance with specified Business Day Convention.

Section 3.4. Initial Exchange Date. "Initial Exchange Date" means, in respe of a Swap Transaction and a party, the date specified as such or, if a date is not s specified and an Initial Exchange Amount is specified, the Effective Date, whic Initial Exchange Date shall be subject to adjustment in accordance with th Following Business Day Convention unless otherwise specified in a Confirmatio

Section 3.5. Final Exchange Date; Exchange Date; Maturity Date; Value Dat "Final Exchange Date", "Exchange Date", "Maturity Date" or "Value Date means, in respect of a Swap Transaction and a party, each date specified as suc or, if no date is so specified and a Final Exchange Amount or an Exchange Amou is specified, the Termination Date, which date shall be subject to adjustment i accordance with the Modified Following Business Day Convention unles otherwise specified in a Confirmation.

Section 3.6. Trade Date. "Trade Date" means, in respect of a Swap Transactio the date on which the parties enter into the Swap Transaction.

ARTICLE 4

CERTAIN DEFINITIONS RELATING TO PAYMENTS

Section 4.1. Initial Exchange Amount. "Initial Exchange Amount" means, in respect of a Swap Transaction and a party, an amount that is specified as such for that party and, subject to any applicable condition precedent, is payable by that party on the Initial Exchange Date.

Section 4.2. Final Exchange Amount; Exchange Amount. "Final Exchange Amount" or "Exchange Amount" means, in respect of a Swap Transaction and a party, an amount that is specified as such for that party and, subject to any applicable condition precedent, is payable by that party on an applicable Final Exchange Date.

Section 4.3. Fixed Amount. "Fixed Amount" means, in respect of a Swap Transaction and a Fixed Rate Payer, an amount that, subject to any applicable condition precedent, is payable by that Fixed Rate Payer on an applicable Payment Date and is specified in a Confirmation or is determined as provided in Article 5 of these Definitions or as provided in a Confirmation.

Section 4.4. Floating Amount. "Floating Amount" means, in respect of a Swap Transaction and a Floating Rate Payer, an amount that, subject to any applicable condition precedent, is payable by that Floating Rate Payer on an applicable Payment Date and is determined by reference to a Floating Rate Option as provided in Article 6 of these Definitions or pursuant to a method specified in a Confirmation.

Section 4.5. Currency Amount. "Currency Amount" means, in respect of a party and any Calculation Period for a Swap Transaction involving more than one currency, the amount specified as such for the Swap Transaction or that party.

Section 4.6. Notional Amount. "Notional Amount" means, in respect of a party and any Calculation Period for a Swap Transaction involving one currency, the amount specified as such for the Swap Transaction.

Section 4.7. Notional Quantity. "Notional Quantity" means, in respect of a party and any Calculation Period for a Swap Transaction, the quantity, expressed in relevant units, specified as such for that party or the Swap Transaction.

Section 4.8. Calculation Amount. "Calculation Amount" means, in respect of a Swap Transaction and a party, the applicable Notional Amount, Currency Amount or Notional Quantity, as the case may be.

Section 4.9. Payment Date. "Payment Date" means, in respect of a Swap Transaction and a party,

(a) if "Delayed Payment" or "Early Payment" is not specified for the Swap Transaction or that party and Payment Dates are specified or otherwise predetermined for the Swap Transaction or that party, each day during the

Term of the Swap Transaction so specified or predetermined and the Termination Date;

(b) if "Delayed Payment" or "Early Payment" is not specified for the Swap Transaction or that party and the parties specify that Payment Dates for the Swap Transaction or that party will occur in accordance with the FRN Convention at a specified interval of calendar months, each day during the Term of the Swap Transaction at the specified interval, determined in accordance with the FRN Convention, and the Termination Date;

(c) if "Delayed Payment" and a period of days are specified for the Swap Transaction or that party and Period End Dates are established for the Swap Transaction or that party, each day that is the specified number of days after an applicable Period End Date or after the Termination Date; or

(d) if "Early Payment" and a period of days are specified for the Swap Transaction or that party and Period End Dates are established for the Swap Transaction or that party, each day that is the specified number of days before an applicable Period End Date or before the Termination Date;

except that (i) in the case of subsections (a), (c) and (d) above, each Payment Date shall be subject to adjustment in accordance with the Modified Following Business Day Convention unless another Business Day Convention is specified to be applicable to Payment Dates in respect of the Swap Transaction or that party and (ii) in the case of subsection (a) above, a Payment Date in respect of a Fixed Rate Payer may be a specified day prior to the Effective Date where the Floating Amounts payable by the Floating Rate Payer are calculated by reference to a cap rate, cap price, floor rate or floor price.

Section 4.10. Period End Date. "Period End Date" means, in respect of a Swap Transaction and a party,

(a) if Period End Dates are not established for the Swap Transaction or that party, each Payment Date of that party during the Term of the Swap Transaction;

(b) if Period End Dates are specified or otherwise predetermined for the Swap Transaction or that party, each day during the Term so specified or predetermined; or

(c) if it is specified for the Swap Transaction or that party that Period End Dates will occur in accordance with the FRN Convention and an interval of calendar months is specified, and if "Delayed Payment" or "Early Payment" is specified for the Swap Transaction or that party, each day during the Term at the specified interval, determined in accordance with the FRN Convention;

except that, in the case of subsection (b) above, each Period End Date shall be subject to adjustment in accordance with the Modified Following Business Day Convention unless (x) another Business Day Convention is specified to be applicable to Period End Dates in respect of the Swap Transaction or that party,

§ 4.10

n which case an adjustment will be made in accordance with that Business Day Convention, or (y) "No Adjustment" is specified in connection with Period End Dates for the Swap Transaction or that party, in which case no adjustment will be made, notwithstanding that the Period End Date occurs on a day that is not a Business Day.

Section 4.11. FRN Convention; Eurodollar Convention. "FRN Convention" or "Eurodollar Convention" means, in respect of either Payment Dates or Period End Dates for a Swap Transaction and a party, that the Payment Dates or Period End Dates of that party will be each day during the Term of the Swap Transaction that numerically corresponds to the preceding applicable Payment Date or Period End Date, as the case may be, of that party in the calendar month that is the specified number of months after the month in which the preceding applicable Payment Date or Period End Date occurred (or, in the case of the first applicable Payment Date or Period End Date, the day that numerically corresponds to the Effective Date in the calendar month that is the specified number of months after the month in which the Effective Date occurred), except that (a) if there is not any such numerically corresponding day in the calendar month in which a Payment Date or Period End Date, as the case may be, of that party should occur, then the Payment Date or Period End Date will be the last day that is a Business Day in that month, (b) if a Payment Date or Period End Date, as the case may be, of the party would otherwise fall on a day that is not a Business Day, then the Payment Date or Period End Date will be the first following day that is a Business Day unless that day falls in the next calendar month, in which case the Payment Date or Period End Date will be the first preceding day that is a Business Day, and (c) if the preceding applicable Payment Date or Period End Date, as the case may be, of that party occurred on the last day in a calendar month that was a Business Day, then all subsequent applicable Payment Dates or Period End Dates, as the case may be, of that party prior to the Termination Date will be the last day that is a Business Day in the month that is the specified number of months after the month in which the preceding applicable Payment Date or Period End Date occurred.

Section 4.12. Business Day Convention. (a) "Business Day Convention" means the convention for adjusting any relevant date if it would otherwise fall on a day that is not a Business Day. The following terms, when used in conjunction with the term "Business Day Convention" and a date, shall mean that an adjustment will be made if that date would otherwise fall on a day that is not a Business Day so that:

(i) if "Following" is specified, that date will be the first following day that is a Business Day;

(ii) if "Modified Following" or "Modified" is specified, that date will be the first following day that is a Business Day unless that day falls in the next calendar month, in which case that date will be the first preceding day that is a Business Day; and

§ 4.14

(iii) if "Preceding" is specified, that date will be the first preceding day that is a Business Day.

(b) The Business Day Convention applicable to a date that is specified in these Definitions or in a Confirmation to be subject to adjustment in accordance with an applicable Business Day Convention shall be the Business Day Convention specified for that date in these Definitions or in that Confirmation or, if a Business Day Convention is not so specified for that date but a Business Day Convention is specified for a Swap Transaction, shall be the Business Day Convention specified in a Confirmation for that Swap Transaction.

Section 4.13. Calculation Period. "Calculation Period" means, in respect of a Swap Transaction and a party, each period from, and including, one Period End Date of that party to, but excluding, the next following applicable Period End Date during the Term of the Swap Transaction, except that (a) the initial Calculation Period for the party will commence on, and include, the Effective Date, and (b) the final Calculation Period for the party will end on, but exclude, the Termination Date.

Section 4.14. Calculation Agent. "Calculation Agent" means the party to a Swap Transaction (or a third party) designated as such for the Swap Transaction and responsible for (a) calculating the applicable Floating Rate, if any, for each Payment Date or for each Calculation Period or Compounding Period (b) calculating any Floating Amount payable on each Payment Date or for each Calculation Period, (c) calculating any Fixed Amount payable on each Payment Date or for each Calculation Period, (d) calculating a Currency Amount by reference to a Currency Amount in another currency on or prior to the Effective Date of the Swap Transaction, (e) giving notice to the parties to the Swap Transaction on the Calculation Date for each Payment Date or for each Calculation Period, specifying (i) the Payment Date, (ii) the party or parties required to make the payment or payments then due, (iii) the amount or amounts of the payment or payments then due and (iv) reasonable details as to how the amount or amounts were determined, (f) if, after notice is given, there is a change in the number of days in the relevant Calculation Period and the amount or amounts of the payment or payments due for that Payment Date or for that Calculation Period, promptly giving the parties to the Swap Transaction notice of those changes, with reasonable details as to how those changes were determined, and (g) determining whether a Market Disruption Event exists on any Reset Date. Whenever the Calculation Agent is required to select banks or dealers for the purpose of making any calculation or determination or to select any exchange rate, the Calculation Agent will make the selection in good faith after consultation with the other party (or the parties, if the Calculation Agent is a third party), if practicable, for the purpose of obtaining a representative rate that will reasonably reflect conditions prevailing at the time in the relevant market or designating a freely convertible currency, as the case may be.

Section 4.15. Calculation Date. "Calculation Date" means, in respect of any ayment Date or any Calculation Period, the earliest day on which it is practicable provide the notice that the Calculation Agent is required to give for that Payment ate or for that Calculation Period, and in no event later than the close of business ♦ the Business Day next preceding that Payment Date or the Payment Date for at Calculation Period (unless that preceding Business Day is a Reset Date, then no event later than the latest time that will permit any payment due on that ♦yment Date to be made on that Payment Date).

Section 4.16. Day Count Fraction. "Day Count Fraction" means, in respect of Swap Transaction and the calculation of a Fixed Amount, a Floating Amount, a ompounding Period Amount or an FRA Amount,

(a) if "Actual/365" or "Actual/Actual" is specified, the actual number of days in the Calculation Period or Compounding Period in respect of which payment is being made divided by 365 (or, if any portion of that Calculation Period or Compounding Period falls in a leap year, the sum of (A) the actual number of days in that portion of the Calculation Period or Compounding Period falling in a leap year divided by 366 and (B) the actual number of days in that portion of the Calculation Period or Compounding Period falling in a non-leap year divided by 365);

(b) if "Actual/365 (Fixed)" is specified, the actual number of days in the Calculation Period or Compounding Period in respect of which payment is being made divided by 365;

(c) if "Actual/360" is specified, the actual number of days in the Calculation Period or Compounding Period in respect of which payment is being made divided by 360;

(d) if "30/360", "360/360" or "Bond Basis" is specified, the number of days in the Calculation Period or Compounding Period in respect of which payment is being made divided by 360 (the number of days to be calculated on the basis of a year of 360 days with 12 30-day months (unless (i) the last day of the Calculation Period or Compounding Period is the 31st day of a month but the first day of the Calculation Period or Compounding Period is a day other than the 30th or 31st day of a month, in which case the month that includes that last day shall not be considered to be shortened to a 30-day month, or (ii) the last day of the Calculation Period or Compounding Period is the last day of the month of February, in which case the month of February shall not be considered to be lengthened to a 30-day month)); and

(e) if "30E/360" or "Eurobond Basis" is specified, the number of days in the Calculation Period or Compounding Period in respect of which payment is being made divided by 360 (the number of days to be calculated on the basis of a year of 360 days with 12 30-day months, without regard to the date of the first day or last day of the Calculation Period or Compounding Period unless, in the case of the final Calculation Period or Compounding Period, the

§ 5.2(b)

Termination Date is the last day of the month of February, in which case the month of February shall not be considered to be lengthened to a 30-day month).

Section 4.17. IMM Settlement Dates. "IMM Settlement Dates" means, in respect of a Calculation Period and a currency or a Floating Rate Option for which contracts are written on the International Money Market Section of the Chicago Mercantile Exchange, each day during that Calculation Period that is specified by the Chicago Mercantile Exchange, pursuant to its contract specifications, as a "1st Delivery Date" for such currency or Floating Rate Option.

ARTICLE 5

FIXED AMOUNTS

Section 5.1. Calculation of a Fixed Amount. The Fixed Amount payable by a party on a Payment Date will be:

(a) if an amount is specified for the Swap Transaction as the Fixed Amount payable by that party for that Payment Date or for the related Calculation Period, such amount; or

(b) if an amount is not specified for the Swap Transaction as the Fixed Amount payable by that party for that Payment Date or for the related Calculation Period, an amount calculated on a formula basis for that Payment Date or for the related Calculation Period as follows:

$$\text{Fixed Amount} = \text{Calculation Amount} \times \text{Fixed Rate} \times \text{Fixed Rate Day Count Fraction}$$

Section 5.2. Certain Definitions Relating to Fixed Amounts. For purposes of the calculation of a Fixed Amount payable by a party:

(a) "Fixed Rate" means, for any Payment Date or for any Calculation Period in respect of a Payment Date, a price, expressed as a price per relevant unit, or a rate, expressed as a decimal, equal to the price or the per annum rate specified as such for the Swap Transaction or that party.

(b) "Fixed Rate Day Count Fraction" means, in respect of any calculation of a Fixed Amount,

(i) if a Price Option or a method for determining a price is specified for the Swap Transaction or the Fixed Rate Payer, and a Fixed Rate Day Count Fraction is not specified, 1/1; and

(ii) in all other cases, the Fixed Rate Day Count Fraction specified for the Swap Transaction or the Fixed Rate Payer.

§ 6.1

ARTICLE 6

FLOATING AMOUNTS

Section 6.1. Calculation of a Floating Amount. The Floating Amount payable by a party on a Payment Date will be:

(a) if Compounding is not specified for the Swap Transaction or that party, an amount calculated on a formula basis for that Payment Date or for the related Calculation Period as follows:

$$\begin{array}{ccccc} \text{Floating} \\ \text{Amount} \end{array} = \begin{array}{c} \text{Calculation} \\ \text{Amount} \end{array} \times \begin{array}{c} \text{Floating} \\ \text{Rate} \\ \pm \text{ Spread} \end{array} \times \begin{array}{c} \text{Floating} \\ \text{Rate} \\ \text{Day Count} \\ \text{Fraction} \end{array}$$

(b) if Compounding is specified to be applicable to the Swap Transaction or that party and Flat Compounding is not specified, an amount equal to the sum of the Compounding Period Amounts for each of the Compounding Periods in the related Calculation Period; or

(c) if "Flat Compounding" is specified to be applicable to the Swap Transaction or that party, an amount equal to the sum of the Basic Compounding Period Amounts for each of the Compounding Periods in the related Calculation Period plus the sum of the Additional Compounding Period Amounts for each such Compounding Period.

Section 6.2. Certain Definitions Relating to Floating Amounts. For purposes of the calculation of a Floating Amount payable by a party:

(a) "Floating Rate" means, for any Calculation Period in respect of a Payment Date, for any Compounding Period or for any Reset Date, a price, expressed as a price per relevant unit, or a rate, expressed as a decimal, equal to

(i) if the Confirmation (or the agreement between the parties governing the Swap Transaction) either (x) specifies a cap price or a floor price or (y) does not contain or incorporate paragraph 2 of the May 1989 Addendum to Schedule to Interest Rate and Currency Exchange Agreement for Interest Rate Caps, Collars and Floors, or provisions equivalent thereto; and

(A) if a cap rate or cap price is specified, the excess, if any, of a rate or price determined pursuant to subparagraph (ii) below over the cap rate or cap price so specified; or

(B) if a floor rate or floor price is specified, the excess, if any, of the floor rate or floor price so specified over a rate or price determined pursuant to subparagraph (ii) below; and

(ii) in all other cases and for purposes of subparagraphs (A) and (B) above:

(A) if a price or a per annum rate is specified for the Swap Transaction or that party to be the Floating Rate applicable to that Calculation Period, Compounding Period or Reset Date, the Floating Rate so specified;

(B) if only one Reset Date is established for the Swap Transaction or that party during (or in respect of) that Calculation Period or Compounding Period, the Relevant Rate for that Reset Date;

(C) if more than one Reset Date is established for the Swap Transaction or that party during (or in respect of) that Calculation Period or Compounding Period and the "Unweighted Average" method of calculation is specified, the arithmetic mean of the Relevant Rates for each of those Reset Dates;

(D) if more than one Reset Date is established for the Swap Transaction or that party during (or in respect of) that Calculation Period or Compounding Period and the "Weighted Average" method of calculation is specified, the arithmetic mean of the Relevant Rates in effect for each day in that Calculation Period or Compounding Period calculated by multiplying each Relevant Rate by the number of days such Relevant Rate is in effect, determining the sum of such products and dividing such sum by the number of days in the Calculation Period or Compounding Period; or

(E) if more than one Reset Date is established for the Swap Transaction or that party during (or in respect of) that Calculation Period or Compounding Period and neither the "Unweighted Average" nor the "Weighted Average" method of calculation is specified, a Floating Rate determined as if "Unweighted Average" had been specified as the applicable method of calculation.

(b) "Reset Date" means each day specified as such (or determined pursuant to a method specified for such purpose) for the Swap Transaction or that party, subject to adjustment in accordance with any applicable Business Day Convention which, if a Business Day Convention is not specified in a Confirmation as being applicable to Reset Dates, shall be (i) if a Price Option or a method for determining a price is specified for that Reset Date, the Following Business Day Convention or (ii) if any other Floating Rate Option is specified for that Reset Date, the Business Day Convention applicable to Floating Rate Payer Payment Dates in respect of that Swap Transaction, unless an adjustment in accordance with that Business Day Convention would cause a Reset Date to fall on the Payment Date in respect of the Calculation Period to which that Reset Date relates, in which case that Reset Date shall be adjusted in accordance with the Preceding Business Day Convention.

(c) "Relevant Rate" means (subject to the effect of any applicable Rate Cut-off Date), for any day, a price, expressed as a price per relevant unit, or a per annum rate, expressed as a decimal, equal to

(i) if such day is a Reset Date, the price or rate determined with respect to that day for the specified Floating Rate Option as provided in Article 7 of these Definitions or as provided in a Confirmation or as provided in any agreement between the parties governing the Swap Transaction; or

(ii) if such day is not a Reset Date, the Relevant Rate determined pursuant to clause (i) above for the next preceding Reset Date.

(d) "Rate Cut-off Date" means each day specified as such (or determined pursuant to a method specified for such purpose) for the Swap Transaction or that party. The Relevant Rate for each Reset Date in the period from, and including, a Rate Cut-off Date to, but excluding, the next applicable Period End Date (or, in the case of the last Calculation Period, the Termination Date) will (solely for purposes of calculating the Floating Amount payable on the next applicable Payment Date) be deemed to be the Relevant Rate in effect on that Rate Cut-off Date.

(e) "Spread" means the per annum rate, expressed as a decimal, or the price, expressed in relevant units, if any, specified as such for the Swap Transaction or the party. For purposes of determining a Floating Amount, a Compounding Period Amount or a Basic Compounding Period Amount, if positive the Spread will be added to the Floating Rate and if negative the Spread will be subtracted from the Floating Rate.

(f) "Floating Rate Day Count Fraction" means, in respect of any calculation of a Floating Amount,

(i) if a Floating Rate Day Count Fraction is specified for the Swap Transaction or the Floating Rate Payer, the Floating Rate Day Count Fraction so specified;

(ii) if a Price Option or a method for determining a price is specified for the Swap Transaction or the Floating Rate Payer or if the "FRF-TAM-CDC" or "FRF-T4M-CDC-COMPOUND" Floating Rate Option is specified as the applicable Floating Rate Option, and a Floating Rate Day Count Fraction is not specified, 1/1; and

(iii) in all other cases,

(A) if any "USD-TBILL" Floating Rate Option is specified as the applicable Floating Rate Option or if the "FRF-TAG-CDC" or "FRF-TAG-CDC-COMPOUND" Floating Rate Option is specified as the applicable Floating Rate Option, "Actual/365";

(B) if any "AUD-BBR", "CAD-BA", "CAD-TBILL", "BEF-BIBOR", "GBP-LIBOR" or "HKD-HIBOR" Floating Rate

Option is specified as the applicable Floating Rate Option, "Actual/365 (Fixed)"; and

(C) if any other Floating Rate Option defined in Section 7.1 of these Definitions is specified as the applicable Floating Rate Option, "Actual/360".

(g) "Floating Rate Option" means, in respect of a Swap Transaction and the calculation of a Floating Amount, the Floating Rate Option specified as such, which may be specified by reference to a Rate Option or a Price Option or may be specified by defining the Floating Rate Option in the related Confirmation or in any agreement between the parties governing that Swap Transaction.

(h) "Rate Option" means, in respect of a Swap Transaction and the calculation of a Floating Amount, any of the terms defined in Section 7.1 of these Definitions.

(i) "Price Option", means, in respect of a Swap Transaction and the calculation of a Floating Amount, any of the terms defined in Section 7.2 of these Definitions.

Section 6.3. Certain Definitions Relating to Compounding. For purposes of the calculation of a Floating Amount where "Compounding" is specified to be applicable to a Swap Transaction:

(a) "Compounding Period" means, in respect of a Calculation Period, each period from, and including, one Compounding Date to, but excluding, the next following applicable Compounding Date during that Calculation Period, except that (i) each initial Compounding Period for a Swap Transaction will commence on, and include, the Effective Date and (ii) each final Compounding Period for a Swap Transaction will end on, but exclude, the Termination Date.

(b) "Compounding Date" means each day during the Term of a Swap Transaction specified as such (or determined pursuant to a method specified for such purpose) for the Swap Transaction or a party, subject to adjustment in accordance with the Business Day Convention applicable to Period End Dates in respect of that Swap Transaction or party.

(c) "Compounding Period Amount" means for any Compounding Period an amount calculated on a formula basis for that Compounding Period as follows:

$$
\begin{array}{l}
\text{Compounding} \\
\text{Period} \\
\text{Amount}
\end{array}
=
\begin{array}{l}
\text{Adjusted} \\
\text{Calculation} \\
\text{Amount}
\end{array}
\times
\begin{array}{l}
\text{Floating} \\
\text{Rate} \\
\pm \text{ Spread}
\end{array}
\times
\begin{array}{l}
\text{Floating} \\
\text{Rate} \\
\text{Day Count} \\
\text{Fraction}
\end{array}
$$

(d) "Adjusted Calculation Amount" means (i) in respect of the first Compounding Period in any Calculation Period, the Calculation Amount for that Calculation Period and (ii) in respect of each succeeding Compounding Period in that Calculation Period, an amount equal to the sum of the Calculation Amount for that Calculation Period and the Compounding Period Amounts for each of the previous Compounding Periods in that Calculation Period.

(e) "Basic Compounding Period Amount" means for any Compounding Period an amount calculated as if a Floating Amount were being calculated for that Compounding Period, using the formula in Section 6.1(a).

(f) "Additional Compounding Period Amount" means for any Compounding Period an amount calculated on a formula basis for that Compounding Period as follows:

$$\text{Additional Compounding Period Amount} = \text{Flat Compounding Amount} \times \text{Floating Rate} \times \text{Floating Rate Day Count Fraction}$$

(g) "Flat Compounding Amount" means (i) in respect of the first Compounding Period in any Calculation Period, zero and (ii) in respect of each succeeding Compounding Period in that Calculation Period, an amount equal to the sum of the Basic Compounding Period Amounts and the Additional Compounding Period Amounts for each of the previous Compounding Periods in that Calculation Period.

ARTICLE 7 *

CALCULATION OF RATES AND PRICES
FOR CERTAIN FLOATING RATE OPTIONS

Section 7.2. Price Options. For purposes of determining a Relevant Rate:

(a) *S&P 500.* "S&P 500" means that the price for a Reset Date will be the value of the Standard & Poor's 500 Composite Stock Price Index at the close of business, New York time, on that Reset Date, as calculated and published by Standard & Poor's Corporation.

(b) *FT-SE 100.* "FT-SE 100" means that the price for a Reset Date will be the value of the FT-SE (Financial Times-Stock Exchange) 100 Share Index at the close of business, London time, on that Reset Date, as calculated and published by The International Stock Exchange.

(c) *NIKKEI 225.* "NIKKEI 225" means that the price for a Reset Date will be the value of the Nikkei Stock Average Index at the close of business, Tokyo time, on that Reset Date, as calculated and published by Nihon Keizai Shimbun Inc.

* **Section 7.1.** on rate options has been deleted from this reproduction of the ISDA definitions.

(d) *TOPIX.* "TOPIX" means that the price for a Reset Date will be the value of the Tokyo Stock Price Index at the close of business, Tokyo time, on that Reset Date, as calculated and published by the Tokyo Stock Exchange.

(e) *DAX.* "DAX" means that the price for a Reset Date will be the value of the Deutscher Aktienindex at the close of business, Frankfurt time, on that Reset Date, as calculated and published by the Frankfurter Wertpapierbörse.

(f) *CAC-40.* "CAC-40" means that the price for a Reset Date will be the value of the CAC-40 Index at the close of business, Paris time, on that Reset Date, as calculated and published by the Société des Bourses Françaises.

(g) *Oil.* "OIL-WTI-NYMEX" means that the price for a Reset Date will be the closing price per barrel of oil on the NYMEX on that Reset Date of the WTI contract for the Contract Month, stated in U.S. Dollars, as reported by the NYMEX. If no such price is reported by the NYMEX on that Reset Date, but a range of two prices per barrel of WTI on a delivery basis, for delivery in the Contract Month, is published under the heading "Spot Crude Price Assessments" in the issue of Platt's Oilgram Price Report that reports prices effective on that Reset Date, the price for that Reset Date will be the average of those two prices as published in that issue. If a range of two prices is not published in the relevant issue of *Platt's Oilgram Price Report*, the Calculation Agent will request the Reference Dealers to provide bid and asked quotations for the relevant WTI contract. If four quotations are provided as requested, the price for that Reset Date will be the arithmetic mean of the average of the bid and asked quotations provided by each Reference Dealer, without regard to the averages having the highest and lowest values. If exactly three quotations are provided as requested, the price for that Reset Date will be the average of the bid and asked quotations provided by each Reference Dealer that remains after disregarding the averages having the highest and lowest values. If fewer than three quotations are provided as requested, the price for that Reset Date will be determined by the Calculation Agent in good faith after consultation with the other party (or both parties, if the Calculation Agent is a third party), if practicable, for the purpose of obtaining a representative price for the relevant WTI contract that will reasonably reflect conditions prevailing at the time in the WTI market.

Section 7.3. Certain Published and Displayed Sources.

(a) "H.15(519)" means the weekly statistical release designated as such, or any successor publication, published by the Board of Governors of the Federal Reserve System.

(b) "Composite 3:30 P.M. Quotations for U.S. Government Securities" means the daily statistical release designated as such, or any successor publication, published by the Federal Reserve Bank of New York.

(c) "Reuters Screen" means, when used in connection with any designated page and any Floating Rate Option, the display page so designated on the Reuter

§ 7.3(c)

Monitor Money Rates Service (or such other page as may replace that page on that service for the purpose of displaying rates or prices comparable to that Floating Rate Option).

(d) "Telerate" means, when used in connection with any designated page and any Floating Rate Option, the display page so designated on the Dow Jones Telerate Service (or such other page as may replace that page on that service, or such other service as may be nominated as the information vendor, for the purpose of displaying rates or prices comparable to that Floating Rate Option).

(e) "FHLBSF" means the Federal Home Loan Bank of San Francisco or its successor.

Section 7.4. Certain General Definitions Relating to Floating Rate Options.

(a) "Representative Amount" means, for purposes of any Floating Rate Option for which a Representative Amount is relevant, an amount that is representative for a single transaction in the relevant market at the relevant time.

(b) "Designated Maturity" means the period of time specified as such for a Swap Transaction or a party.

(c) "Reference Banks" means (i) for purposes of the "AUD-BBR-BBSW" Floating Rate Option, the financial institutions authorized to quote on the Reuters Screen BBSW Page, (ii) for purposes of any "BIBOR" Floating Rate Option, four major banks in the Brussels interbank market, (iii) for purposes of the "CAD-BA" and "CAD-TBILL" Floating Rate Options, four major Canadian Schedule A chartered banks, (iv) for purposes of any "LIBOR" Floating Rate Option, four major banks in the London interbank market, (v) for purposes of the "DKK-CIBOR" Floating Rate Option, four major banks in the Copenhagen interbank market, (vi) for purposes of the "DEM-FIBOR-ISDB", "DEM-FIBOR-FIBO" and "DEM-FIBOR-Reference Banks" Floating Rate Options, four major banks in the Frankfurt interbank market, (vii) for purposes of the "DEM-FIBOR-GBA" or "DEM-FIBOR-FIBP" Floating Rate Option, the banks nominated through the German Banking Association to the German Bundesbank (or such other bank or monetary authority as may replace the Bundesbank) which calculate and publish that rate, (viii) for purposes of the "NLG-AIBOR" Floating Rate Option, four major banks in the Amsterdam interbank market, (ix) for purposes of any "FIM-HELIBOR" Floating Rate Option, five major banks in the Helsinki interbank market, (x) for purposes of any "PIBOR" Floating Rate Option, four major banks in the Paris interbank market, (xi) for purposes of the "HKD-HIBOR" Floating Rate Option, four major banks in the Hong Kong interbank market, (xii) for purposes of any "LUXIBOR" Floating Rate Option, four major banks in the Luxembourg interbank market, (xiii) for purposes of the "NZD-BBR" Floating Rate Option, four major banks in the New Zealand money market, (xiv) for purposes of any "NKR-NIBOR" Floating Rate Option, four major banks in the Oslo interbank market, (xv) for purposes of the "SPP-MIBOR" Floating Rate Option, four major banks in the Madrid interbank market, (xvi) for purposes of any "EDOR" Floating Rate Option, four major banks in the Stockholm interbank market, (xvii) for purposes of the "USD-TIBOR" Floating Rate Option, four major banks in the Tokyo interbank market and (xviii) for purposes of the "USD-Prime" Floating Rate Option, three major banks in New York City, in each case selected by the Calculation Agent or specified for the Swap Transaction.

(d) "Reference Dealers" means (i) for purposes of the "USD-TBILL" Floating Rate Option, three primary United States Government securities dealers in New York City, (ii) for purposes of the "USD-CD" Floating Rate Option, three leading nonbank dealers in negotiable U.S. Dollar certificates of deposit in New York City, (iii) for purposes of the "USD-CP" Floating Rate Option, three leading dealers of U.S. Dollar commercial paper in New York City, (iv) for purposes of the "USD-Federal Funds" Floating Rate Option, three leading brokers of U.S. Dollar Federal funds transactions in New York City, (v) for purposes of the "USD-BA" Floating Rate Option, three leading dealers of U.S. Dollar bankers acceptances in New York City and (vi) for purposes of the "OIL-WTI-NYMEX" Floating Rate Option, four leading dealers in oil futures, in each case selected by the Calculation Agent or specified for the Swap Transaction.

(e) "Bond Equivalent Yield" means, in respect of any security with a maturity of six months or less, the rate for which is quoted on a bank discount basis, a yield (expressed as a percentage) calculated in accordance with the following formula:

$$\text{Bond Equivalent Yield} = \frac{D \times N}{360 - (D \times M)} \times 100$$

where "D" refers to the per annum rate for the security, quoted on a bank discount basis and expressed as a decimal: "N" refers to 365 or 366, as the case may be, and "M" refers to, if the Designated Maturity approximately corresponds to the length of the Calculation Period or Compounding Period for which the Bond Equivalent Yield is being calculated, the actual number of days in that Calculation Period or Compounding Period and, otherwise, the actual number of days in the period from, and including, the applicable Reset Date to, but excluding, the day that numerically corresponds to that Reset Date (or, if there is not any such numerically corresponding day, the last day) in the calendar month that is the number of months corresponding to the Designated Maturity after the month in which that Reset Date occurred.

(f) "Money Market Yield" means, in respect of any security with a maturity of six months or less, the rate for which is quoted on a bank discount basis, a yield (expressed as a percentage) calculated in accordance with the following formula:

$$\text{Money Market Yield} = \frac{D \times 360}{360 - (D \times M)} \times 100$$

where "D" refers to the per annum rate for a security, quoted on a bank discount basis and expressed as a decimal; and "M" refers to, if the Designated Maturity

§ 7.4(f)

approximately corresponds to the length of the Calculation Period or Compounding Period for which the Money Market Yield is being calculated, the actual number of days in that Calculation Period or Compounding Period and, otherwise, the actual number of days in the period from, and including, the applicable Reset Date to, but excluding, the day that numerically corresponds to that Reset Date (or, if there is not any such numerically corresponding day, the last day) in the calendar month that is the number of months corresponding to the Designated Maturity after the month in which that Reset Date occurred.

(g) "Contract Month" means, in respect of the determination of the "OIL-WTI-NYMEX" Price Option, the month and year specified (or determined pursuant to a method specified for that purpose) for the Swap Transaction.

(h) "Exchange" means, in respect of a Price Option or a Swap Transaction (i) the stock or commodity exchange indicated for the following Price Options:

Price Option	Exchange
S&P 500	New York Stock Exchange
	American Stock Exchange
	NASDAQ
FT-SE 100	The International Stock Exchange
NIKKEI 225	Tokyo Stock Exchange
TOPIX	Tokyo Stock Exchange
DAX	Frankfurt Stock Exchange
CAC-40	Paris Bourse
OIL-WTI-NYMEX	NYMEX

and (ii) any other stock or commodity exchange specified for a party or a Swap Transaction in the related Confirmation.

(i) "NASDAQ" means the National Association of Securities Dealers Automated Quotation National Market System.

(j) "The International Stock Exchange" means The International Stock Exchange of the United Kingdom and the Republic of Ireland Limited.

(k) "WTI" means light sweet domestic crude oil (West Texas Intermediate) deliverable in satisfaction of futures contract delivery obligations under the rules of NYMEX.

(l) "NYMEX" means the New York Mercantile Exchange.

(m) "Market Disruption Event" means, in respect of a Swap Transaction and the determination of a Relevant Rate by reference to a Price Option, in addition to any events specified in the related Confirmation and unless otherwise provided in the related Confirmation, either of the following events, the existence of which shall be determined in good faith by the Calculation Agent:

(i) suspension or material limitation of trading (excluding daily settlement limits in the normal course of trading) in any commodity, or affecting any index,

§ 7.5(e)

on all Exchanges specified in a Confirmation as relevant to the determination of the Relevant Rate; or

(ii) in respect of any Price Option calculated by reference to values or components, suspension or material limitation of trading (excluding daily settlement limits in the normal course of trading) in a material number of the components of that Price Option on all Exchanges specified in a Confirmation as relevant to the determination of the Relevant Rate.

Section 7.5. Corrections to Published and Displayed Rates and Prices. For purposes of determining the Relevant Rate for any day:

(a) in any case where the Relevant Rate for a day is based on information obtained from the Reuter Monitor Money Rates Service or the Dow Jones Telerate Service, that Relevant Rate will be subject to the corrections, if any, to that information subsequently displayed by that source within one hour of the time when such rate is first displayed by such source;

(b) in any case where the Relevant Rate for a day is based on information obtained from H.15(519) or Composite 3:30 P.M. Quotations for U.S. Government Securities, that Relevant Rate will be subject to the corrections, if any, to that information subsequently published by that source within 30 days of that day;

(c) in any case where the Relevant Rate for a day is based on information obtained from Composite 3:30 P.M. Quotations for U.S. Government Securities, that Relevant Rate will be subject to correction based upon the applicable rate, if any, subsequently published in H.15(519) within 30 days of that day;

(d) in any case where the Relevant Rate for a day is based on information obtained from the Reuters Screen CDCR Page, that Relevant Rate will be subject to the corrections, if any, published for the applicable Reset Date, no later than the last day of the calendar month during which the Reset Date occurred, in the publication entitled "Cote Officielle" opposite the heading "Taux annuel monetairè" (if the applicable Floating Rate Option is FRF-TAM-CDC), or under the heading "TMM" (if the applicable Floating Rate Option is FRF-T4M-CDC-COMPOUND or FRF-T4M-CDC) or under the heading "TMP" (if the applicable Floating Rate Option is FRF-TMP-CDC AVERAGE);

(e) in any case where the Relevant Rate for a day is based on an index or price on an Exchange or published in *Platt's Oilgram Price Report*, that Relevant Rate will be subject to correction based upon the applicable index or price, if any, subsequently calculated and published by the person responsible for that calculation and publication within one Banking Day of the original publication in the place of original publication; and

§ 7.5(f)

(f) in the event that a party to any Swap Transaction notifies the other party to the Swap Transaction of any correction referred to in subsections (a), (b), (c), (d) or (e) above no later than 15 days after the expiration of the period referred to in such subsection, an appropriate amount will be payable as a result of such correction (whether such correction is made or such notice is given before or after the Termination Date of the Swap Transaction), together with interest on that amount at a rate per annum equal to the cost (without proof or evidence of any actual cost) to the relevant party (as certified by it) of funding that amount for the period from, and including, the day on which, based on such correction, a payment in the incorrect amount was first made to, but excluding, the day of payment of the refund or payment resulting from such correction.

Section 7.6. Certain Adjustments in Indices. Unless otherwise specified in a Confirmation, in determining a price for any Reset Date with respect to any Price Option calculated and published by any person, if that person discontinues calculation and publication of the index on which such price is based, or if the information necessary for that person to perform the necessary calculation is not available to it, but a comparable successor to that index acceptable to both parties is calculated and is published by another person on that Reset Date, the price for that Reset Date will be the value of that successor index as calculated and published by that person at the close of business, at the place specified for that Price Option, on that Reset Date. If a comparable successor to that index is not available on that Reset Date, or if the method of calculation of that index or the value thereof is changed in a material respect so that the price on that Reset Date does not fairly represent the value of that index as calculated and published on the Trade Date of the Swap Transaction, then the Calculation Agent shall make such adjustments in respect of such calculation in good faith after consultation with the other party (or both parties, if the Calculation Agent is a third party), if practicable, for the purpose of obtaining a value at the close of business, at the place specified for that Price Option, on that Reset Date, that produces a price based on an index that is comparable to the index as last calculated and published or as calculated and published immediately prior to such change.

Section 7.7. Effect of Market Disruption Event. In the event that a Market Disruption Event exists on any Reset Date and an alternative method for determining the Relevant Rate in the event of a Market Disruption Event has not been specified by the parties, such date shall not be considered a Reset Date. In such event the next succeeding Business Day on which a Market Disruption Event does not exist shall be considered the Reset Date and a price shall be obtained for that Reset Date in accordance with the terms of the relevant Price Option. If a Market Disruption Event exists on each of the five Business Days immediately following the original Reset Date, a price shall be determined based on the latest available quotation for the relevant Price Option, whether or not a Market Disruption Event exists on that date.

ARTICLE 8

OPTIONS

Section 8.1. Option. "Option" means any Swap Transaction that is identified in the related Confirmation as an Option and provides for the grant by Seller to Buyer of (i) the right to cause an Underlying Swap Transaction to become effective, (ii) the right to cause Seller to pay Buyer the Cash Settlement Amount, if any, in respect of the Underlying Swap Transaction on the Cash Settlement Payment Date, (iii) the right to cause the Optional Termination Date to become the Termination Date and, if so specified in the related Confirmation, the Final Exchange Date of the Related Swap Transaction or (iv) any other right or rights specified in the related Confirmation. An Option may provide for the grant of one or more of the foregoing rights, all of which can be identified in a single Confirmation.

Section 8.2. Certain Definitions and Provisions Relating to Options. When used in respect of an Option, the following terms have the indicated meanings:

(a) **Underlying Swap Transaction.** "Underlying Swap Transaction" means a Swap Transaction, the terms of which are identified in the Confirmation of the Option, which Underlying Swap Transaction shall not become effective unless (i) "Physical Settlement" is specified to be applicable to the Option and (ii) the right to cause that Underlying Swap Transaction to become effective has been exercised.

(b) **Related Swap Transaction.** "Related Swap Transaction" means a Swap Transaction, the terms of which are identified in the Confirmation of the Option, for which an Optional Termination Date is or may be specified.

(c) **Physical Settlement.** If "Physical Settlement" is specified to be applicable to the Option, it means that Seller grants to Buyer pursuant to the Option the right to cause the Underlying Swap Transaction to become effective.

(d) **Cash Settlement.** If "Cash Settlement" is specified to be applicable to the Option, it means that Seller grants to Buyer pursuant to the Option the right to cause Seller to pay Buyer the Cash Settlement Amount, if any, in respect of the Underlying Swap Transaction on the Cash Settlement Payment Date.

(e) **Optional Termination.** If "Optional Termination" is specified to be applicable to the Option, it means that Seller grants to Buyer pursuant to the Option the right to cause the Optional Termination Date to become the Termination Date and, if so specified in the related Confirmation, the Final Exchange Date of the Related Swap Transaction.

(f) **Optional Termination Date.** "Optional Termination Date" means, in respect of an Option to which Optional Termination is specified to be applicable, the date or dates specified in or pursuant to the related Confirmation.

(g) **American Option.** "American Option" means a style of Option pursuant to which the right or rights granted are exercisable during an Exercise Period that consists of more than one day.

(h) **European Option.** "European Option" means a style of Option pursuant to which the right or rights granted are exercisable during an Exercise Period that consists of only one day.

Section 8.3. Parties. (a) **Buyer.** "Buyer" means, in respect of an Option, the party specified as such in the related Confirmation.

(b) **Seller.** "Seller" means, in respect of an Option, the party specified as seller or as writer in the related Confirmation.

Section 8.4. Terms Relating to Exercise. (a) **Exercise Period.** "Exercise Period" means, in respect of an Option, each of the periods specified in or pursuant to the related Confirmation, which, in the case of a European Option, shall consist of one day.

(b) **Notice of Exercise.** "Notice of Exercise" means, in respect of an Option, irrevocable notice delivered by Buyer to Seller (which may be delivered orally (including by telephone) unless the parties specify otherwise in a Confirmation with respect to a specific Option) of its exercise of the right or rights granted pursuant to the Option, which notice becomes effective between the hours specified in a Confirmation on a day during the Exercise Period that is a Banking Day in the city in which Seller is located for purposes of receiving notices and in any financial centers relevant to the Underlying Swap Transaction and which notice must include the Exercise Terms, if any. Buyer may exercise the right or rights granted pursuant to the Option only by delivering a Notice of Exercise.

(c) **Exercise Terms.** "Exercise Terms" means those terms of an Underlying Swap Transaction or a Related Swap Transaction which are identified in or pursuant to the Confirmation of an Option as terms that must be specified by Buyer in the Notice of Exercise.

(d) **Effectiveness of Notices.** Any notice or communication given, and permitted to be given, orally (including by telephone) in connection with an Option will be effective when actually received by the recipient.

(e) **Written Confirmation.** If "Written Confirmation" is specified to be applicable to the Option or if demanded by Seller (which demand, notwithstanding any provisions regarding notice applicable to the Option, may be delivered orally (including by telephone)), Buyer will (i) execute a written confirmation confirming the substance of the Notice of Exercise and deliver the same to Seller or (ii) issue a telex to Seller setting forth the substance of the Notice of Exercise. Buyer shall cause such executed written confirmation or telex to be received by Seller within one Banking Day (in the city in which Seller is located for purposes of receiving notices) following the date that the Notice of Exercise or Seller's demand, as the case may be, becomes effective. If not received within such time, Buyer will be deemed to have satisfied its obligations under the immediately preceding sentence at the time that such executed written confirmation or telex becomes effective.

Section 8.5. Terms Relating to Premium. (a) **Premium.** "Premium" means, in respect of an Option, an amount, if any, that is specified as such in or pursuant to the related Confirmation and, subject to any applicable condition precedent, is payable by the Buyer on the Premium Payment Date or Dates.

(b) **Premium Payment Date.** "Premium Payment Date" means, in respect of an Option, the date or dates specified as such in or pursuant to the related Confirmation, subject to adjustment in accordance with the Modified Following Business Day Convention or, if another Business Day Convention is specified to be applicable to the Premium Payment Date, that Business Day Convention.

Section 8.6. Terms Relating to Cash Settlement. (a) **Cash Settlement Amount.** "Cash Settlement Amount" means, in respect of an Option to which Cash Settlement is specified to be applicable, an amount, if any, that, subject to any applicable condition precedent, is payable by the Seller on the applicable Cash Settlement Payment Date and is determined by a method specified in or pursuant to the Confirmation of the Option or the agreement governing such Option.

(b) **Cash Settlement Payment Date.** "Cash Settlement Payment Date" means, in respect of an Option to which Cash Settlement is specified to be applicable, the date specified as such in the Notice of Exercise or determined pursuant to the related Confirmation, subject to adjustment in accordance with the Modified Following Business Day Convention or, if another Business Day Convention is specified to be applicable to the Cash Settlement Payment Date, that Business Day Convention.

Section 8.7. Currency Options. In respect of an Option for which the Underlying Swap Transaction involves an exchange of amounts in different currencies, the following terms shall have the indicated meanings:

(a) **Call.** "Call" means an Option entitling, but not obligating, the Buyer to purchase from the Seller at the Strike Price a specified quantity of the Call Currency.

(b) **Put.** "Put" means an Option entitling, but not obligating, the Buyer to sell to the Seller at the Strike Price a specified quantity of the Put Currency.

(c) **Additional Terms.** "Call Currency", "Call Amount", "Put Currency", "Put Amount" and "Strike Price" shall each have the meanings specified as such for the Option in a Confirmation. The Put Amount is the Final Exchange Amount for the Buyer of the Option and the Call Amount is the Final Exchange Amount for the Seller of the Option.

(d) **Expiration Date.** The "Expiration Date" of an Option shall be the date specified as such in a Confirmation, which date is the last date on which the Option can be exercised, which date, unless otherwise specified, shall be subject to adjustment in accordance with the Following Business Day

§ 8.7(d)

Convention. The "Expiration Time" of an Option shall be the time specified as such in a Confirmation, which time is the latest time on the Expiration Date on which the Seller will accept a Notice of Exercise.

(e) **Expiration Settlement Date.** The "Expiration Settlement Date" of an Option is the date specified as such in the related Confirmation and shall be the last date on which an Option that has been exercised can be settled.

(f) **Price.** In addition to specifying the Premium as an amount, the Premium can be specified in a Confirmation as a price, which shall be stated as a percentage of the Put Amount or the Call Amount, as the case may be.

ARTICLE 9

ROUNDING; INTERPOLATION; DISCOUNTING

Section 9.1. Rounding. For purposes of any calculations referred to in these Definitions (unless otherwise specified), (a) all percentages resulting from such calculations will be rounded, if necessary, to the nearest one hundred-thousandth of a percentage point (*e.g.*, 9.876541% (or .09876541) being rounded down to 9.87654% (or .0987654) and 9.876545% (or .09876545) being rounded up to 9.87655% (or .0987655)), (b) all U.S. Dollar amounts used in or resulting from such calculations will be rounded to the nearest cent (with one half cent being rounded up), (c) all Yen amounts used in or resulting from such calculations will be rounded downwards to the next lower whole Yen amount, (d) all Italian Lira and Spanish Peseta amounts will be rounded to the nearest Italian Lira or Spanish Peseta (with one half Italian Lira or Spanish Peseta being rounded up) and (e) all amounts denominated in any other currency used in or resulting from such calculations will be rounded to the nearest two decimal places in such currency, with .005 being rounded upwards (*e.g.*, .674 being rounded down to .67 and .675 being rounded up to .68).

Section 9.2. Interpolation. In respect of any Calculation Period to which "Linear Interpolation" is specified to be applicable, the Relevant Rate for the Reset Date in respect of that Calculation Period or any Compounding Period included in that Calculation Period shall be determined through the use of straight-line interpolation by reference to two rates based on the relevant Floating Rate Option, one of which shall be determined as if the Designated Maturity were the period of time for which rates are available next shorter than the length of the Calculation Period or Compounding Period (or any alternative Designated Maturity agreed to by the parties) and the other of which shall be determined as if the Designated Maturity were the period of time for which rates are available next longer than the length of the Calculation Period or Compounding Period (or any alternative Designated Maturity agreed to by the parties).

Section 9.3. Discounting. (a) In respect of any Swap Transaction to which "Discounting" is specified to be applicable, a discounted Fixed Amount or Floating Amount for any Calculation Period not longer than one year shall be calculated by dividing the Fixed Amount or the Floating Amount, as the case may be, for that Calculation Period by an amount equal to:

$$1 + \left\{ \text{Discount Rate} \times \frac{\text{Discount Rate}}{\text{Day Count Fraction}} \right\}$$

(b) For any Swap Transaction to which "FRA Discounting" is specified to be applicable, an FRA Amount in respect of any Calculation Period not longer than one year shall be calculated, in lieu of calculating a Fixed Amount and a Floating Amount for that Calculation Period, in accordance with the following formula:

$$\text{FRA Amount} = \frac{\text{Calculation Amount} \times \left\{ \begin{array}{l}(\text{Floating Rate} \pm \text{Spread}) \\ - \text{Fixed Rate}\end{array} \times \frac{\text{Floating Rate}}{\text{Day Count Fraction}} \right\}}{1 + \left\{ \text{Discount Rate} \times \frac{\text{Discount Rate}}{\text{Day Count Fraction}} \right\}}$$

If the FRA Amount for any Calculation Period is positive, the Floating Rate Payer shall pay to the Fixed Rate Payer the FRA Amount on the Payment Date in respect of that Calculation Period and the Fixed Rate Payer shall not be obligated to pay any FRA Amount in respect of that Calculation Period. If the FRA Amount for any Calculation Period is negative, the Fixed Rate Payer shall pay to the Floating Rate Payer the absolute value of the FRA Amount on the Payment Date in respect of that Calculation Period and the Floating Rate Payer shall not be obligated to pay any FRA Amount in respect of that Calculation Period.

(c) "Discount Rate" means (i) if a rate is specified as such, the rate so specified, expressed as a decimal, (ii) if a Discount Rate is not specified and "Discounting" is specified to be applicable to the Swap Transaction, the Fixed Rate or Floating Rate used to calculate the amount being discounted, or (iii) if a Discount Rate is not specified and "FRA Discounting" is specified to be applicable to the Swap Transaction, the Floating Rate for that Calculation Period plus or minus the Spread.

(d) "Discount Rate Day Count Fraction" means (i) if a Discount Rate Day Count Fraction is specified as such in the Confirmation, the Day Count Fraction so specified, (ii) if a Discount Rate Day Count Fraction is not specified and "Discounting" is specified to be applicable to the Swap Transaction, the Day Count Fraction used to calculate the amount being discounted or (iii) if a Discount Rate Day Count Fraction is not specified and "FRA Discounting" is specified to be applicable to the Swap Transaction, the Floating Rate Day Count Fraction.

§ 10.1

ARTICLE 10

PAYMENTS

Section 10.1. Relating Payments to Calculation Periods. Unless otherwise provided for a Swap Transaction or a party, (a) where the Fixed Amount or Floating Amount is calculated by reference to a Calculation Period, the Fixed Amount or Floating Amount applicable to a Payment Date will be the Fixed Amount or Floating Amount calculated with reference to the Calculation Period ending on, but excluding, the Period End Date that is (or is closest in time to) that Payment Date or, in the case of the final Calculation Period, ending on, but excluding, the Termination Date and (b) a Discounted Amount applicable to a Payment Date will be the Discounted Amount calculated with reference to the Calculation Period commencing on, and including, the Period End Date that is (or is closest in time to) that Payment Date or, in the case of the initial Calculation Period, commencing on, and including, the Effective Date.

ISDA Standard Letter Agreement Confirming a Swap Transaction

This appendix presents the latest issue of the ISDA's standard letter agreement confirming a Swap transaction.

EXHIBIT I
[Draft—June 12, 1992]

Heading for Letter

[Letterhead of Party A]

[Date]

Transaction

[Name and Address of Party B]

Heading for Telex

Telex

Date:

To: [Name and Telex Number of Party B]

From: [Party A]

Re: Commodity Swap Transaction—Cash Settled

Dear   :

The purpose of this [letter agreement/telex] is to confirm the terms and conditions of the Transaction entered into between us on the Trade Date specified below (the "Transaction"). This [letter agreement/telex] constitutes a "Confirmation" as referred to in the ISDA Master Agreement specified below.

The definitions and provisions contained in the 1992 ISDA Commodity Derivative Definitions[1] (as published by the International Swap Dealers Association, Inc.) are incorporated into this Confirmation. In the event of any inconsistency between those definitions and provisions and this Confirmation, this Confirmation will govern.

1. This Confirmation supplements, forms part of, and is subject to, the ISDA Master Agreement dated as of [date], as amended and supplemented from time to time (the "Agreement"), between you and us. All provisions contained in the Agreement govern this Confirmation except as expressly modified below.

2. The terms of the particular Transaction to which this Confirmation relates are as follows:

Notional Quantity per
Calculation Period :[2]   [Specify quantity in relevant units of commodity
                                            (*e.g.*, barrels)] (Total Notional Quantity: [   ])

Commodity:

Trade Date:

Effective Date:

Termination Date:

Calculation Period(s):

[Period End Date(s):]

Fixed Amount Details:

Fixed Price Payer: [Party A/B]

---

[1] If the Transaction contemplates one party paying a price based on a Commodity Reference Price and the other party paying a price based on a rate, such as Libor, the parties may also wish to incorporate the 1991 ISDA Definitions and specify the priorities in the event of any conflict between the definitions.

[2] The parties may specify a different Notional Quantity for each party. In addition, the parties may specify a different Notional Quantity (or a formula for determining that Notional Quantity) for each Calculation Period.

Fixed Price Payer [Settlement] [Payment] Dates:

[, subject to adjustment in accordance with the [Following/Modified Following/Nearest/ Preceding] Business Day Convention]

Fixed Amount [or Fixed Price]:

Floating Amount Details:

Floating Price Payer:

[Party B/A]

Floating Price Payer [Settlement] [Payment] Dates:

[, subject to adjustment in accordance with the [Following/Modified Following/Nearest/ Preceding] Business Day Convention]

Calculation Period(s):

Commodity Reference Price:[3]

[Commodity:
Unit:
Price Source/Exchange:
Currency:],[4]

[Specified Price:]

[Specify whether the price will be the bid price, the asked price, the average of the high and low prices, the morning fixing, etc.]

[Delivery Date:]

[Specify whether the price will be the spot price, the First Nearby Month, the Second Nearby Month, etc.]

Determination Date(s):[5]

[, subject to adjustment in accordance with the [Following/Modified Following/Nearest/ Preceding] Commodity Business Day Convention]

[Method of Averaging:]

[Market Disruption:]

[Market Disruption Event(s):]

[Disruption Fallback(s):]

[Alternate Price Source:]

Calculation Agent:

3. Account Details:

Payments to Party A:

Account for payments:

Payments to Party B:

Accounts for payments:

---

[3] The parties may either (i) specify one of the Commodity Reference Prices defined in the ISDA Commodity Derivative Definitions or (ii) create a Commodity Reference Price by specifying a Commodity, a Unit, a Price Source or an Exchange and, if relevant, a Currency.

[4] Delete if a Commodity Reference Price is specified above.

[5] The parties must specify the date or dates, or the means for determining the date or dates, on which a price will be obtained for purposes of calculating the Floating Amount, *e.g.*, each Commodity Business Day during the Calculation Period or the last three Commodity Business Days in each Calculation Period.

[4. Offices:

(a) The Office of Party A for the Swap Transaction is   ; and

(b) The Office of Party B for the Swap Transaction is   .]

[5. Broker/Arranger:]

Closing for Letter

Please confirm that the foregoing correctly sets forth the terms of our agreement by executing the copy of this Confirmation enclosed for that purpose and returning it to us or by sending to us a letter or telex substantially similar to this letter, which letter or telex sets forth the material terms of the Transaction to which this Confirmation relates and indicates agreement to those terms.

Yours sincerely,

[PARTY A]

By: _____

    Name:

    Title:

Confirmed as of the date
first above written:

[PARTY B]

By: _____

    Name:

    Title:

Closing for Telex

Please confirm that the foregoing correctly sets forth the terms of our agreement by sending to us a letter or telex substantially similar to this telex, which letter or telex sets forth the material terms of the Transaction to which this Confirmation relates and indicates agreement to those terms, or by sending to us a return telex substantially to the following effect:

"Re:

We acknowledge receipt of your telex dated [   ] with respect to the above-referenced Transaction between [Party A] and [Party B] with an Effective Date of [   ] and a Termination Date of [   ] and confirm that such telex correctly sets forth the terms of our agreement relating to the Transaction described therein. Very truly yours, [Party B], by [specify name and title of authorized officer]."

Yours sincerely,

[PARTY A]

By: _____

    Name:

    Title:

Glossary

30/360 day count: See *bond basis*.

accreting Swap: A Swap whose notional amount increases over time.

actual/360 day count: The number of days in the period divided by 360. With an actual/360 option, you pay an extra five days' interest each year.

actual/365 day count: The number of days in the period divided by 365.

American-style option: An option that can be exercised at any point during the option period.

amortizing Cap: A Cap whose notional amount decreases over time.

amortizing Swap: A Swap whose notional amount decreases over time.

annuity: Periodic stream of constant payments.

assignments: An unwind that is done with a third party rather than the original counterparty.

basis point: One hundredth of one percent.

basis risk: Risk that the spread between the item being hedged and the hedging vehicle will change.

basis Swap: A floating/floating Swap; the exchange of one floating index for another.

benchmark issue: An on-the-run issue.

Bermuda-style option: An option that can be exercised on several days.

blended rate Swap: A Swap that is the combination of several different rates.

bond basis: Assumes 12 months of equal length (30 days).

Boston option: An option for which the premium is paid at the end of the option period rather than at the inception.

BP: Basis point.

callable Swap: A Swap with an option embedded in it that allows it to be called.

cancelable Swap: A Swap with an option embedded in it that allows it to be canceled after a certain time period.

Caps: An option that gives the purchaser protection against rates rising above a certain level.

Caption: An option on a Cap.

cash settle: A transaction that is settled in cash rather than by the actual delivery of the product.

collars: The combination of a Cap and a floor.

collateralized Swap: Swap where securities are put up to "collateralize" mark-to-market losses or potential mark-to-market losses.

Commodity Business Day: A day in which the agreed-on index is published or the agreed-on exchange is open.

commodity Swap: A Swap with the exchange of a fixed and floating commodity price.

compound: Process by which rate is increased to take into account the passage of time.

compound option: An option on an option.

confirm: A telex that lists all the details of each derivative transaction.

contingent Swap: A Swap for which one contingent on a certain rate or event happens in order for the Swap to be activated. The most common type of a contingent Swap is a Swaption.

corporate start: The start of an obligation five business days after the terms are agreed on rather than the two days in a spot start. Not used often in the Swap market.

counterparty: One of the parties to a Swap or derivatives transaction.

credit-enhanced Swap: A Swap where one counterparty, the one with the weaker credit, puts up some "enhancement," usually collateral, to induce the first party to enter into the Swap. Sometimes, letters of credit or other credit supports are used.

cross-index Swap: A Swap where Libor in one currency is swapped for Libor in another currency plus or minus a spread.

currency Swap: Exchange of one currency for another.

day count: The method of calculating the number of days in determining interest payments.

decompound: Process by which rate is decreased to take into account a shorter time period.

deferred start Swap: A Swap that does not start immediately.

deferred Swap: See *deferred start Swap.*

delayed Libor reset Swap: A Swap in which the Libor is not set at the beginning of each floating reset period.

delta: The correlation between the movement in the price of an option and the price of the underlying security.

Determination Date: The date on which relevant price is determined in a commodity Swap.

diagrams: Pictures drawn to show the actual cashflows between two or more parties.

Diff: A Libor differential Swap.

difference option: An option that focuses on the difference between two indices (i.e., the spread between the 2-year Treasury and 30-year Treasury).

differential Swap: A Libor differential Swap.

discounting: Bringing the future value of something to the present.

Disruption Event: An event that prevents the determination of a price in a commodity Swap. For example, this can be the failure of a price source to publish a price, a trading disruption, or a trading suspension.

equity Swap: The exchange of a return linked to a stock index with another rate such as Libor.

escalating rate Swap: A Swap in which the fixed rate increases over time at an agreed-on level.

European-style option: An option that can only be exercised on one day.

exchange-traded: Vehicles traded on established exchanges.

Exercise Date: The date on which an option can be exercised.

Expiration Date: The last day of an option period.

exploding option: An option that disappears or "explodes" when a certain price level is reached.

final exchange of principal: The exchange of the two previously agreed-on currency amount at the end of a currency Swap.

fixed rate: The combination of a Treasury level plus a spread.

floating/floating Swap: See *basis Swap.*

floating rate: The leg of the Swap that gets periodically reset based on a moving index.

floor: An option that gives the purchaser protection against rates falling below an agreed-on level.

Floortion: An option on a floor.

foreign exchange Swap: See *currency Swap*.

forward start Swap: A Swap that starts at some date in the future rather than immediately.

FRA: Forward rate agreement.

Fraption: An option on an FRA.

FSA: Forward spread agreement. A spread lock that starts at a future date.

futures: Organized exchange where commodities and other financial instruments are traded.

high coupon Swap: An off-market Swap with an above-market fixed rate.

in the money: A position with intrinsic value.

initial exchange of principal: The exchange of the two previously agreed-on currency amounts at the beginning of a currency Swap. In actuality, this initial exchange may not take place.

interest rate Swap: The exchange of a fixed interest rate payment for a floating payment; the combination of a Cap and a floor.

interpolation: Technique for using on-the-run Treasury levels to determine the exact rate to be used for some intermediate date.

investor collar: The purchase of a floor while simultaneously selling a Cap.

ISDA: International Swap Dealers Association.

level: Price.

Libor: London Interbank Offer Rate.

Libor differential Swap: Basis Swap with one floating Libor payment exchanged for another in a different currency.

Libor in arrears Swap: Libor reset at the end of the period instead of at the beginning.

lottery ticket: An option with every likelihood of being exercised. Premiums are very low and returns are big if the option gets exercised.

low coupon Swap: An off-market Swap with a below-market fixed rate.

Main Street: Application or product suitable for the average consumer rather than large corporations.

mark to market: A technique that values the portfolio to the current market value.

mark-to-market Swap: A Swap that is periodically valued; the out-of-the-money counterparty pays the in-the-money counterparty. Occasionally, settling only goes one way.

market-linked deposits: Investments offered by several banks which offer a return equal to a return of some index, say the S&P, along with the guarantee of the return of the initial principal invested. Such investments offered by commercial banks also carry FDIC insurance up to $100,000.

master Swap agreement: A negotiated document that governs all Swap transactions between the two parties.

matched book: A completely hedged position.

modified American-style option: An option that can be exercised on more than one date.

money market basis: Assumes an extra five days (six in leap year) in each year.

naked Swap: A Swap with no offsetting loan.

notional amount: The face amount on Swap contracts.

novation: The creation of a new Swap document while simultaneously canceling an old one.

off-market Swap: A Swap with a fixed rate that is either above or below the current market rates.

on-the-run Treasuries: Benchmark issues.

OTC: Over the counter.

out-of-the-money: A position with no intrinsic value.

participating Cap: Same as participating Swap.

participating Swap: A Swap plus a Cap.

payor: The fixed-rate payor.

payor's Swaption: Option that lets the purchaser enter into a Swap as the fixed-rate payor.

premium: The option price.

puttable Swap: A Swap that gives the fixed-rate payor the right to cancel the Swap after an agreed-on time. Another combination of a Swap and Swaption.

quanto Swap: A Diff.

receiver: The floating-rate payor.

receiver's Swaption: Option that lets the purchaser enter into a Swap as a floating-rate payor.

reset date: The date to which the floating-rate component is reset.

reverse Swap: A new Swap that is executed to unwind an existing position. The new Swap is at current market levels and has a tenor that equals the remaining life on the first Swap. The fixed-rate payor of a reverse Swap becomes the floating-rate payor and vice versa.

reversible Swap: A Swap plus a Swaption for twice the notional amount of the underlying Swap. The Swaption is written so that a fixed-rate payor could convert to a floating-rate payor and vice versa.

roller coaster Swap: A Swap in which the fixed- and floating-rate payors switch every other period.

Specified Price: The floating index used in a commodity Swap.

spot start: The contract that starts two days after terms are set.

spread: The component added to the interpolated Treasury yield to determine the fixed Swap rate.

spreadlock: The obligation to enter into a Swap at some future date at the spread level "locked in" at an agreed-on level and the Treasury level in effect when the obligation is exercised.

staged drawdown Swap: A Swap for which the notional amount increases over time. The increases are agreed on in advance.

step-up Swap: A Swap in which the fixed rate "steps up" over time.

strike: Exercise price on an option.

stub period: The short period at the beginning or the end of a contract.

Swap annuities: A Swap unwind paid over time rather than up front.

Swaption: An option on a Swap.

TED spread: The difference between the T-bill rate and the Eurodollar rates.

terminations: An unwind of a Swap contract.

tick: One thirty-second of one percent. A term used in bond prices.

tranche: A piece of a transaction.

Treasury lock: The obligation to enter into a Swap at some future date at the Treasury level "locked in" at an agreed-on level and the Swap spread in effect when the obligation is exercised.

two-sided price: Both the bid and the offer.

underlying: The commodity on which an option is written.

unwinds: Termination of the Swap contract.

up-front fees: Fees paid at the inception of the contract.

volatility: Measures the rate of change over time.

wi bond: When issued bond.

wi note: When issued note.

yield: The current rate rather than the initial rate offered on a debt or equity instrument. Usually yield to maturity (ytm) or sometimes yield to call date.

yield curve Swap: A Swap in which the two indexes are set at different points on the yield curve.

zero cost collars: Combination (i.e., purchase and sale) of a Cap and a floor struck at such levels that there is no premium paid.

zero coupon Swap: An interest rate Swap in which no payments are made on one or both legs of the transaction until maturity.

zero coupon yield curve: A yield curve that brings forward each payment at its own zero coupon rate.

About the Author

Mary S. Ludwig has been actively involved in the Swap markets since 1985. As a corporate financial risk manager, she has executed Swap transactions in excess of $4 billion. Ms. Ludwig was Corporate Cash Manager at Olympia & York Companies (USA) and Assistant Treasurer at the Equitable Life Assurance Society. She is a member of The Financial Women's Association.

Index